MW00759930

A Just and Righteous God

18 Sermons

(13 previously unpublished)

by

JONATHAN EDWARDS

Compiled and Edited by Dr. Don Kistler

SOLI DEO GLORIA PUBLICATIONS

. . . for instruction in righteousness . . .

Soli Deo Gloria Publications
A division of Ligonier Ministries, Inc.
P.O. Box 547500, Orlando, FL 32854
(407)333-4244/FAX 333-4233
www.ligonier.org

This compilation of sermons entitled *A Just and Righteous God* is
© 2006 by Soli Deo Gloria Publications.
All rights reserved. Printed in the USA.

ISBN 1-56769-059-9

Library of Congress Cataloging-in-Publication Data

Edwards, Jonathan, 1703-1758.
A just and righteous God : 18 sermons / by Jonathan Edwards ;
compiled and edited by Don Kistler.– 1st modern ed.
    p. cm.
ISBN 1-56769-059-9 (alk. paper)
1. God–Righteousness–Sermons. 2. Congregational churches–
Sermons. 3. Sermons, American. I. Kistler, Don. II. Title.

BT145.E39 2005
252'.058–dc22

                                        2005021263

Contents

CHAPTER ONE

God Is a Just and Righteous God

"*Righteous art Thou, O Lord, and upright are Thy judgments.*"

PSALM 119:137

"*He is a Rock. His work is perfect; all His ways are judgment; a God of truth without iniquity, just and right is He.*"

DEUTERONOMY 32:4

oses begins this song by taking notice of the greatness and majesty of the God of Israel, which he had mentioned more generally in the foregoing verse, and describes, particularly in this, wherein he takes notice of the power, holiness, faithfulness, and

1

justice of God. The expressions are such that several attributes are implied. First, God is a Rock, which implies His power. A rock is a place of strength, a place for defense. He who dwells upon a high and steep rock is not easily come at by his enemy. Hereby also is signified the faithfulness of God, since one may safely trust in a strong Rock, being able to defend and preserve him as a fortress that will not fail him. So we may safely trust in God.

Second, he says that His work is perfect, which seems principally to respect the holiness of His works. The word "perfect" signifies "holy" oftentimes in Scripture, perfect so that it cannot be blamed. This seems more evident by the following words: "for all His ways are judgment, a God of truth, and without iniquity; just and right is He." These expressions are much of the same significance, the more strongly to signify the justice and righteousness of God.

DOCTRINE: God is a just and righteous God.

Under this doctrine I shall, first, explain what the righteousness of God is; second, prove that He is righteous; and, third, show under several propositions wherein His righteousness appears.

1. As to the nature of the righteousness of God, it may be thus defined: It is a natural, necessary, and unchangeable disposition of the divine nature to render to everyone their own. It is not in strictness different from the divine nature and essence itself, but only in our way of conceiving. Being and disposition, or inclination, aren't different in God. In ourselves we distinguish between our selves and souls and the disposition or inclination of our souls; the one is a substance, the other

a property of that substance. But there is no such distinction in God of substance and property. This is opposite to the simplicity of God's nature; but all that is in God is God. God is all thought and He is all love. God is all joy, all that disposition that we call justice, and all that disposition which we call mercy, which is indeed the same disposition in God. He is an infinitely powerful love and wise love. He is an infinitely wise justice. He is an all comprehensive, simple, and unchangeable thought or idea.

Those attributes of the holiness, faithfulness, and justice of God are near akin in our manner of conception; we conceive of His justice as being a part of His holiness, and of His faithfulness as being part of His justice. They are all comprehended in that more general disposition of doing those things that are pure, amiable, and righteous.

When we speak of justice and holiness and a disposition or inclination of the nature of God, it is not to be distinguished from the will of God. Justice is God's constant will of giving to everyone what is according to a regular equality. But yet in some things we are forced, in our way of conceiving, to distinguish between the free will of God and the unalterable inclination of His nature. God wills to be infinitely merciful and gracious, and yet He is not necessarily merciful to everyone; but He is necessarily just to all. He can't be otherwise than just to every particular person, but He is so necessarily and unalterably just that He can't be otherwise to anyone. 'Tis a contradiction to the very nature and being of God to suppose that He could do one unjust act. God can as soon cease to be, or to be and not be at the same time, as that He could do an unjust act. And 'tis as supposable that God should not render unto everyone his own.

All things are God's, and He is the mighty Possessor of

heaven and earth; men and angels are not their own, and nothing that they have is their own any otherwise than by God's gift. Yet by God's disposition there is an equality and regularity in things in their own nature that has the nature of God as its origin. And God orders all things in the moral and rational world according to that beautiful and harmonious equity and proportion, that equality that we call justice. So the laws that God makes are most harmonious and equal, and God distributes rewards and punishments in an exact proportion to their fitness and preparedness for those laws, and the agreeable preparation between them and the nature, habits, or actions of the receivers. Positive constitutions are of God, so the laws and covenants of God themselves are said to be just and righteous. Deuteronomy 4:7: "For what nation is there so great that hath statutes and judgments so righteous as all this law which I set before you this day?" Now the law and covenant of God are not called righteous because they are agreeable to the law and covenant, but because they are exactly agreeable to the most wise proportion and equality, the fitness of things.

The original rule of righteousness is the nature and wisdom of God; the wisdom of God weighs things in exact and even balances, and proportions them according to the beautiful excellency of His own nature; but the law and covenants of God are a copy of this original. And once given, they are a rule of righteousness not only to us, but to God. God Himself is bound by His covenant; thereby man can challenge things promised by Him as their own; and He has bound Himself to bestow them. Now if evil and not good belongs to us by the covenant of God, God has obliged Himself by His Word that He will bring it on us.

2. We shall prove that God must of necessity be perfectly just and righteous by the following arguments:

• From God's infinite understanding. A Being who knows all things can't be unrighteous because all disposition to injustice arises from ignorance and mistake. All unright men are drawn into unrighteousness by being deceived; the understanding must first be corrupted and blinded before it is possible to induce the will to choose wrong; if a man's understanding is right, his will must be right. Men must of necessity be made to believe that such or such a thing is most eligible before it is possible to persuade them to will it. Men love injustice, choose it, and will it because they are mistaken; the deceived have a mistaken notion about it; they are poor, ignorant, blinded, deluded creatures, and that makes 'em put darkness for light and light for darkness, bitter for sweet and sweet for bitter. They are drawn into the commission of sin and unrighteousness as a poor, ignorant, weak, ignorant child may be drawn aside to folly.

But a Being who is of infinite understanding, who knows all things, 'tis impossible that He should be deceived or in any way mistaken, and His understanding can't be perverted; for the will and understanding in man are not very different, but in God they are the very self-same thing. But if we in the least reflect and aren't stupid, we can't but be convinced that God knows all things. All who own any such thing as the being of a God will also own that He is the Creator of the world that He has made all things. And if He made all things, then He made not only every star above, every man and angel, every tree and plant, every man, beast, fowl, fish, or insect, every spire of grass, every hair, vein, and fibre. And if He made them and upholds them, then doubtless He does it knowingly and He must know all things, and know all their circumstances, all their powers, and properties; for He has given them their circumstances, powers, and properties, and

He must see all their dispositions and relations.

Again, all who don't deny the being of God will own that He is infinite or He is not God; for if He isn't infinite, there is no distinction between God and angels, or other beings. But if He is infinite, He must be everywhere present; and wherever His being is, there His knowledge is; and therefore He must necessarily have a full and perfect prospect of all things in heaven and on earth. And if He knows all things, He knows what things are most fitting, most excellent, and most desirable. He can't be deceived and made to think that injustice and wickedness are good and lovely and to be desired. Men love and do injustice because they are deceived and think it is lovely and desirable to be done, either because 'tis lovely in itself or will be some advantage to them. God can't be thus deceived. He can't think it will be of any benefit to Him, for He who is infinite can't be added to. He can't think that it is lovely and desirable in itself because He isn't blind. He perfectly knows the true nature of all things.

• It is impossible that God could be under any temptation to do unrighteously. Men are unrighteous because they are tempted to unrighteousness from some prospect of self-interest; they have a view to promote their own wealth, of enriching themselves, or of additions of pleasure, of being better off some way or another. But it is impossible that God should be under any such temptation, for it is impossible that He could want any addition to His happiness or pleasure.

This appears because He is eternal and the cause of all things; and therefore He must be independent and self-existent. 'Tis allowed that He is independent in His essence, and, if so, must also be independent as to His happiness. 'Tis as absurd to suppose that He could receive any additions from His own creature, that He could want anything from them who first received all from Him.

Again, He is infinitely powerful. He can do what He pleases, as is very evident by what He has done in creating heaven and earth, and His daily governing the world. Now, if He is infinitely powerful, 'tis impossible that He could stand in need of anything of profit or pleasure; for if He wants something, He can immediately procure it with infinite ease. He has no need to do injustice to procure because, by His infinite power, He can procure it without being unjust—so that He can't be under any temptation to be unjust from the prospect of in any way advantaging Himself either by any sort of additions to His wealth or pleasure or by being in any way bettered by it. Nor can He hope to get some thing by it when indeed He can't because, as I have shown already, He can't be mistaken.

• To suppose that God is unjust contradicts all the attributes, and so the very being of God. It contradicts His all-sufficiency, for how can an all-sufficient Being be tempted with hopes of any benefit by being unjust. And if God isn't all-sufficient, He must be dependent, and stands in want of anything from creatures. He must be dependent, for a Being who is independent and self-existent can't be dependent on others for anything; and if God is dependent, He can't be eternal. He must be dependent for His being, and so must be made; it is absurd to suppose that a dependent being exists only of Himself; and if He doesn't exist of Himself He must be made by some other, and so must have a beginning.

If He is unjust He can't be infinite, for we have shown that if He does unjustly, it must be with a prospect of some addition to Himself. But if He is infinite, He can't be added to. If He is unjust He can't be unchangeable; for imperfection implies malableness; that which is in an imperfect state may be added to or taken from, and so can be changed. If He is unjust He can't be Almighty. He can't do what He pleases, for if He can do what He pleases He can't be under any temptation to be unjust for any end whatsoever. I have shown already that if He is unjust, He can't be omniscient. He must be a fallible, foolish, ignorant being. If He is unjust, He is far from being a holy being or a faithful being; if He is unrighteous, He is not a merciful Being, for to be good and gracious it is a further degree than being merely just. He who is not righteous, instead of being gracious and merciful, is rather cruel and delights in injuring others. So that to suppose that God is not righteous is to suppose Him to be destitute of all those things we used to call the divine attributes, and therefore is not God at all; for that being that is neither infinite nor eternal nor unchangeable nor almighty nor omniscient, nor yet holy nor just nor good, but a being that is made by another, dependent upon others, finite, weak, foolish, wicked, unjust, and cruel is not God. If this is the case the dispute is not whether God is just or not, but whether there is any God at all or not.

3. I will show wherein God's righteousness appears.

• It appears in His giving so righteous and equal a law. The law of God, as we find it delivered to us in the Holy Scriptures, is a most perfect rule of righteousness. All proper, equal, and suitable duties are commanded towards both God and our fellow creatures. Some human lawgivers have been famed for the justice and righteousness of their laws, but none of them are to be compared with the law of God. All manner of unrighteousness in both heart and in life is prohibited; the least unjust thought or desire, or so much as the appearance of unrighteousness, is condemned. The rules and laws of men were given by mere human lawgivers or philosophers without the help of divine revelation. There were among them many things that were imperfect, not according to perfect righteousness. There were many good rules laid down, but they were not sufficient to guide a man to a suitable behavior towards God and man. But all rules of righteousness that are to be found among them all are all collected in the written law of God, and all their defects are left out.

In the law of God we are commanded to love God—the supreme Being, the Creator of the world and our Maker, and He who takes the care of us every day and bestows all good things upon us—with all our hearts, with all our souls, and with all our strength. We are to serve Him with fear and submission, trust, praise, adoration and obedience. And what can be more righteous than that we should do so?

In His law we are commanded to love our neighbors as ourselves, to do by them as we would that they should do by us. We are not to look on our own things, but on the things of others. And what can be more just and righteous than that we should do? And all the laws of God are of this tenor; therefore well might it be said as in Deuteronomy 4:5–8: "Behold, I have taught you statutes and judgments, even as the LORD my God commanded me, that ye should do so in the land whither ye go to possess it. Keep therefore and do them; for this is your wisdom and your understanding in the sight of all the nations, which shall hear all these statutes and say, 'Surely this great nation is a wise and understanding people. For what nation is there so great, who hath God so nigh unto them, as the LORD our God is in all things that we call upon Him for? And what nation is there so great that hath statutes and judgments so righteous as all this law, which I set before you this day?' "

• God's righteousness and justice appear in that He always

performs His promises. He is a faithful God, a God who never fails of His Word; what has once gone out of His mouth shall never be recalled. God cannot lie (Titus 1:2). He cannot repeal the promises He has made. Numbers 23:19: "God is not a man that He should lie, nor the son of men that He should repent. Hath He said, and shall He not do it? Or hath He spoken and shall He not make it good?"

He shows His justice in keeping covenant unto thousands of those who love Him. In forging a strict observance of the covenant of grace, God made a covenant with Jesus Christ before the foundation of the world that, upon condition of His assuming the human nature, performing the law, and laying down His life, He would see His seed and would be a means of saving particular persons. And Christ, having performed the condition, God is righteous to perform His promises unto Christ. God is obliged to Jesus. He has bound Himself to Jesus Christ to give repentance, faith, and salvation to such and such persons; and He is righteous to perform His promises. So He never fails to effectually call and save those whom in this covenant He has given to Christ. He is bound in justice.

So He has engaged by covenant with mankind to justify and save them who believe on the Lord Jesus Christ and accept Him as their only Savior. And all those who accept Christ, God is bound in justice to save and glorify; so that He manifests His justice in saving believers. He doesn't only manifest His mercy, but His justice in it. Romans 3:25-26: "Whom God hath set forth to be a propitiation through faith in His blood, to declare His righteousness for the remission of sins that are past through the forbearance of God, to declare, I say, at this time His righteousness that He might be just and the Justifier of him that believes in Jesus." Seeing that Christ has purchased our salvation and paid the full price that justice demanded, it is no more than just that salvation should be bestowed upon believers.

• God's righteousness appears in justly punishing sin. Herein God acts the part of a just Judge and Ruler, of a Governor. It belongs to Him who is the supreme Judge of the world to distribute to every one rewards and punishments according to their deserts, and not to suffer sin to go without an equitable punishment. We call him a just judge who clears the innocent and condemns the guilty. God, the sovereign of the world, will by no means depart from this rule, that the person on whom the guilt lies must suffer. 'Tis the immutable will of God that all sin receive its due punishment.

This justice appears in the instances that God gives of His vengeance here in the world, in those terrible destructions with which God has punished wicked men, such as the destruction of the old world. And sometimes there is a terrible vengeance that follows particular persons here in this world. We have many instances in Scripture, such as Cain, Err, Onan, Ananias and Sapphira, and many of whom common histories give an account.

Oh, but more especially God shows the strictness of His justice in the punishment of ungodly men in the world to come, because those judgments that God inflicts in this world aren't equal to the desert of sin; but in another world He punishes sin as it deserves, with eternal punishment— those who have sinned more with a greater punishment and those who have sinned less with a lesser one, but all with an exceedingly great and intolerable misery, as all sin deserves. God shows His justice in this to the admiration of the angels of heaven in that all who die as unbelieving sinners shall by no means escape the punishment of hell. Whatever shrieks, cries, and moans the punished may make, there is no escaping because God is strictly just and will by no means depart from the strict rule of justice. The majesty and glory of God will appear to be wonderful to those who are in heaven by this, that they see such a marvelous display of the awful majesty and justice of God in the righteous inflictions of His dreadful wrath.

There will be a more remarkable discovery of the justice of God at the Day of Judgment when all shall be judged in the most open and solemn manner possible, with all the inhabitants of heaven and earth present. Then God will wonderfully display His justice in acquitting believers and in rewarding righteous men who are legally innocent, and rewarding holy men according to His promise in fulfilling and completing all those good things to them that He so often spoke of to them.

He will then remarkably display His vindictive justice in so open and solemn a manner, condemning and punishing men and devils; in punishing the princes of darkness and the great men of this world, the wicked, proud kings and emperors, princes and noblemen; in punishing those rulers who gathered themselves against Him when He was on earth. God's justice in those many things now lies hidden, as it were, but then it will come forth into the light and will be wonderfully discovered. The justice of God will then regulate all those irregularities that have been in the world since the foundation of it. But there is in some respects the most glorious discovery of Gods' vindictive justice in the work of redemption by Jesus, in God's punishing sin when imputed to His one and only Son who is intimately near and dear to Him. Rather than justice not have its course, God would bring such sore and dreadful misery, such pain, distress, and wrath upon the Son of His eternal and infinite delight. This shows the severity and inflexibleness of God's justice beyond anything else, and as nothing else can do.

Just men are very apt to be partial to their own children if they are zealous against iniquity; yet they are many times very loathe that justice should take place with respect to their own children. But God was so just and righteous that He gave the full cup to His own Son. He gave the very dregs of it for Him to wring out, and would not abate one jot or tittle of the punishment of all the sins that were imputed to Him, because God would by no means clear the guilty. God was unchangeably resolved that sin, wherever it was imputed, should have its full recompense, that the uttermost farthing of the debt should be paid.

APPLICATION

1. Hence we may learn that we can't be accepted of God without a righteousness. If God is a just and righteous God, He loves righteousness and hates iniquity. He can never be a friend to unrighteousness. Psalm 45:7: "Thou lovest righteousness and hatest iniquity." Psalm 5:4: "For Thou art not a God that hast pleasure in unrighteousness, neither shall evil dwell with Thee." Unrighteousness is a thing that God never can be reconciled to; and therefore, if ever we are accepted, it must be for the sake of some righteousness or other that we are entitled to. God will never take pleasure in us without a righteousness.

And it must not only be some righteousness, but it must be a perfect righteousness. God will never accept any person unless it is for a perfect righteousness. It is the eternal rule that God proceeds by, with both men and angels, that the condition of their being accepted with Him should be that they have a perfect righteousness. He has not departed, nor ever will He depart, from this rule. The guilt of one sin is sufficient to effectually block the way to God's favor and acceptance; for every sin is infinitely odious to God, and if there is the guilt of it upon the soul it is enough to render that soul odious in God's sight.

Nor is it enough that persons should merely be free from the guilt of sin that they should be entitled to happiness in God's favor; but they must have a positive, perfect righteousness. Such a righteousness must in some way or another be ours. Either we ourselves must perform such a righteousness or such a righteousness must be imputed to us and we must in some way or another become entitled to it so that it should be ours in the sight of God.

Let no person, therefore, ever hope to be saved and go to heaven without a perfect righteousness. 'Tis folly for any to have dependence upon a righteousness that is imperfect, that comes short of full perfection and that is mixed with sin; for God will have no regard at all to it, but will reject it and cast it as dung in our faces if we pretend to bring it and offer it to Him. He is so righteous and holy a Being that He will not accept such an offering.

2. Hence we learn the necessity we stand in of a Savior. We have heard that God, as He is the sovereign King and Judge of the world, will by no means clear the guilty. He will surely execute vengeance upon all sin. No sin shall escape its deserved wrath. God is inflexibly and unalterably a righteous Judge, and therefore is inflexibly determined to punish sin according to its deserts.

Therefore, as we fallen men have been guilty of much sin,

'tis impossible but that our sin must be punished; and unless we have a Mediator who is able and willing to bear our punishment for us and to go through it, 'tis impossible but that we ourselves must suffer all the punishment that we have deserved; 'tis impossible but that we must be cast into prison and continue there till we have paid the uttermost farthing.

And neither is it sufficient that our sins should merely satisfied for in order to our being made happy in God's favor; but be we must have a positive, perfect righteousness, as we have heard in the foregoing inference. Therefore we have a necessity that some other person, worthy to be accepted by God on our account, should perform that righteousness for us, and that we should believe in that righteousness and should close with those offers which are made of His righteousness, and with all our hearts receive it. If we do not have such a Savior to suffer the vindictive righteousness of God for us and to perform an active righteousness for us, we may conclude that justice will have its course upon us; for divine justice always must and will take place. We must suffer the vindictive justice of God for us. We must be miserable when we die; we must be condemned at the Day of Judgment, and there will remain no more sacrifice for sin. For as Christ once offered Himself, so it is appointed to man once to die, and after this the judgment (Hebrews 9:26–27).

3. Let this doctrine be of awakening unto sinners. God is a just and righteous Judge, and when He comes to judge them He will judge them according to their works. He is so just that you can't bribe Him; nothing that you can do or offer to Him can be of force to persuade Him to judge you favorably. If you offer Him prayers, tears, or blood it is all one. You will never persuade God to depart from a strict rule of justice.

When He comes to try you, you must be dealt with according to your works.

God is a true God, and what He has spoken that He will make good. He has said that He will destroy the workers of iniquity, and that the wicked shall be cast into hell. He has said that neither whoremongers, nor adulterers, nor sorcerers, nor drunkards, nor effeminate, nor covetous, nor railers, nor liars should ever enter into the kingdom of heaven, but should be cast into the lake of fire that burns with fire and brimstone forever and ever. He has said that all them who offend and do iniquity shall be cast into a furnace of fire where there shall be weeping and gnashing of teeth. All these things have gone forth of out of the mouth of God, and He is a God who will not lie, for He is not a man that He should lie, nor the son of man that He should repent. What God has once said you may assuredly expect that He will fulfill.

Consider this, that if it should be so that you should be found outside of a Savior at last, the justice of God obliges Him to punish every one of your sins; for the least of your sins you deserve eternal burnings, and for the least sin that ever you committed you will find a dreadful reckoning. You must suffer for it to all eternity. How dreadful then will your misery be, which will be a compilation of all the punishments that all your innumerable transgressions have deserved.

4. Be persuaded to own and submit to the justice of God. You have heard it proved that God must be a perfectly just and righteous Being, that it is impossible that He should be otherwise, that if God isn't a just Being it will follow that He has no divine perfections at all, and so that there is no God. Wherefore, whatever little objections may be started in your mind against the justice of God, don't

think that you have reason to suspect whether or not God is righteous. There is reason why this should be an established principle with you, as we have shown, so established that nothing should be sufficient in the least to shake it.

It becomes you, therefore, to own this justice of God. However we may fear the effects of it, yet it becomes us to own that we are naturally in such a state that it would be just for God to reject us, and all our prayers and services, to cast us into hell, and to make us drink of the wine of His fierceness and wrath. It will do no good to quarrel and find fault, and to try to pick flaws in God's justice; for let us do what we will, God's justice will take place. So it becomes persons, when they are under affliction, to own that it is just, that it is far less than our iniquities have deserved. Lamentations 3:39: "Why doth a living man complain, a man for the punishment of his sin?"

5. Let us study to imitate God in this point. As God our heavenly Father is righteous, so let us be righteous. We have the law of God (which is a transcript of the perfect justice of His nature) for our rule. Let us walk according to it. If you would walk with God and would have Him walk with you, and not contrary to you, you must be as righteous as He is. Endeavor to recover your righteousness of nature, that original righteousness that we had in our first estate, and seek always to behave according to strict principles of justice, to observe rules of justice and honesty towards your neighbor. Carefully avoid everything that is contrary to that rule of doing to others as you would that they should do to you; thus you must do if you would be a child of Him whose ways are judgment, who is a God of truth and without iniquity.

CHAPTER TWO

It Is Crime Enough to Render Any Man a Cursed Person Not to Love Jesus Christ

"If any man love not the Lord Jesus Christ,
let him be Anathema, maranatha."

1 CORINTHIANS 16:22

The apostle, after writing to the Corinthians about many things, concludes his letter with a blessing and a curse: a curse upon all who do not love the Lord Jesus Christ, not fixing it to any particular person in this verse, and a blessing to the Church at Corinth in the two next verses: "The grace of our Lord Jesus Christ be with you, my love be with you all in Christ Jesus." He calls the curse and blessing both together his salutation, as in the verse foregoing: "The salutation of me, Paul, with mine own hand."

It is observable that he first denounces a curse to all them who don't love Christ, and yet, in the next verse, blesses the whole Corinthian church: "The grace of the Lord Jesus Christ be with you, my love be with you all." Doubtless there were some in that church who did not love Jesus Christ—the Corinthians who professed the Christian religion but did not really love the Lord Jesus Christ—and the apostle at this time had particular reason to be afraid of 'em upon several accounts. He manifests himself as being much afraid of 'em upon the account of many enormities that he had heard of among them. But yet, as they are visible Christians, they are visibly lovers of the Lord Jesus Christ. And so the apostle denounces a curse against them who don't love Christ, yet he blesses them as looking upon them in a judgment of charity to be lovers of Christ. All who are visible Christians, who haven't in some way forfeited the charity of God's saints, are to be looked upon and treated as lovers of Christ.

It is usual for the apostle to conclude his epistles with a blessing to those whom he writes to; but it is not usual for him to join the curse of hypocrites with it. The reason for his doing it here was very probably that the occasion of this epistle, what he had heard of the scandals and disorders in doctrine that were among them. He mentions the divisions there were among them, the contentions in going to law with one another, the breaking out of gross uncleanness in the case of the incestuous persons, and their great disorders at the Lord's Table. Those things made the apostle doubt whether there was not a number of 'em who were hypocrites who had no love to Jesus Christ. He puts this curse here in so solemn a manner to awaken such, if there were any, and to put them upon serious consideration and examination of themselves, whether they had any love for Christ or not. It is a awful sentence that is here spoken by the apostle: "If any man love not the Lord Jesus Christ, let him be Anathema, maranatha."

These terms were probably such as they knew the meaning of. They signify the final and eternal curse of God, not only a temporal calamity or chastisement, but a full and everlasting infliction of God's wrath. The word "anathema" is a Greek word that is derived from "anatithemi," which signifies "to set apart," or "devoted." The "anathema" signified that which was devoted to destruction.

"Maranatha" was originally a Syrian word and, according to interpreters, signifies "the Lord cometh." So this word threatens everlasting condemnation when Christ the Lord comes to judgment. Such a curse was denounced by God through Enoch against the ungodly in Jude 14–15: "And Enoch also, the seventh from Adam, prophesied of those saying, 'Behold, the Lord cometh . . . to execute judgment upon all that are ungodly.'"

DOCTRINE: It is crime enough to render any man a cursed person not to love Jesus Christ.

Let the man be outwardly never so religious and devout, never so exact in rules of justice and honesty; let him take never so much pains in religion; let him bestow never so much to the poor and to pious uses; let him suffer never so much in religion—yet if he doesn't love Jesus Christ, that is enough to render him accursed, whatever he has done and whatever he has suffered. Many men in their own minds hardly call this any crime at all. It is not a terrifying consideration to 'em that they have no love to Christ; they aren't ashamed of it, nor do they feel guilty on the account of it, notwithstanding that it is so highly resented by God, or that God shows such high resentments of it in His Word, and that there are such dreadful curses denounced against it, as in our text.

In speaking to this doctrine I shall:

1. Show what it is to be an accursed person.
2. Show that they who don't love Jesus Christ highly deserve to be so accursed.
3. Show that such shall actually have the curse executed upon them.
4. Then make application.

1. I am to show what it is to be a accursed. It is to be devoted by God to His wrath. The word "anathema," as I have shown, signifies a thing that is set apart or devoted. For man to curse is to invoke the wrath of God on any one; for God to curse is to devote His wrath onto someone or something. Thus the ground was cursed after the fall, that is, God would everywhere impress the signatures of His wrath upon this world by making it a world of misery, sorrow, and calamity, and at last burning it up with all the wicked of it. So Jericho and Ai and others cities were accursed by God in Joshua 6:17, so that all who were in it, except Rahab the harlot, were to be destroyed without mercy, and the city was to be forever a heap, to be never again built, in token of God's wrath against it. The cattle were all to be killed and the silver and gold were not to be used in token of God's wrath. He who was hanged on a tree was cursed because God appointed this sort of death for none but those whom He made special examples of His wrath and vengeance. So it was in the instance that we have in Numbers 25:3–4: "And Israel joined himself unto Baal Peor, and the anger of the Lord was kindled against Israel. And the Lord said unto Moses, 'Take all the heads of the people and hang them up before the sun.'" So the kings of those cities of Canaan who divided the spoil that was cursed were hanged on trees. So Achitophel hanged

himself, for he was cursed by David in the name of the Lord. And it was so ordered that Absalom was hanged in an oak for his rebellion against his father; it was written that he was cursed who set light by father or by mother. So the seven sons of Saul were hanged to remove God's curse from the nation, and Judas hanged himself, having the curse of the wrath of God against him declared by Jesus Christ. And Jesus Christ, the dear Son of God, was hanged on a tree, was made a curse for sinners and bore the very wrath of God on the cross.

The curse of God sometimes signifies the calamities and miseries that arise from God's wrath in this world when there is a blast upon their affairs and concerns; but it is generally to be understood of devoting someone to misery, to everlasting destruction, or to that which is equivalent to it. Thus Jericho was said to be an accursed city; it was destroyed and appointed to be a desolation forever, and never to be built again. Jesus Christ bore the everlasting curse of the law and utter destruction. Jesus Christ, who was made a curse, did not indeed suffer everlasting destruction, but he bore that which was the equivalent of it. So to be accursed is to be devoted to utter destruction by God's eternal wrath.

2. The second thing is to show that those who don't love Jesus Christ highly deserve to be thus accursed. All sin deserves God's wrath, but this in an eminent manner, a special manner, and in a high degree. As God of old used to make manifest His curse to those who were guilty of some special provoking iniquity by ordering them to be hanged on trees, so those who don't love the Lord Jesus Christ deserve the curse in a like high degree and special manner. This will appear by the following considerations:

All will allow that a person may have so much reason to love another that it will be the highest and most intolerable degree of baseness not to love him. We may conceive of thousands of such cases in our own minds. A person may be so excellent in himself in every way, so amiable in himself, and his excellencies may appear so plainly and shine so brightly and be represented to such advantage, he may stand in such a relation to us and we may have such a dependence upon him that we have the highest reason to take notice of his excellency. And withal he may be so kind, compassionate, and bountiful, his kindness may be attended with such peculiar circumstances of our distress, extremity, and our undeservedness, that disinterestedness of it and the great difficulty and suffering that it is attended with, together with the vast advantage that may accrue to us from it in an exceedingly happy change of condition, that it may be more than brutal baseness not to love such an extraordinary person. We can hardly think of it; one can't imagine a crime more abominable and provoking that tends more to raise the indignation of human nature that may be thought of in this kind.

The heathens themselves used to look upon ingratitude as the worst and most detestable of vices; and if all ingratitude is not so, yet when ingratitude is in the highest degree that can be imagined, nothing can be more worthy of being abhorred. Men are generally very sensible what a provoking thing it is in their own cases. What will sooner enrage a man than to have their kindness slighted when they have laid themselves out much for the relief or benefit of others? Yea, they will take it very grievously if their dignity and good qualifications aren't respected. If they see what they think is excellent being slighted and despised by others, it makes 'em their enemy; they hate those who don't think of that for which they think they ought to be respected and admired. And above all, if they think that both their excellency and their kindness are disregarded, if they think they ought to have love from everybody, if they have no love from them, 'twill be an unpardonable crime.

It is especially so with great men, when their kindness towards inferiors is slighted and their persons disregarded. But however men, through their pride, resent such things towards themselves, there is some ground for it. Yet if they were really so excellent and so much to be loved, as they think themselves to be, it would be base indeed and to be exceedingly abhorred. This shows the truth of this assertion that one person may have so much reason to love another that it is the most detestable and provoking degree of baseness not to love them.

There can be nothing that renders any person deserving of our love, nor any possible degree of it, but what is to be found in Jesus Christ. He has in Him all possible excellency. He has infinite majesty as He is the great God and Creator of the world. He has infinite holiness. He has infinite wisdom and boundless grace and goodness. There is nothing that is an excellency but it is in Him in an infinite degree. It is impossible but that it should be so, because all that is excellent, all that is beautiful and desirable in the whole creation, He is the Fountain of it. And if it isn't enough that He has all divine excellency, which indeed comprehends all possible excellency, He also has in His person all human excellencies, such as charity, meekness, patience, and humility, joined with great wisdom and holiness. We can't devise any qualification that is endearing in any man but it is in Christ's human nature to an immensely greater degree than it ever was in any other man, and greater than in any other creature.

The man Christ Jesus is the firstborn of every creature, the brightest and most beautiful part of all the works of creation. His lovely qualifications are exceedingly and clearly set before us and brightly represented to us. His excellencies aren't what we have only just accidentally heard of, but Christ has manifested Himself in various ways unto mankind, from the very first creation and fall of man. At length He came down and dwelled among us and familiarly conversed with men for a long time, manifesting Himself not only in visions and by His prophets, but by appearing Himself personally. We have an account of His life, His birth, His conversation, His speeches, His sufferings, death, resurrection, and His ascension very particularly represented by four several histories. Besides these, we have the revelations of Himself by the Holy Ghost to the apostles after He was ascended into heaven.

We in this land of light have the excellencies of Christ continually set before us from our very infancy by education, and by the constant preaching of the Word. We have Christ set before our eyes by sensible signs in the Sacraments, and we also see the glory of Christ set before us in the many instances of the success of the gospel and the holy lives of His people. God has used an abundance of methods to set before us the excellency of His Son. The light clearly shines all around us and breaks forth from every quarter. God has exercised His infinite wisdom in contriving to set forth His Son's excellency in a glorious light.

And then He stands in such a relation to us, and we have that dependence upon Him that we have all that reason to take notice of His excellency that can be conceived of. He exhibits Himself to us as our Savior, as our Deliverer from all misery, and as the Author of all our happiness. We stand in the greatest necessity of Him. We shall perish forever without Him. Neither can we have any other help, but we have such a dependence upon Him that He is our all and our only hope.

As there is no possible excellency but what is in Him, so there is no possible kindness that can be in anyone to oblige love than there is to found in Him. Neither is it possible that the kindness of anyone should be attended with circumstances that do more than enhance the obligation than His kindness is attended with. His love and grace exceed in degree all that ever was. He loved men so greatly that He aimed at nothing less than their eternal happiness with Him, their near relation to Him, union and communion with Him, and their being co-heirs with Him of eternal happiness in the Father's love. He loved them so that He was willing to lay Himself out exceedingly to accomplish these things. His love was such as brought Him down from heaven to the earth, and made Him willing to be incarnate and appear in a low condition to undertake great labors and undergo great sufferings, and even to lay down His life. There can be no greater love conceived of, whether you measure the love by the benefit or by the manner of procuring it; there can be no greater benefit than deliverance from eternal misery, and the conferring of eternal happiness. And it is impossible that there could be greater expressions of love in procuring this benefit. Merely doing a great deal without expense is not so great a manifestation of love as suffering; and none can show his love by suffering more than by dying. There are degrees of suffering even in death, yet there is no greater degree that can be thought of than what Christ suffered in His death. The kind of death was most tormenting and disgraceful, but besides outward torment, there was torment in His mind, the part that is most capable of misery. Both His bloody sweat and His crying out show the greatest degree of suffering; and as it is impossible that there could be a greater kindness in anyone, so it is impossible that any kindness could be attended with circumstances that more increase our obligation, whether we consider His greatness and infinite superiority or His independence in any way from us. It is impossible that any person could be greater or stand in less need of us.

Therefore, if it is possible that one person may have so much reason to love another that it will be the highest degree of baseness not to love him, then it follows that its is the utmost and most provoking degree of baseness in men not to love Jesus Christ. And therefore, if any sin deserves that God should be so provoked as to devote them to His wrath, doubtless this sin is such that persons who are guilty of it, however little troubled their consciences are about it, yet doubtless they deserve to be forever cursed of God.

I shall offer one consideration more. The abuse offered to God the Father in not loving Jesus Christ is equal to that offered to the Son. We may well conclude that this sort of sin, baseness toward the Redeemer whom God has sent into the world, is the most provoking to God of any whatsoever. The Father took pity upon us after we had sinned against Him, and brought ourselves thereby into the greatest misery. Though we brought it upon ourselves through our own folly and baseness towards Him, yet, when He saw what a miserable, doleful condition we were in, His bowels yearned towards us. Yea, He pitied us and loved us so that He sent His own Son to suffer in our stead, to bear what justice and the law required in our room.

Now to have those persons upon whom He had such pity, and to whom He had showed such kindness, be base towards the Son whom He sent to save us, to slight Him and disregard His love and kindness is a great abuse offered to the Father, to not so much as to love or thank Him for it, doubtless is provoking to the Father.

It is a provoking thing to God when men are base to any of His messengers who come in His name. Though they are but His servants, He expects that they should be treated with the respect becoming them who come in the name of so glorious a

Being. But God takes it abundantly more heinously when they are base to His own Son.

The Son is infinitely dear to the Father; therefore He is often called God's dear Son. God declares from heaven that Christ is His beloved Son, and Christ said to God, "Thou lovedst Me before the foundation of the world." And therefore, what baseness is offered to the Son of God is equally provoking to the Father, both because the love of the Father towards men in sending His Son is as great as that of the Son in coming, and because the Son is infinitely dear to the Father. So when He is abused, 'tis as near to the Father as the Son, for the Father and the Son are one.

3. The third thing under the doctrine is that those who never have any love for the Lord Jesus Christ shall be forever cursed by God for their baseness. All who now have no love for Christ are now under the curse upon that account, and they who never do love Christ in this life will be cursed to all eternity. They are cursed men while they are here in this world; but they shall know what it is to be cursed in the world to come. There are many fruits of God's curse that come upon those who don't love Jesus Christ before they die; they are cursed in soul, in their body, and in all their affairs. God curses their souls oftentimes by giving them up to hardness of heart and blindness of mind by suffering their lusts greatly to prevail, by giving them up to worldly-mindedness, to sensuality, to pride and maliciousness, and oftentimes to erroneous principles and a cavilling spirit at the doctrines of Christianity, oftentimes to some particular vice, to drunkenness, uncleanness, dishonesty, profaneness, or some other. Some are given up to many vices. God often curses their souls by turning Satan loose against them by suffering 'em to fall into frequent and strong temptations. God gives them to the devil in a sense while they are alive.

There is a blast upon the Word and ordinances that they enjoy; they do them no good, but rather harden them. They are made a savor of death to them; they are like the ground that let the rain fall upon it or sun shine upon it. It will bring forth nothing but briars and thorns, which is nigh unto cursing. Their outward enjoyments are made curses to them; their table is made a snare and a trap to them; if they are in prosperity, they are like an ax that is being fatted for the slaughter. This is the curse that Jeremiah denounced by God's Spirit against those who had God far from their reins, that is, who did not love Him. Jeremiah 12:2–3: "Thou art near in their mouth, but far from their reins; pull them out like sheep for the slaughter. Let them be prepared for the day of slaughter."

If they are in affliction, it is not Fatherly correction, but their afflictions are the fruits of God's vengeance. Their meat and their drink, their money and their land, their good and their evil, is all cursed to them. Those curses stand good against all those that are written. Deuteronomy 28:16–19: "Cursed shalt thou be in the city and cursed shalt thou be in the field. Cursed shall be thy basket and thy store. Cursed shalt be the fruit of thy body and the fruit of thy land, the increase of thy kin and the flocks of thy sheep. Cursed shalt thou be when thou comest in and cursed shalt thou be when thou goest out." And in verse 20: "The Lord shall send upon thee cursing, vexation, and rebuke in all that thou settest thine hand unto until thou be destroyed, until thou perish quickly, because of the wickedness of thy doings whereby thou hast forsaken Me." All that they receive will be for their destruction in another world until they are destroyed. And then, as I said before, they'll know what it is to be cursed by God. Oftentimes men are cursed in this world, and yet are merry and jocund. But then they will feel the weight of it. They will be forever devoted to God's wrath and fiery vengeance that shall be poured out upon them without mixture for their not loving Jesus Christ.

APPLICATION

USE OF CONVICTION. This use is for natural men, to convince them that they have no righteousness. If the doctrine is true, then how vain and unreasonable are they who have no love at all for Jesus Christ, and yet think that they do, and that may well recommend 'em to God's favor. They think they are so righteous that they attract God's gracious respect towards them. Yet there are multitudes of such men who have no more hearty respect and love for Christ than they have to the Emperor of Turkey. And yet they think that their prayers, their striving and diligence, lay so much obligation upon God that it would be hard if He should have no respect to 'em. If God won't show 'em some mercy after they have done so much, they can't but look upon it as very hard. But how unreasonable is it in men to look upon God as obliged to 'em for the pains they take purely out of respect for themselves. They show no sort of respect to Him, and do nothing in the least from any love for Him or for Jesus Christ.

In Isaiah 58:3 is the language of the abundance of men's hearts: "Wherefore have we fasted, and Thou seest not? Wherefore have we afflicted our souls and Thou takest no notice?" They think themselves greatly abused; they keep complaining of it. But hear what God says to such in Zechariah 7:5–6: "Speak unto all the people of the land, and to the priests, saying, 'When ye fasted and mourned in the fifth month, and in the seventh month, even those seventy years, did ye at all fast unto even unto Me? And when ye did eat and when ye did drink, did not ye eat for yourselves and drink for yourselves?" The people used to keep fasts in the time of the seventy years' captivity; but it was not from a true sense of their sin or for the glory of God, but their only end was that they might be redeemed out of captivity again and be restored to their own land. So when carnal men fast and pray, it is to themselves and for themselves, only that they may be delivered from hell. God is no more obliged to men for going to meetings for themselves, for reading for themselves, and for praying for themselves than He is obliged to 'em for plowing for themselves and getting money for themselves. They have as little respect for God in their religion and prayers and striving as they have in their striving to get money.

Why don't they look upon it as hard that God doesn't love 'em for being so diligent and industrious to get a great estate? The only reason is because they know they do that for their own interest and not from any love for God. And for the same reason it is unreasonable to think that God will love 'em the better for their religious works, for they are done as much from selfishness as the other. God is no more obliged to a man for having a mind not to go to hell than He is for their having a mind not to be poor.

Our doctrine also shows us the unreasonableness of carnal men's trusting their own works upon another account: They think that they lay God under some obligation to be favorable to 'em at the same time that they are guilty of so provoking a crime as not loving Jesus Christ. They provoke God every day and every hour by the utmost degree by being so base as not to love Christ Jesus, which I have shown is the lowest degree of baseness, and highly merits that God should devote such persons to His eternal wrath. God has declared that He will devote them to it. How vain, therefore, is it for such persons nevertheless to think that they and their works are lovely in the sight of God, and worthy of His acceptance.

Surely this doctrine lays conviction enough before those who don't love Christ, and shows them that they deserve hell and nothing but hell. Don't these arguments that have been offered prove that this crime carries in it the blackest and most horrid baseness? And surely, to be base to God the Father and God the Son is worse than to be base to any creature. This crime alone, I have shown, is enough to make a man a cursed creature. Then, if so, certainly they who are not only guilty of this crime, but innumerable others, deserve hell, though they pray, read, and seek to avoid going to hell purely from love for themselves.

Yea, this crime of not loving Jesus Christ, going along with all else that they do, so far from placing any obligation upon God to show mercy to 'em, it renders their works abominable to God. It may justly be a new provocation to God when they come to meetings and pretend to worship Christ, when they hear the Word of Christ without any love for Him. When they go to prayer in secret without any love for Christ, when they pretend to pray in the name of Christ and have no sort of love for Christ, there is reason that God should be highly provoked by these things; for God appointed these duties to be exercises of love and true devotion. These duties ought always to be performed with love. And there is the highest reason that they should be done so.

When therefore they are not, it is a high provocation; the duties of religion were appointed that God might be honored by them. But they who attend 'em without love don't honor Him; for how can that be an honor to God that is done without any sort of true respect for Him? And if God isn't honored by 'em, why should He take any delight in 'em? Why should He take any delight in the prayers of a carnal man, though he prays often and earnestly, as long as He has no honor by them? And if there is no reason why He should take delight in them, how can there be any reason that He should accept them, or look upon the performers of these acts as being any the better for them?

I entreat you to consider the reasonableness of these things, and don't be so unreasonable as anymore to imagine that you make yourself lovely in God's sight by your works, or lay any sort of obligation upon Him to be merciful to you by them.

USE OF EXAMINATION. Let us examine ourselves whether we have any true love for Jesus Christ or not. And we may try ourselves by the same rules as we try whether or not we have any true love for anyone else.

1. If we have true love for God we shall prize His favor for its own sake, that is, not only for the sake of any benefits that God is able to bestow. If one person loves another, truly he'll desire and prize the love of the beloved person for its own sake. Whether he ever has any benefit or is made the richer or more honorable by the love of the other, or has more honor or any other benefit from their love, yet he will desire and prize their love. To be loved by them will seem most desirable. Whatever benefit he has from him, it won't satisfy him unless he is assured that he is loved; that is a benefit in itself. So those who truly love Christ will find being loved by Christ to be a benefit itself, to be prize enough. His love will be riches and happiness of itself without any other. Those who truly love Christ don't only prize His love for the sake of being delivered from hell by Him, or for being brought to heaven by Him; they would earnestly desire the love of Jesus Christ if there was neither heaven nor hell, nor any other benefit than only to be loved by Him. And if that man

could have all that his heart could wish for besides, it would not satisfy him if he was not sure that Christ loved him.

2. When one person has true love for another, he desires communion with them for its own sake, to be with them, to see them, to be with them and to converse with them will be desired and prized for the sake of the sweetness and pleasantness of their conversation. Whether he expects any other benefit by it or not, whether he thinks their company is any honor to him or not, yet he will desire their company. So they who truly love Christ will desire His company for its own sake, just to have the communication of His Spirit—to see Him spiritually in this world, to see Him face to face in the world to come, and to be with Him and to dwell in His presence forever, these things will appear in themselves as exceedingly desirable. If a Christian were to live in this world always, he would desire communion with Christ; if he were to live in great prosperity in this world, he would desire the communion of Christ; and if he were to live in a dungeon, he would desire communion with Christ; and if he went to another world, his desire there would be to enjoy Christ.

3. When one person loves another with a true love, he loves their honor for its own sake; he can't bear to see them dishonored or hear of them being ill reflected upon. He seeks their honor and endeavors to get a good opinion of them in others. If they are respected and promoted, he rejoices without any respect to any interest of his own. So it is with those who truly love Jesus Christ: they love His glory; they seek and prize it; they are jealous over it. It rejoices their hearts when any honor is done to the name of Christ, and they lay themselves out so that He may be honored and glorified, whether the honor of Christ is in any way to his advantage or not.

4. He who has a true love for another is willing to suffer for them whether he ever has any benefit or recompense for it. True lovers and friends are willing to suffer for one another; and it seems to be compensation enough if they can in any way by suffering promote the interest of the beloved one. So those who love Christ have a spirit to suffer for Christ and His cause, to suffer reproach, loss, and pain if they can but truly promote the interest and kingdom of Christ.

CHAPTER THREE

God Carries His People Along Through the World to Their Glory Far Above the Reach of All Their Enemies or Anything that Might Hinder Their Blessedness

*"Ye have seen what I did to the Egyptians, and how
I bare you on eagles' wings and brought you to Myself."*

EXODUS 19:4

These are the first words that God spoke to Moses or
the children of Israel after they came to Mt. Sinai.
God had spoken to Moses from Mt. Sinai before
alone, and that was when He kept the flock of his father-in-law.

God appeared to Him in the burning bush and bid him loose his shoe from off his foot because the place where he stood was holy ground, of which we have an account in chapter 3 of this book. God then told Moses that He would certainly be with him, and that this would be a token to him that He had sent him, and that when He had brought forth the people out of Egypt they should worship Him in that mountain (Exodus 3:12).

Here we have an account that in the third month after the children of Israel came out of Egypt, they came unto the wilderness of Sinai and camped before this same mountain. Then Moses went up unto God, and these were the first words that were spoken by God from this mountain after the children of Israel came there. Moses went up to God and the Lord called unto him out of the mountain saying, "Thus shalt thou say to the house of Jacob and tell the children of Israel, Ye have seen what I did to the Egyptians, and how I bare you on eagles' wings and brought you to Myself.' "

There are three things God here puts them in mind of concerning His wonderful acts and manifestations towards them, and His great mercy and distinguishing favor towards them:

1. His severity towards their enemies: "Ye have seen what I did to the Egyptians." Such had been God's distinguishing, great favor to them that He had executed terrible wrath upon them who hated and injured them. He plagued the Egyptians with many sore plagues, and at last He destroyed all the firstborn of Egypt, from the firstborn of Pharaoh on the throne to the firstborn of the captives in the dungeon. And at last He overthrew Pharaoh and all his host in the Red Sea. These things were now fresh in their memories.

2. God's great care of their safety in His providences towards

'em: "how I bare you on eagles' wings on high and far above the reach of your enemies, or anything that might hurt you." An eagle is a very loft bird in her flight, and when soars as she flies aloft she goes where she desires and is out of the reach of all them who are here below. Those below can't reach her to hurt her or to interrupt her in her progress. So did God carry the children of Israel, as it were, high and aloft in the air where their enemies could not reach them to annoy them. They could see 'em and could wish ill to 'em, but they could not reach 'em to hurt them or to hinder their going where God would carry them. Thus God kept and carried 'em in safety from all who threatened them.

The Egyptians sought to destroy them by killing all the male children, but they multiplied the more for all that. They sought to diminish the Israelites by oppression and hard bondage but they could not; the more they oppressed them, the more they multiplied. Pharaoh with his army pursued them and thought to destroy them, but God kept 'em out of their reach. When they were in sight, God kept 'em from coming nigh for a whole night by taking the pillar of cloud that was before them and putting it between them and the Egyptians. He kept the Egyptians from overtaking them by taking off their chariot wheels so that they dragged heavily and then drowned them in the Red Sea.

The power was on the side of their enemies, and the people had nothing to defend them but their God; yet they were strangely kept out of their reach so that they could not hurt them. It was if they had been carried on eagles' wings high in the air where they could not come at them. And as their enemies could not destroy them, so neither could they stop them or hinder them from going where God would carry them, as you can't stop an eagle that flies high in the air.

The Egyptians tried to hinder them from going out of Egypt, but they could not. God brought 'em out with a stony hand and an outstretched arm. Pharaoh hung back a long time, but was resolved to hold 'em and not to let 'em go. At last, in a fit of great anger, he opposed God's plagues. Pharaoh bid 'em go and serve God in the land, but Moses told him "no," he must let them go out of the land. Then God inflicted more plagues, and Pharaoh said that he would let the Israelites go, but they should not go far away. Then God inflicted more plagues, and Pharaoh consented to let them go, but they must leave their children behind. Moses told him "no," they must go with their young and their old, their sons and their daughters, along with their herds.

Upon this Pharaoh was angry and swore, and was enraged to have his slaves talk at this rate. However, upon God's plaguing him more, he was brought to consent that they could take their little ones too, but he would have their flocks and their herds. But Moses told him "no," but their cattle must go with them too, and that there should not be a hoof left behind.

Upon this Pharaoh was greatly enraged and bid him to be gone out his presence, and that he would see his face no more. He told him that he would die on the day that he saw his face again. But Moses told him that for all this, he would not only be forced to let him go, but that his great men and servants would be made to come and bow down themselves to Moses and entreat them to go.

This was most contrary to Pharaoh's pride, but they were brought to it; they could not help it; they were glad at last not only to let them go, but to give them silver, gold, and precious stones to get rid of 'em.

When Pharaoh had recovered his courage a little and pursued them, he could not do it. Thus they could no more hinder them. God carried them on eagles' wings so that none could stop them in their flight. Again, they were kept safe from all Egypt's plagues; there were no flies, no hail, no light in their dwellings, not a dog moved his tongue. While Egypt was destroyed with storms and tempests, the children of Israel were on eagles' wings above all and were not hurt. The waters of the sea did not overwhelm them as it did the Egyptians.

3. We may observe what God accomplished by these things. God brought them to Himself in a strange land. They were in an idolatrous country, banished from God's presence, as it were, separated from God. But God brought them out and brought 'em to Mt. Sinai, the place of the special manifestation of His presence and a type of heaven. He brought 'em to Himself and for Himself, to treat them in a correct way and for them to worship and serve Him more freely and truly without corruption. And He was carrying them to Canaan, to His holy habitation, the land He had chosen for this special presence.

DOCTRINE: God carries His people along through the world to their glory far above the reach of all their enemies, or anything that might hinder their blessedness.

PROPOSITION 1. God designs His people for glory. God had chosen the children of Israel for His own peculiar treasure; and it was His design to bring 'em out of Egypt to Himself, to bring 'em to Mt. Sinai, and to bring 'em to Canaan, to His holy habitation, for He was determined and resolved upon it. So it is His design to bring all His spiritual Israel to the heavenly Canaan and Mt. Zion so that there they may dwell in glory forever. The glory of the saints consists in God's bringing them to Himself, His bringing them into the nearest union to Himself, His bringing them to a perfect and sinless conformity to Himself, His bringing them to His immediate, glorious presence, His bringing them to see Him, and His bringing them to the full enjoyment of His love.

In these things consists the highest possible blessedness of the rational creature. And to this blessedness God is immediately determined to bring all His saints. 'Tis what He purposed in Himself from before the world was, and He has often declared this purpose, and in various ways, ever since the world began. 'Tis what He has often promised to them, and He has confirmed His promise with an oath the more to manifest the immutability of His counsel.

Whatever men design with respect to God's people, yet this is God's design; their enemies often design other things. Satan designs quite the contrary; wicked men often design nothing but their calamity and misery—but God designs their perfect and immortal glory and blessedness. They are vessels prepared forordained to glory (Romans 9:23).

PROPOSITION 2. While God's people are in this world, God is carrying them along towards this blessedness in all His providences towards them. God designs them for glory to bring them to Himself as their last end, and their highest and ultimate happiness. And unto this God, as it were, aims and levels all His providences that happen to them and all His providences concerning them. 'Tis for this end that they are continued in this world, that here they may be prepared to be brought to God. And this therefore is the work at which all God's dispensations towards them are aimed, and the great event in which they will issue. The motion of every wheel is so ordered and directed so as to bring this about. The present life is but a journey, and all the changes and events of it are but as so many steps onwards towards their journey's end.

God, who is infinitely wise, knows the way to their blessedness, and He'll carry 'em along in that way. The saints oftentimes meet with things where they can't see how they could in any way be for their furtherance on their way to glory, or how their happiness could issue from it—but God knows. The children of Israel did not know the way through the wilderness to Canaan, but God did. He knew where to lead 'em. Once a man has believed in Christ, God makes it His own care and business to carry them along towards glory; and He does it continually every day. God is pursuing this work of carrying them to glory. Whatever providences they happen to meet with at any time, the saints may comfort themselves with this thought: This has happened to me to bring me still nearer to my heavenly Father's house. Hence Romans 8:28: "All things work together for good for them that love Him."

PROPOSITION 3. God thus carries them along through the world far above the reach of their enemies, and all that might hinder their blessedness. They are carried far above their reach in two respects:

First, nothing can by any means reach them to make them miserable. 'Tis impossible that anyone who is a true saint could be ruined or made miserable. If all the kings of the earth should combine, yea, the whole world of mankind; yea, if all the devils in hell should rise up together and set out to ruin one truly godly person or make him miserable, though it was only a child, they could not do it. You can as soon pull down the sun or a star out of the firmament as you can procure the ruin of a godly man.

If the earth were removed, the mountains were cast into the midst of the sea, and the waters thereof tossed t hemselves and rose, yet the godly man would be safe (Psalm 46:2–3). If the heavens and earth should be dissolved and the world should be all on fire, such would be out of reach. Neither angels nor principalities can ever make one of God's to be a miserable man.

A godly man never needs to be afraid. Psalm 46:2–3: "Therefore will not we fear, though the earth be removed, and though the mountains be carried into the midst of the sea; though the waters thereof roar and be troubled, though the mountains shake with the swelling thereof." Psalm 112:7: "He shall not be afraid of evil tidings; his heart is fixed, trusting in the LORD." Psalm 125:1: "They that trust in the LORD shall be as Mt. Zion, which cannot be removed, but abideth forever." Psalm 91:7: "A thousand shall fall at thy side, and ten thousand at thy right hand; but it shall not come nigh thee."

Second, they can't so reach 'em as to hinder their happiness; they not only cannot ruin and undo them or make them miserable, but they can't hinder them from being exceedingly happy and blessed. They can't hinder them from being in a happy state and condition here; neither can they possibly keep 'em out of heaven, as the Egyptians could not keep the children of Israel from going to Canaan by all that they could do.

If a man believes in Christ, he must be happy whatever happens; he must and will be happy in spite of all that earth and hell can do to hinder it. But to descend a little to particulars as to how God carries 'em above:

• They are above the reach of the changes of the world in those respects mentioned. The saints live here in an evil world, and one thing that makes it so that is a world that is so full of changes. 'Tis upon this account that it is such a dangerous world; it is like the foam on the surface of the water, exceedingly changeable and unstable, fluctuating and unstable. 'Tis a world very full of storms and tempests. But whenever changes happen in the world, however great and many, yet they can't reach them. The world's changes may be such as to overthrow the mightiest kings, the strongest kingdoms, and the greatest empires.

They may alter the whole face of the world, yet they can't overthrow one saint. If God's judgments are abroad in the earth and there are overflowing scourges, if it is a time of public calamity, yet the godly are out of reach. Thus, when God sent the prophet Isaiah to warn of approaching judgments, He directed him to tell the righteous man that it would be well with him (Isaiah 3:10).

The righteous may be afflicted; they may be sorely afflicted, and yet they may be said to be out of the reach of afflictions. Afflictions can't reach their main interest; they can't hurt 'em as to that. The afflictions and calamities of the world are like floods of water, but the godly won't sink. They can't sink in these floods. Let them come in never such an abundance, yet the godly man won't sink; he'll be borne up atop, as it was with Noah. When all the world was drowned, he was borne up on the top of the deluge. Though the flood waters overwhelmed the tops of the highest mountains, yet they could not overwhelm him. Afflictions may be like fire, the flames of which may rage very fiercely, yet they shall not kindle upon the godly, as God has promised. Isaiah 43:2: "When thou passest through the waters, I will be with thee; and through the rivers, they shall not overflow thee; when thou walkest through the fire, thou shalt not be burned; neither shall the flame kindle upon thee."

God carries His people on eagles' wings so high that they are, as it were, above the clouds; so high that they are as far above the storms and tempests of the world that they cannot reach them.

- The malice of wicked men can't reach them. Wicked men may hate them, they may wish their ruin, and may endeavor it, but they can't effect it. Though they are kings and mighty potentates, they can't effect it. Wicked men may reproach and revile them, though they may persecute them, though they can kill the body, yet they can't reach them. None of these things really hurt . They don't make 'em miserable; nor will it at all hinder their blessedness; nay, it shall be so ordered that it shall promote their blessedness. Wicked men can do no more to make a godly man truly miserable or to hinder their true happiness than they can to put out the brightness of the sun or hinder its future shining.

Fourth, Christ has bid them not to fear them who can kill the body and have no more that they can do. They need not fear what men can do to them (Psalm 56).

- They are above the reach of all the devils in hell. The devils have a great spite against all mankind, but especially against the godly and would fain make them miserable if they could; they would hinder their happiness and make them miserable if they could. But the godly are out of their reach; they are carried on angels' wings so high that the devil, that roaring lion, though he sees them and longs for their blood, yet cannot catch them to make a prey of them.

Satan can tempt them but, by his temptation, he never can persuade them to forsake God and desert the cause of Jesus Christ; he can afflict them, but he can't destroy them; his afflictions will be made to turn to their good. A believer in Jesus Christ is more out of the reach of Satan than our first parents were in their innocence. Satan found means to procure their fall and to work their ruin; but this is impossible with respect to a believer in Christ.

- Death can't hurt them; they may truly be said, in a good

sense, to also be above the reach of death; they aren't under the power of death as are all the rest of mankind. Death is rather under their power and is their servant. This king of terrors can't reach them with his venom and sting; he can't reach them so as to do them any hurt. Death is one of the enemies of the saints (1 Corinthians 15: 22). But the godly get the victory over their enemy and triumph over it, saying, "Death, where is thy sting?"

2. I am come briefly to show how that it is in God that they are then above their reach, give the reasons why they are above the reach of those enemies and evils, and to show how they are safe from them in God.

The love of God is inalienable from them. He has loved them from eternity, and it is not from their loveliness. He loves them though they sin. Romans 8:31: "If God be for us, who can be against us?" And verse 38: "For I am persuaded that neither death, nor life, nor angels, nor principalities, nor powers, nor things present, nor things to come, nor height, nor depth, nor any other creature, shall be able to separate us from the love of God, which is in Christ Jesus our Lord." Jeremiah 31:3: "I have loved thee with everlasting love." John 13:1: "Having loved His own, He loved them to the end."

God's covenant is sure, and all things shall work together for the good of them who love Him. Christ has said that "none shall pluck them out of My hands" (John 10:28). 2 Thessalonians 3:3: "The Lord is faithful who shall establish you and keep you from evil."

His power is sufficient to keep you safe. We are "kept by the power of God through faith" (1 Peter 1:5).

Christ is all always at the right hand of God to make intercession for them. This is what He prayed for on earth in John 17:11: "Father, keep through Thine own name those whom Thou hast given Me." And verse 15: "I pray not that Thou shouldest take them out of the world, but that Thou shouldest keep them from the evil." Hebrews 7:25 speaks of Christ as being He "who ever liveth to make intercession."

APPLICATION

USE OF EXHORTATION. Let this influence sinners to turn to God and embrace a life of holiness. If you do so you will be embraced by God, and what peculiar favor you will be admitted to upon it; how mercifully God will deal with you. He will carry you on eagles' wings, which intimates the great love and tenderness God will have for you, the regard He will have for your welfare as a Father in thus carefully protecting you and carrying you through the world to your blessedness. The expression holds forth the like tender regard and care as that of Christ from Matthew 23:37: "How often would I have gathered thy children together, even as a hen gathereth her chickens under her wings." And Deuteronomy 32:11–12, which is parallel to that text: "As an eagle stirreth up her nest, fluttereth over her young, spreadeth abroad her wings, taken them, beareth them on her wings, so the LORD alone did lead him, and there was no strange god with him."

What a privilege and happiness it is to have God thus take care of man's welfare, to secure us from all harm, and to carry us safely through the world. This shall be your happiness if you will forsake your sins and turn to God. God will take care of you as an eagle does her young ones, and will carry you along through the world towards your eternal blessedness, far out of the reach of all enemies and danger. Here consider:

- How many, how strong, and how cruel your enemies are.

The world is full of your enemies who are against you and seek your destruction. They seek no less than your life; nor is it a mere, temporal death that they seek to bring upon you, but eternal death. All the devils in hell are your enemies, and doubtless there are thousands and millions of 'em; and there is not one of 'em but what would be glad for your ruin. And they are seeking to bring it about by all the means that they can. Doubtless there are many consultations in hell on how to make sure of your ruin.

Those enemies aren't only in hell, but they are roaming to and fro on the earth; the air swarms with them; the air is full of 'em. Therefore Satan is said to be the prince of the power of the air. They are forever vigilant and active; they are about you night and day, watching for opportunities, contriving snares, plying and endeavoring to work your ruin. They encompass you before and behind, longing to satiate their cruelty in your destruction. The mouths of these lions that skulk around you thirst for your blood; they long to rend and devour you and make prey of you.

Wherever you go, you do, as it were, walk among serpents, every one of which is a thousand times more venomous and cruel than the viper or rattlesnake. How dreadful it is to be lost of God, defenseless among all these, and how highly privileged are they whom God carries on eagles' wings, far above their reach. If God doesn't protect you, these enemies have a great advantage against you; for the world is full of instruments for 'em to make use of, and your own hearts are full of lusts to betray you to them.

How terrible an enemy death is when it has its sting, and persons are left to its power; what horrors, just amazement, and dire, dreadful issues attend it. How dreadful death is when it is an inlet to eternal death, and how blessed they are who are carried above its reach. If you had but a little sense of the strength and cruelty of your enemies and of how greatly you are exposed to them, then you would be sensible that it is an unspeakable privilege thus to be safeguarded by God.

• Consider what great blessedness God will carry you to. He won't only keep you safe from enemies, but will bring you to Himself. And how much better is this for you. You shall not only go through the world in safety from your enemies, but when you have gotten through, then you shall enter into a state of eternal rest and joy, into a world where there are no more enemies who seek your hurt and ruin, where your peace never more shall be disturbed nor your joy interrupted.

How happy it is when you have gotten through the world to be received up with songs into immortal glory. How much better this is than to be swallowed up by your enemies, to be a prey to the roaring lion, to be fixed by devils, to be hurried down to hell, there to dwell, to be tormented by him and to be tormented with him to all eternity.

Why, how good will it be, after you have gotten through all the harms and tempests in your voyage, to enter with full sails into a fair, calm, and serene heaven, and to land on the heavenly shore. How much better this is than to sink and be swallowed up in the whirlpools of the bottomless gulf of woe and misery.

• Consider how happy and great a privilege it is to be in such a state as to have an infallible security of eternal glory, to be so carried along through the world towards glory that nothing can in any way reach you to hinder your going there. This is a greater privilege than our first parents had when they never had been guilty of any sin at all. They were not infallibly secure of eternal life, as is proved by the event.

Yea, this is a greater privilege than the angels in glory had in the state wherein they were created, a greater privilege than those who are now angels of light had, than any archangel in heaven had before they were confirmed. Those were all capable of failing of eternal life, and were not infallibly sure that they would not fail till they were confirmed in it.

Here I will mention two things you must do in order to obtain those great privileges which, if you do, you shall obtain them. First, you must choose that spiritual happiness that is to be had in God for your portion. If you choose this happiness for your portion, God will carry you safely through the world to it; you shall infallibly have it; nothing shall hinder your being brought to it; no, all the devils in the hell shall not hinder it. But you must prefer this before all; you must set your heart chiefly on this; you must sell all for this.

Second, you must put your trust in God for safety; this is all that God requires. If you will come to God through Christ and commit yourself to His care and rest in His sufficiency and faithfulness, you shall be safe. Proverbs 29:25: "Whoso putteth his trust in the LORD shall be safe."

USE OF CONSOLATION. Let this doctrine be of consolation to the godly under the troubles they meet with in the world. Make sure of this under all the outward afflictions, reproaches, ill will of men, persecutions, and buffetings from Satan, though he sometimes seems as though he will swallow you up. Consider this when it seems as if God is hiding His face, when you are under fears of death, or in the immediate approaches of it.

The godly have this glorious end to think of, that God is carrying them to glory, their eternal blessedness, though they can't see how. And 'tis your duty to rejoice in all things.

CHAPTER FOUR

The Grace of God in the New Covenant Eminently Appears in that We Are Justified Only by Faith

f

"Therefore it is of faith that it might be by grace."

ROMANS 4:16

The apostle in this chapter is arguing for the truth of the doctrine of justification by faith only from the instance of Abraham. The apostle mentions this instance as that which would be most likely to be of weight with the Jews who were the principal opposers of this doctrine because the thing that they so highly valued in themselves was that they were the children of Abraham, and supposed that they had a right to the blessings of the covenant of Abraham by virtue of their being circumcised and their observance of other legal rites that were peculiar to the children of Abraham according to the flesh.

The apostle, therefore, to convince them, shows that Abraham himself, to whom God first gave the ordinance of circumcision, was not justified by works, but by faith only. And this he evinces in several ways: First, in that the Scripture says expressly that Abraham believed God and it was counted to him for righteousness. Second, he was justified before circumcision, the work which the Jews above all others built upon for justification. Romans 4:10: "How was it then reckoned? When he was in circumcision, or in uncircumcision? Not in circumcision, but in uncircumcision." And in verse 11 he argues that circumcision was so far from being that by which he was justified that it was a seal of the justification which he had already received; it was a seal of the righteousness of faith which he had yet being uncircumcised. Third, he argues that Abraham was not justified by the works of the law, but by faith, because the promise that he would be the heir of the world was not to Abraham or to his seed through the law, but through the righteousness of faith. 'Tis in this promise that God's covenant with Abraham chiefly consisted; and this promise was not through the law. That is evident because it was a gracious promise; it was a promise made of God's mere pleasure and sovereign grace. If the promise were made through the law the promise would be of no effect because the law works wrath; there are none of the seed of Abraham who could ever perfectly keep the law. And so, if the covenant was made through the law, the promise never would have been fulfilled to us, as we see in verses 13–15. But the promise was not through the law, but of faith; and so it was a gracious promise of sovereign grace that surmounts our transgressions and unworthiness. It is sure to all the seed; otherwise none of the seed of Abraham would have obtained it. "Therefore it is of faith that it might be by grace to the end that the promise might be sure to all the seed."

DOCTRINE: The grace of God in the New Covenant eminently appears in that, according to the tenor of that covenant, it proposes that we are justified only by faith.

The goodness of God appeared in the first covenant, which proposed justification by works. It was an act of God's goodness and condescension towards man to enter into any covenant at all with him, and that He would become engaged to give eternal life to him upon his perfect obedience. But the second covenant that God has entered into with us since we broke the first one, may, by way of distinction, be called the covenant of grace. The free, sovereign, and rich grace of God appears in a manner very distinguishing; and the grace of God in it appears eminently in that it proposes justification by faith alone.

In order to clear up this doctrine, we will, first, inquire what justification is; second, what justifying faith is; third, what is meant when it is said that we are justified by faith alone; and, fourth, how free grace eminently appears in this way of justification.

Upon the first of these inquiries, as to what justification is, I shall not insist, but shall only say that nothing else seems to be intended by it than a man's being looked upon by God as having righteousness belonging to him, and God's judging it as meet that he should be dealt with as such. There is a two-fold righteousness: There is a negative righteousness, which consists only in a freedom from guilt. Such a righteousness Adam had; therefore, when God justifies a man, He looks upon him as being free from guilt. Therefore one part of the justification of a fallen man consists in the pardon of sin, or imputing Christ's death and sufferings to him.

Then there is a positive righteousness. This is something more than a mere freedom from guilt, and consists in the actual fulfillment of a law, such as Adam would have had if he had withstood the temptation and had persevered in obedience. Therefore, another part of our justification consists in the imputation of perfect obedience to us. If God looks upon a man as having such a righteousness, both negative and positive, belonging to him, He therein justifies him whether this righteousness belonging to him is performed personally—as Adam, our first parent, would have been justified had he stood firm, and as the elect angels have been justified—or whether some other person has performed it for him, whose act God sees fit to accept for him. Justification then pertains not only to God's determination that righteousness belongs to a man, but His giving them an answerable treatment, that is, the enjoyment of His favor and eternal life.

2. The next inquiry concerns the nature of justifying faith and what it is. I don't here speak of the grace of faith in its most general extent; there are acts and exercise of faith considered in its more general nature that yet aren't such exercises. The grace of faith in its more general nature is a sense and conviction of the truth and goodness of divine revelation, in general, God's sufficiency and His truth, and so of the truth and goodness of all revelation. Thus it is by faith that we believe that the worlds were made (Hebrews 11:3). But this act of faith is not justifying. Justifying faith is a sense and conviction of the reality and excellency of Christ as a Savior that entirely inclines and unites the heart to Him. This is the act of the whole soul, of every faculty, entirely embracing and acquiescing in the gospel that reveals Jesus Christ as our Saviour. The soul that

truly believes in Christ asserts, accords, and symphonizes with the revelation of Christ as our Redeemer. There is an entire yielding of the mind and heart to it, a closing with it with the belief, with the inclination, and with the affection. It being the complex act of the whole soul, and of each faculty together, it is difficult to perfectly describe it in a few words. We will therefore briefly consider it by the parts:

There is in justifying faith an entire sense and conviction of the reality of Christ as a Savior, which the understanding embraces and acquiesces to. There is a full conviction of the truth of the gospel, and a realizing sense of things that are declared in it concerning Jesus the Redeemer and His salvation, concerning Jesus' acts and sufferings; indeed, that these things are true, and that Jesus is the Son of God and that He is the Savior of mankind; that the way of salvation by Him as declared in the Word of God is the very way of life, and that what God tells us of the designs of His grace in Christ is true; that the promises of the gospel are really true; that the account we have of the scheme and contrivance for the redemption of mankind is not fable, but a great reality, a conviction of the reality of Christ.

Believing the truth of the gospel is a great and a main thing that constitutes justifying faith, as is evident by many passages of Scripture. One in particular is John 20:31: "These things are written that ye might believe that Jesus is the Christ, the Son of God, and that believing ye might have life through His name." John 8:24: "I said therefore unto you that ye should die in your sins; for if ye believe not that I am He, ye shall die in your sins." 2 Thessalonians 2:13: "God hath chosen you to salvation through sanctification of the Spirit and belief of the truth."

But it is not any kind of believing the truth of the gospel that is justifying faith, for there may be a sort of assent to the truth of the gospel without any true grace. The devils believe and tremble; persons have a belief from education; and the thing may appear plausible and probable from moral arguments. But these things will never make the soul have a sense of the reality and certainty of the gospel. He who savingly believes the gospel believes it from it intrinsic evidence; they see those intrinsic characters of divinity in it; they see it to be divine; they see that it is from God, for they see God in it. Thus the disciples believed and were sure that their Master was the Christ, the Son of the living God (John 6:69). They were not convinced so much by ratiocination merely, for flesh and blood had not revealed it to 'em, as Christ tells Peter in Matthew 16:17. But the Father in heaven had revealed to 'em the divine glory of their Master.

This brings me to the second thing about justifying faith: It is a sense and conviction of the excellency of Christ as a Savior. There is a sense of the goodness of Christ as well as a sense of the truth about Christ. Justifying in Scripture is sometimes called "knowing Christ" because it is being acquainted with His excellency as Savior that is generally understood. Isaiah 53:11: "By His knowledge shall My righteous Servant justify many." John 17:3: "This is eternal life, that they may know Thee, the only true God, and Jesus Christ whom Thou hast sent."

'Tis not so much a sense of the excellency of Christ's person absolutely considered, as His excellency as a Saviour—though that includes a sense of the excellency of His Person. This includes a sense of the need we stand in of this Savior. We aren't sensible of His excellency as our Savior if we think that He is a needless Savior. There is therefore a sense of our helplessness and unworthiness. Matthew 15:26–28: "Truth, Lord; yet the dogs eat of the crumbs which fall from their master's table. Then Jesus answered and said unto her, 'O woman, great is thy faith.' " So also Luke 7:6 and following, concerning the centurion, where he says, "I am not worthy that thou shouldest enter under my roof." Whereupon Christ says, "I have not found so great faith, no, not in Israel."

There also belongs a sense of Christ's sufficiency as a Savior, His fitness for the work. The sufficiency of a Savior is a great part of His excellency. Thus the woman who had the issue of blood said within herself, "If I may but touch the hem of His garment I shall be whole." And Christ bids her to be of good comfort, for her faith had made her whole (Matthew 9:21–22). In Romans 4:21 Abraham's faith is commended: "that he was fully persuaded that what God had promised He was able also to perform."

There is in faith a sense of the sufficiency of Christ's righteousness, of His power and grace. John 16:8: "When that Holy Ghost is come He shall convince the world of righteousness and of judgment." To the excellency of Christ as a Savior belongs also a sense of the excellency of His way of salvation. The believing soul has a sense and conviction of this. The way of salvation by the mediation and righteousness of Christ appears glorious, excellent, and lovely in His eyes, such as is suitable to his case, excellently adapted to the needs of His soul. The Person of the Savior appears excellent, as it did to Thomas, whose faith was drawn forth and he said, "My Lord and my God."

This salvation that He wrought out, the blessedness that He purchased, consists much in holiness and the enjoyment of God. The faith of God's people partly consists in that they embrace with high esteem the salvation and glory that Christ has purchased.

Third, this sense and conviction entirely inclines and unites the heart to Christ as Savior. It is evident by the Word of God that justifying faith is not only an act of the understanding, but also of the heart and inclination; there is consent as well as assent. Matthew 23:37: "How often I would have gathered you to Myself, but ye would not." It is gladly receiving the gospel (Acts 2:41). 'Tis often called "obeying the gospel" or "obeying from the heart the form of doctrine," which signifies something more than the assent of the understanding. It implies a yielding of the whole soul. 'Tis receiving the love of the truth (2 Thessalonians 2:10). It is the opposite of disallowing or rejecting Christ, as is evident by 1 Peter 2:7: "Unto you which believe, He is precious; but to them which are disobedient, the stone which the builders disallowed . . . ." It is a true conviction of the reality and excellency of Christ; it causes an adherence of the soul to Him. It brings the soul that before was remote to close with Him; and therefore 'tis expressed by coming to Christ, by looking to Him, by opening the door to let Him in, by hearing His voice and following Him.

To believe is to have the heart drawn to Christ. John 6:44: "None can come unless the Father draweth him." The believing soul rests in Christ as being a Savior who is entirely suitable to his inclination; he is satisfied and hungers nor thirsts any more. The heart cleaves to Him and rests in Him in dependence.

Believing is trusting in Him. Romans 15:12: "In Him shall the Gentiles trust." 2 Timothy 1:12: "I know whom I have believed, and I am persuaded that He is able to keep that which I have committed unto Him." Therefore it was typified by flying to the city of refuge of old.

3. We come now to inquire what is meant when it is said that we are justified by faith only. This inquiry divides itself into two parts: How we are justified by faith, and how we are not justified by works.

What is meant when it is said that we are justified by faith? 'Tis generally said that faith justifies as the condition. God has fixed this as the condition of justification. But this doesn't perfectly explain the matter because there is something of ambiguity in the expression. In one sense of the word, Christ alone performs the condition of our justification. He has performed that which God looks upon as necessary to belong to the fallen creature in order that he should be freed from an obligation to punishment, and have a right to eternal life. In another sense of the word, there are other graces besides faith that may be the condition of justification—if we mean by "condition" anything that may be put into a conditional proposition, or that with which we shall be justified, and without which we shall not. Such is love for God; and so obedience is a condition of justification; so repentance is a condition of justification. And therefore we often find these things put into conditional propositions in Scripture, such as "he that confesseth and forsaketh his sin shall find mercy." And "the Lord hath promised a crown of life to them that love Him." And "if ye forgive men their trespasses, your heavenly Father will forgive you."

Faith is that upon the account of which God judges it meet that they should be looked upon as having Christ's righteousness belonging to 'em. God sees it meet that some men rather than others should have Christ's righteousness imputed to 'em, or should be looked upon as having Christ's righteousness belonging to 'em. And it is doubtless upon actually belonging to 'em. This is the qualification that God has respect to in our own faith, upon the account of which God in His wisdom, sees it proper that they should have an actual communion with Christ in His righteousness, and that because faith is the grace that most directly and immediately unites the soul to Christ as a Savior. It is the proper act of receiving Him or closing with Him as a Savior; and though we can't be justified without other graces, yet we are not and shall not be justified without them, but we are not justified by them because they are not what God has respect to, or that upon the account of which He judges it proper that men should be looked upon as being in Christ, and so having an interest in His righteousness.

It may next be inquired how we are not justified by works. This inquiry needs to be made in order to know how far faith influences in the matter of justification, because the act of faith itself is a work. Therefore, when it is said that we are not justified by works, nothing else is implied than that nothing that we do procures acceptance for us with God. The justification of God does not come to us by virtue of any goodness, comeliness, or profitableness in us; 'tis not by reason of any influence we have; nothing that we do can move God's favorable respect, or attract Him, or influence Him, or incline Him to abate His anger or receive us into favor.

In the first covenant, respect was had to the goodness or loveliness of works in fixing them as the condition of life. But 'tis not so under the second covenant. God doesn't justify us on the account of faith, on the account of its loveliness, but only because it is that by which we receive Christ and have our souls united to Him. And so, having so received Christ, and being so united to Him, God judges it proper, in His wisdom and sovereignty, that we should be looked upon as being in Him, and so having His righteousness to be ours.

4. We now come to show how the free grace of the New Covenant eminently appears in that it proposes justification only by faith. We are taught that we are justified freely through grace (Romans 3:24), and it appears in that we are justified only by faith. Ephesians 2: 7–8: ". . . that in the ages to come He might show the exceeding riches of His grace in His kindness towards us through Jesus Christ, for by grace are ye saved through faith." And that will appear if we consider wherein the

freedom of a gift consists.

There are but three things that contribute to the freedom of a gift: First, when a gift is given to an offender without satisfaction being made by him. But our being justified by faith in the satisfaction of another evidently shows that it is not so upon the account of any satisfaction made by ourselves. Second, when the gift is given without any expectation that the giver will receive any profit by it. This also appears by our being justified only by faith. God has not been in time past obliged by the receipt of any benefit from us; it is not given in recompense for any kindness we have done; for then it is not only and merely by faith, but works. It shows that it is not from any expectation of benefit hereafter inasmuch as faith is only the soul's receiving of Christ and His salvation. Third, when it is given without worthiness or without any excellency in our persons or actions to move the giver to bestow love and beneficence; for it certainly shows the more abundant and overflowing goodness or inclination to communicate good by how much less loveliness and worthiness there is to attract beneficence. For one with but little goodness may be drawn by abundant beauty to do good. But he whose goodness is more abundant can find in his heart to do good to the less deserving. Justification's being only by faith shows that it is not for any excellency or loveliness of ours, seeing that it is only for receiving the salvation that is offered to everyone who believes. It is, as it were, offered to everyone who will accept it without any consideration of their worthiness or unworthiness. Revelation 22:17: "Whosoever will, let him come and take of the waters of life freely."

APPLICATION

1. How much do those doctrines derogate from the glory of
the New Covenant that teach justification in any other way than
that of faith alone? Notwithstanding the fact that Scripture is
so plain and full in this matter, there have been and are many
who maintain contrary doctrines, and who despise those who
do maintain this doctrine and call them "soli-fidians." Though
they own the Scriptures to be the Word of God and affirm that it
is true, yet they pervert its meaning by their subtle explications;
they so explain it as to make it speak what they would.

The great part of the Church of Rome denies this doctrine;
the Socinians deny it in the sense in which it has now been
explained. Likewise, 'tis also vehemently opposed and ridiculed
by the Arminians in the sense in which it has been explained;
they maintain justification upon the account of sincere obedience. They hold that, seeing we have broken the first
covenant that proposed perfect obedience as the condition of
justification, now God has given us another covenant wherein
sincere obedience is proposed in its place. And herein they
suppose the grace of the New Covenant appears in that, seeing
we have made ourselves incapable of performing perfect
obedience, God will take up with sincere though imperfect
obedience in place of it. They suppose that Christ has satisfied
for the imperfections of our obedience and has purchased an
abatement of the strictness of the terms of justification, that is,
the perfection of obedience for us, and has made God willing
to accept imperfection in the place of it. They hold indeed that
faith has something to do in the affair of justification, but 'tis
principally as a good work, as a part of evangelical obedience,
and not merely as a reception of Christ.

If our doctrine is true, they exceedingly derogate from the

glory of the gospel, or New Covenant, which so much consists in the grace of it. Was it not a great and main design of God in the gospel to magnify the riches and sovereignty of His grace? Doubtless, therefore, such doctrines are very displeasing to God.

2. See how much they dishonor the gospel who trust in their own righteousness for justification. They rob it of its main glory to recommend them to God's acceptance. Thus do all they who entertain hopes of recommending themselves to God's acceptance by any excellency or loveliness of their persons or actions. Their practice therein is directly opposite to this doctrine, whether they directly hope, by their goodness or love-liness, to move God to pass by all their sins and to accept them to eternal life, or only hope in some measure to move God to abate something of His anger and to make Him somehow more placable and to draw His pity. If they only expect that God should be moved by their works to be willing to give 'em faith, or that they may have something to be justified by, or that Christ may be more willing to accept them when they come to Him by faith—if they only do thus, yet this is in effect trusting in their own righteousness for justification, because if God is inclined by their righteousness to give 'em faith so that they may be justified, that argues that He has already in some measure accepted them to favor for their own righteousness' sake, inasmuch as He is inclined to show them mercy and to give 'em faith for it. And if He is more ready to accept 'em when they come to Him by faith for their goodness, then He doesn't accept them merely because they believe, but partly for their own excellency.

3. What cause we have we to praise God, seeing that His grace so eminently and gloriously appears in the manner of justification proposed by it. We have justification offered to

us only for our acceptance of Christ, notwithstanding all our unworthiness and provocations. God is willing to freely pardon and accept us into favor, and to bestow eternal life upon us, on the account of the righteousness of another, that we were at no pains to work out, on the account of sufferings that we had no share in.

Let us be exhorted earnestly to seek that we may be the subjects of the wonderful grace of the New Covenant so that His grace may be manifested and glorified in us. What reason have we to come and praise God the Father, who provided such a redemption for us, and in this way justifies us, as well as to praise the Lord Jesus Christ, who is our righteousness.

4. This doctrine should put us upon examining whether we have ever exercised a justifying faith, so that we may know whether we are the subjects of this wonderful grace of the New Covenant. Let us try ourselves by that description that has been given of justifying faith. Have we ever had a sense and thorough conviction of the reality and excellency of Christ as a Savior? Does the gospel that reveals these things about the Savior seem real and certain to us from the evident characteristics of truth that we see in it, or from the divine glory of it that has been revealed to our souls? Have we ever seen the excellent fullness of Christ? Have we been convinced of the loveliness and suitableness of the way of salvation? Have we had such a sense of those things as has entirely inclined us to Christ Jesus, and to His way of salvation? Has it caused us with our whole hearts to adhere to it and acquiesce in and take complacence in it?

Let us not deceive ourselves by any kind of assent of the understanding to the gospel without the answerable according and symphonizing of the inclination and will, and the yielding of the whole soul. On the other hand, let us not deceive ourselves without any joys and affections that are not accompanied with such a conviction of the understanding of the truth and reality of the gospel from the discoveries of its glory.

5. Let us earnestly seek faith in Jesus Christ, which is the qualification that God has a primary respect to in imparting Christ's righteousness to men. And that we may be successful therein, let us especially do these three things:

First, let us labor after those things that are preparatory to a sense of our sinfulness and misery. Seek for a conviction by the law; think much of divine threatnings and our exposedness to damnation. Daily meditate on the dreadfulness of God's anger and our own helplessness.

Second, let us well improve the means of it: the Word and ordinances.

Third, let us earnestly seek the Author of it. Let us be much and earnest in prayer to God, for faith is the gift of God. Ephesians 2:8: "for by grace are ye saved through faith." Let us beg earnestly of God that He would command the light to shine into our dark hearts and fulfill in us all the good pleasure of His goodness (2 Thessalonians 1:11).

CHAPTER FIVE

Wicked Men's Sins Lie at Their Door

"If thou dost not well, sin lieth at the door."

GENESIS 4:7

*T*hese words are what God says to Cain on the occasion of his being wroth for God's having respect to his brother Abel's offering, and for not having respect to his. He was wroth at God and wroth at his brother. He was wroth with his brother and hated him because he envied him. Abel was his younger brother, and he looked upon himself as superior to him and better than he. He could not bear it that God would prefer his brother, and he hated him upon that account. The like spirit is sometimes seen nowadays: men sometimes have a spirit against their wives, their younger brothers, or other inferiors because God accepts them and

66

shows them mercy to those who are their inferiors and doesn't show mercy to them.

Cain was wroth with God for having respect to his brother's offering and for rejecting his. He had a quarreling spirit towards God that He should accept his younger brother, whom he judged less worthy. It is said that Cain was very wroth and his countenance fell. There is much of the same spirit nowadays in some who quarrel with God for showing mercy to others whom they look upon as less worthy than they, and not showing mercy to them.

God in this verse expostulates with Cain about the unreasonableness of his wrath: "If thou doest well, shalt not thou be accepted? But if thou dost not well, sin lieth at the door."

Cain was displeased with God, as though He were partial and had respect of persons in accepting his younger brother before him. But God argues the unreasonableness of his thus charging God, when the fault was altogether with himself: "If thou doest well, shalt not thou be accepted?" that is, "You shall be accepted as well as Abel if you do well."

Cain thought that he had done well for, in the matter of outward things, their actions were alike. He brought an offering to God of the fruit of the ground; he was a tiller of the ground, and he thought he did well in bringing some of the fruits of it as an offering to God as well as Abel did in bringing some of his flock.

But God, who does not see as man sees, who does not look on the outward appearance, but who looks at the heart, saw a difference. It was not because the fruits of the ground that Cain offered were not good in themselves that God did not accept them, but because the heart that he offered them with was not good. Abel offered his offering with faith and Cain did not. Hebrews

11:4: "By faith Abel offered a more excellent sacrifice than Cain."

Thus God intimates to Cain the reasons of his not being accepted. He offered what he did outwardly, as to the matter of it, yet he did wickedly because he did what he did with an insincere heart; and therefore sin lay at the door to hinder his acceptance and to procure His displeasure.

DOCTRINE: Wicked men's sins lie at their door.

Here I will explain what is implied in this doctrine and give reasons for it.

1. The sins that they have committed, all of them, as to the guilt of them, still remain. The particular sins that they commit, as to the act of them, soon cease and are past; wicked men, very commonly, when the act is over, see nothing but that they are as they were before. Proverbs 30:20: "She eateth and wipeth her mouth, and saith, 'I have done no wickedness.' " Wicked men will often multiply their sins; they will add one sin to another and are little sensible that anything remains of their sin to do them any hurt. Sins, as to the act of them, are vanishing things, but as to the guilt of them, not as to the influence and fruit of them.

When men have sinned, it may be that nothing visible remains. They look as they did before; their sin has not altered their visage or outward appearance; no visible filth or deformity remains; they don't see but that they are as clean and pure as they were before. As there is nothing remaining that they can see, so neither is there anything remaining that they can feel; they don't feel it as when they have wounded themselves. They can feel the pain of it remaining afterwards, but they feel no pain of any wound after they have committed sin.

But there is something invisible that remains; the guilt

of sin remains. There is not one sin that they have ever been guilty of, whether openly or secretly, whether in riper years or in childhood, that has vanished and is done with, though men can't see that it is any otherwise in any respect than if such a sin had never been.

They themselves aren't sensible that anything remains of a lie they told when they were children, or of an idle word, or of an unclean, wicked thought, or a profanation of the Sabbath that they were guilty of long ago. They can't perceive that anything now remains, so that it should not be as though these things had never been. Yet, notwithstanding, the guilt of it all remains; none of it is done away with; the guilt is not all lessened or worn out by length of time. Those sins remain in full force against them. They have as much concern in them now; and their sins remain in full power and influence with the committers of them as the first minute after they were committed.

Though they seem to be but little sins to them, yet, as they were sins, the guilt abides, and they can't remove it; they can't abolish it. Do what they will, those sins are still there.

It may be that they never thought much about them; they never troubled themselves much. But for all that, or if they did something at first, now 'tis so long ago that they have almost forgotten them; yet their sins have as much to do with them now as ever they had. The guilt of sin is not a thing that fades through age; time won't wear it out as it will other things.

However they may have forgotten them, yet God sees them. He saw and took notice of what they did, and He remembers it. Things may fade in their memory, but they won't fade in God's memory; they are written, every one, as in a book. Their account stands; their debts don't cease because they are old and wear out; but their account stands, all of it. None is cancelled. We read in Malachi 3:16 that a book of remembrance in is written of the good deeds of the godly; and so it is concerning the evil deeds of wicked men.

2. The guilt of their sins remains, ready to bring God's judgments and wrath on a fit occasion, as an enemy lies waiting at a man's door to destroy him. Men's sins are their enemies; not only those lusts and sinful habits that are in the heart are a man's enemies by their power and influence to move the heart to sinful acts and alienate it from God. But sinful men's natural actions may be looked upon as a man's dreadful enemies by the guilt that they contract; they seek a man's ruin, mischief, and destruction. Those are the enemies of men; without these other enemies could do them no harm. These are men's enemies, for they have the wrath of God, they have a man's death and damnation in their womb.

These enemies are always lying at a wicked man's door, day and night, watching for his destruction. As a wolf lies in ambush for his prey, and as a mortal enemy waits at a man's door for an opportunity to kill him whenever he comes forth, they are waiting for a convenient opportunity. They are waiting for God's time to destroy them; they hunt for their precious life.

Every one of the sins that ever they have committed lie at their door, waiting till they shall come forth, that is, till God in His wisdom opens the door, when His time comes, for them to do their work of ruining the man; till He sees that it is a fit and convenient time.

Wherever wicked men go, their sins attend them, still watching for their destruction. If they move from one town to another, if they cross the ocean, if they move and live in some other continent, if they move to the opposite side of the globe, their sins follow them and are yet at their heels. The iniquity of their heels compass them about (Psalm 49:5). Wherever they build their house, their sins still lie at their door, watching their destruction. So they have their house haunted with apparitions.

The curse of God and the sword of His vengeance is waiting for them (Job 15:20, 22). The wicked man is waited for by the sword. This is the flaming sword of God's wrath. Again it is said in Job 18:12 that destruction is ready at his side.

Wicked men think that the destruction awaiting their sins is far off because they see nothing. But they are mistaken; the sword is at their right hand, ready to thrust them through whenever God shall give the word.

This again is represented by the axe lying at the root of the tree that doesn't bring forth good fruit (Matthew 3:10). There it lies ready to cut it down whenever God's time comes. Justice will take it up and they shall be hewn down and cast into the fire.

Their sins have already kindled the fire of hell. Their damnation is prepared for them and is waiting for them. Eternal death does, as it were, watch for them; and therefore it is said that wicked men's damnation doesn't slumber (2 Peter 2:3). It is awake, watching and waiting to receive them. Eternal death is watching; it keeps awake; it is watching and waiting to seize them when God shall give the word. It is ready, prepared against them as a warrior is prepared with weapons of destruction, all clad in armor, ready for the battle. Job 15:24: "Trouble and anguish shall make him afraid; they shall prevail against him as a king ready to the battle."

This is again represented by the sword's being whet, the bow being bent, and the arrow being on the string and leveled at their hearts (Psalm 11:2). Nothing is wanting but only for God to give the word.

However little wicked men are sensible of it, their sins follow and pursue them wherever they go more closely than ever Saul did David. While they are eating, when they are working, when they are sleeping, their sins are nigh them, waiting and watching for their destruction. I have read of one in South America who had greatly provoked another by an abuse that he offered. He was so provoked by the ill usage that he had received from another that the governor of the place was desperately resolved to kill him who had affronted him. And accordingly, when the governor's commission expired, he made it his whole business to seek an opportunity for it. The other man, being informed of this, and resolving to avoid his enemy, moved to another place 960 miles distant, supposing that his adversary would not pursue him so far. But in less than 15 days his enemy was there with him. Upon this he took another flight 1200 miles distant from there and in little more than twenty days his adversary was with him there. Upon this he moved another 1500 miles from there. But a few days afterwards, his adversary was with him there. In this manner he pursued him for three years and four months. He who was pursued used the utmost caution to avoid his enemy, always wearing a coat of mail; but his adversary carefully watched for his life, and at last killed him in his own house and in his own bed.

Much more closely does men's guilt follow and their sins pursue them wherever they go. Wicked men's sins still lie at their door, though they may have since reformed that particular sin. Though they have avoided that sin of late, though they have curbed their lusts and denied themselves, yet there lie their old sins still. If their sins of youth were committed long ago and they have long since left them off, and though, since they have grown older, they have been more out of the way of temptation and have grown more sober, yet their sins lie at their door all their days, and lie down with them in the dust.

Job 20:11: "His bones are full of the sins of his youth; they shall lie in the dust."

Their sins lie still at their door, notwithstanding any good deeds they have done since. If they have behaved themselves well of late, if they have become sober and religious persons, yet still their old sins lie at their door. If they have from self ends been sorry for their sins, if they have been sorry that they committed their sins and wished that they never had committed them, yet still they lie at their door.

APPLICATION

USE OF AWAKENING TO SINNERS. Let all who are in an unconverted state consider that their sins lie at their door as mortal enemies, watching for their destruction. All the sins that ever you have been guilty of in your life lie there. Remember what sins you committed at such and such a time, how you yielded at such a time to your lusts, how you went against your light and did that which you knew or had reason at the same time to think was displeasing and provoking to God, and yet ventured to do, so dreadful was your presumption. You preferred a moment's sensual pleasure or a little earthly gain before a good conscience. Consider that these sins now lie at your door.

You who have been secretly guilty of lascivious actions, who have secretly indulged your impure lusts in either impure actions by yourself or wantonness with another; though what you did was in the dark and the world doesn't know of it and so doesn't look upon you the worse for it—yet your sin lies at your door. There it is day and night; it is always ready with destruction at your side, wherever you go.

You who have secretly defrauded and wronged your

neighbor, however you may make light of what you have done, yet you are not done with it; the sin lies at your door; the curse and wrath of almighty God which that sin deserves is impending every day over your head.

Look back and consider what sins you committed in your childhood. Consider what sins you committed in your youth, what sins you have committed alone and what sins you have committed with others; how sinfully you have thought, how wickedly you have talked, how you have sinned with your tongue and with your hands. Be particular in your self-reflections and consider that all these things live on in full strength, power, and force to destroy you. None of these things, as to the guilt of them, are in any measure vanished away.

Any one of your sins is a far worse enemy than any man can be, than any temporal enemy. Temporal enemies only hunt for the temporal life, but your sins seek your eternal damnation. You would be better watched over by a murderer than to have your sins, though it was but one sin, lying at your door because sin, as we observed before, has hell in its womb. The sin that lies at your door is armed with the sword of God's vengeance. Consider:

1. If your sins continue to lie at your door, they will surely do their execution first or last. If you were watched by a murderer, you might possibly use such precaution so that he would have no opportunity to execute his purpose; but the sins that lie at your door, if God doesn't take them away from thence, will surely do their execution. They lie there only waiting for God's time; and God's time will surely come, and then there will be no escaping. All the men in the world can't save you. You can't defend yourself against your sins. If you hide yourself on the top of Carmel or on the bottom of the sea, your sins will find you out. If you fortify yourself with a wall built up to heaven,

there will be no defense against these foes. By your sins you have conceived mischief, and you shall bring forth vanity (Job 15:35). "At the last it shall bite like a serpent and sting like an adder" (Proverbs 23:32).

There will be no such thing as fleeing when God's time comes. You will then be like a man who is encompassed all around by enemies with mortal weapons, and there will be no escaping. You shall be met, whatever way you endeavor to make your escape. Job 20:24: "He shall flee from the iron weapon, and the bow of steel shall strike him through." When this day comes it shall be with them as is described in Isaiah 24:18: "And it shall come to pass that he that fleeth from the noise of the fear shall fall into the pit, and he that cometh up out of the midst of the pit shall be taken in the snare; for the windows from on high are opened and the foundations of the earth do shake." It will be the day of God's wrath and there will be no escaping.

2. Your sins that lie at your door are there waiting for the appointed time of your death; that is the time for them to do their execution. They lie at your door waiting to have you come out so that they may kill you; and when that time comes, then you will come forth; then you must come forth, and then these enemies will seize you.

Wicked men's sins lie at their door when they lie upon their deathbeds. Consider how dreadful this would be if it should be your case: It will make that time a dreadful time to you; the thoughts of it then will be frightful and amazing; it will make the thoughts of approaching death amazing; it will make your hearts to tremble. But when the time comes, you must go. Wicked men are driven away in their wickedness, as Solomon expresses it in Proverbs 14:32. And they are driven from light into darkness and chased out of the world, as it is expressed in

Job 18:18 and following.

Their sins lie down with them in the dust, all the sins that ever they committed in their lives. Job 20:11: "Their bones are full of the sins of their youth." Or, as the Prophet Ezekiel expresses it, "Their iniquity shall be upon their bones" (Ezekiel 32:27).

Wicked men's sins are ready to meet with them in this world upon occasion to bring God's judgments upon them. Many things that wicked men meet with here are fruits of God's curse upon them for their sins; but when they come to die, then will they do their full execution upon them.

3. Consider that you are never safe one moment as long as sin lies at the door. Destruction is waiting for you, and you do not know when it will come upon you. Wicked men walk in slippery places, and destruction oftentimes comes upon them very suddenly. Psalm 73:18–19: "Surely thou didst set them in slippery places. Thou castedst them down into destruction. How are they brought into desolation, as in a moment! They are utterly consumed with terrors."

Oftentimes their destruction is just by when they think it far off. Job 15:23: "He knoweth not that the day of darkness is ready at hand." Their sins sometimes suddenly lay hold on them when they think nothing of it, as if they were caught in a snare that was hidden as they were walking. Job 18:8–10: "For he is cast into a net by his own feet, and he walketh upon a snare. The gin shall take him by the heel, and the robber shall prevail against him. The snare is laid for him in the ground, and a trap for him in the way."

God oftentimes brings their judgment upon them in a way that they don't think of and that they could not possibly foresee. Job 20:26: "A fire not blown shall consume him." God raises a tempest in the night when they are asleep that carries them away. Job 27:20–21: "Terrors take hold on him as waters, a tempest stealeth him away in the night. The east wind carrieth him away, and he departeth; and as a storm hurleth him out of his place."

4. Wicked men's sins often find them out and the wrath of God falls upon them in the midst of their prosperity. Job 15:21: "In prosperity the destroyer shall come upon him." While men are like a flourishing tree, taking root in the ground and spreading forth their branches, the curse comes upon them and suddenly dries up their roots and lops their branches. Job 18:16: "His roots shall be dried up beneath, and above shall his branch be cut off."

Oftentimes their sins that lie at their door seize them and do execution upon them when they are expecting and plotting on prosperity. Job 20:23: "When he is about to fill his belly, God shall cast the fury of His wrath upon him, and shall rain it upon him while he is eating."

So wicked men are never safe, and it is from stupidness that they can lie down in their beds and sleep quietly with their sins lying at their door. If they have any peace, the peace that they have is a stupid and unreasonable peace. They can never have any peace if they exercise their reason.

How can there be any safety for such, for the curse of God lies upon them? Bildad observes that brimstone is scattered upon such a man's habitation (Job 18:15). There the wrath of God abides upon them; the heavens are ready to reveal such a man's iniquity, and the earth to rise up against him (Job 20:27).

USE OF EXHORTATION. Give yourself no rest till you have obtained that your sins should be removed from your door. If they were removed, then you would dwell in safety; then you might go in and out safely, and be quiet from fear of evil. Then God would be at peace with you; then heaven and earth would be at peace with you.

And that you may be directed in this matter, consider that it is by Jesus Christ alone that they can be removed, for the blood of Christ is sufficient to take away the guilt of sin. If you go to Christ and trust in Him, He will take away these enemies from your door. If you are in Him, you shall be free from them as you travel about. It will be a glorious freedom that you enjoy.

Now when you go about, wherever you go, your sins follow you; they compass you about, seeking your destruction. But then you may go about without fear; all those enemies will forever be removed. Psalm 103:12: "As far as the east is from the west, so far hath He removed our transgressions from us." Then when you go about, instead of your sins compassing you about, Christ will be as a wall of fire, a wall of defense around you. Wherever you go, then when you lie down, instead of having your sins watching over you to destroy, you may lie down and sleep. The Lord will sustain you and the angels will pitch their tents round about you.

CHAPTER SIX

The Covenant of Grace Firm and Sure

ℱ

"Yet he hath made with me an everlasting covenant,
ordered in all things, and sure."

2 SAMUEL 23:5

These are some of the last words of David, "the man that was raised up on high, the anointed of the God of Jacob, and the sweet psalmist of Israel," as in the first verse. David had spoken much in his time—or rather the Spirit of God had spoken much by him—concerning divine things in the many psalms and spiritual songs that he composed and sang, as is intimated in his being here called "the sweet psalmist of Israel." But these, we are told, are his last words, which he probably spoke but a little before his death; and he spoke them not of himself, but by the inspiration of the

Spirit of God, as he tells us in the second and third verses.

These last words of his seem to be with relation to the Messiah that God had promised to raise up in his house, and who is the root and the offspring of David. I shall read the whole over to you:

> Now these be the last words of David. David the son of Jesse said, and the man who was raised up on high, the anointed of the God of Jacob, and the sweet psalmist of Israel, said, "The Spirit of the Lord spake by me, and His word was in my tongue. The God of Israel said, the Rock of Israel spake to me, He that ruleth over men must be just, ruling in the fear of God. And he shall be as the light of the morning, when the sun riseth, even a morning without clouds; as the tender grass springing out of the earth by clear shining after rain. Although my house be not so with God, yet He hath made with me an everlasting covenant, ordered in all things, and sure; for this is all my salvation, and all my desire, although He make it not to grow.

When David himself drew near to the time of his dissolution and departure out of the world, he comforted himself with a prospect of that good thing which God had promised him, that should surely be accomplished in his family. Though he was drawing near to the end of his days, yet he remembered with joy that God had promised concerning his offspring.

It was what David's heart was upon above all things, and had his greatest dependence upon. As he says in this verse, "This is all my salvation, and all my desire," that is, this promise was above all things the object of his dependence, and the thing promised above all things the object of his desire. And he shows where his chief dependence was, and what his heart was most upon, by his dying breath.

The whole of this last speech of David, as in the original, is very applicable to the Messiah and His kingdom. What is here translated, "He that ruleth over men must be just, ruling in the fear of God," might have been as well translated, "He that is to be the ruler over men shall be just, ruling in the fear of God"; for the words "must be" are not in the original, agreeable to Isaiah 32:1: "Behold, a king shall reign in righteousness."

And then the following words are very applicable to Christ: "He shall be as the light of the morning, when the sun riseth, even a morning without clouds." This description is very agreeable to many others that we have of Christ and of gospel times: Christ is compared to the sun of righteousness and to the morning. He is the light of the world. And His appearance and the promulgation of the gospel in the world is compared to the light of the morning, to the day-spring from on high, visiting the world, and to the sun's arising with healing in its beams.

And as for these words, "As the tender grass springing out of the earth," the tender grass may signify the souls of believers that flourish under the happy government and influence of Christ, as "by clear shining after rain." And then Christ, the just Ruler over men, is the Sun from whence comes that clear shining. Or the tender grass may well be interpreted of Christ Himself, agreeable to other places where Christ is called a "tender plant" and a "branch of righteousness that grows up unto David"; the man whose name is "the branch," in the original, "that which springs." And this well agrees with the last words in the verse of the text, "Although He make it not to grow." By it being like tender grass by clear shining is meant that it shall be flourishing and beautiful, agreeable to Isaiah 4:2, "The branch of the Lord shall be beautiful and glorious."

In these words observe:

1. What it is that David here comforts himself with the consideration of, and that is the covenant which God had made with him. The covenant he speaks of is that which we have an account of in the seventh chapter:

> And when thy days be fulfilled, and thou shalt sleep with thy fathers, I will set up thy seed after thee, which shall proceed out of thy bowels, and I will establish his kingdom. He shall build a house for My name, and I will establish the throne of his kingdom forever. I will be his Father, and he shall be My son. If he commit iniquity, I will chasten him with the rod of men, and with the stripes of the children of men: But My mercy shall not depart away from him, as I took it from Saul, whom I put away before thee. And thine house and thy kingdom shall be established forever before thee: thy throne shall be established forever (vs. 12–16).

2. The great dependence that David had upon this covenant: "This is all my salvation, and all my desire." When God revealed this covenant by Nathan, David esteemed it a great thing and rejoiced greatly at it, as appears by the prayer that he made upon that occasion (chapter 7:18–29).

3. The difficulties that David's faith in this covenant overcame: "Although my house be not so with God." His house is his family, either those who had already been buried, or those of his posterity who were yet to be born. "Be not so with God" refers to the foregoing words: although they be not just, "ruling in the fear of God," or though they be not "as the tender grass springing out of the earth." David met with great and sore

difficulties and frowns of providence in his family, particularly in Amram and Absalom; and speaking of his posterity who were kings of Judah, few of them were just, "ruling in the fear of God."

"Although He make it not to grow." Upon these accounts, there was no present prospect of that good thing's being accomplished as yet. There was no present appearance of the horn of David budding forth, and the branch of David growing, as the accomplishment of this covenant is elsewhere expressed (see Jeremiah 33:15). But yet for all this, this was all his dependence.

4. The reason why David's dependence on this covenant was so firm: because the covenant was everlasting, ordered in all things, and sure. It was in every way so ordered as to make it sure; it had all the circumstances needed in order to its being firm. As in temporal covenants—they must be so and so ordered—there were these circumstances necessary to be attended in order to their being firm: they must be sealed, and witnesses must be taken. Thus David observes that the covenant God had made with him was ordered in all things so as to make it sure.

DOCTRINE: The covenant of grace is in every way so ordered as is needful in order to its being made firm and sure.

The covenant of grace has all those circumstances and qualifications that tend to make it firm and sure. It is the covenant of grace that is spoken of that is thus "ordered in all things, and sure." For the sure mercies of David are the benefits promised in that covenant, as is evident by Isaiah 55:1, where Christ invites all who thirst to come to the waters, and he who has no money to come, buy, and eat; and by Acts 13:34: "And concerning that He raised Him up from the dead, now no more to return to corruption, He said on this wise, 'I will give thee the sure mercies of David.' "

This will appear by the consideration of the following things:

• The fulfillment of the promises of this covenant made sure by the covenant of redemption, which God Christ from all eternity. God entertained a purpose of redeeming mankind in this way from all eternity; it was a thing that was much upon his heart. And He entered into a covenant with His Son, promising Him that, upon the condition of His coming into the world, fulfilling all righteousness, and suffering death, He would see His seed and justify by His knowledge all those who would know Him and believe on Him (Isaiah 53:10–11).

God in that covenant gave unto Christ all the elect, all those who were to be effectually called to believe on Him, promising that they would be redeemed by Him, accepted for His sake into His favor, and that He would glorify them with Himself. Christ did not undertake this work of redemption, so exceedingly difficult and expensive to Him, without promises of success by the Father; and therefore the grace of God in saving believers is said to be given them in Christ before the world began. 2 Timothy 1:9: "Who hath saved us, and called us with an holy calling, according to His own purpose and grace, which was given us in Christ Jesus before the world began." And in Titus 1:2, it is said that God, who cannot lie, promised eternal life before the world began.

Now what abundant confirmation is this that God certainly will save all those who believe in Jesus Christ. Surely God will fulfill the engagements that He from all eternity entered into with His own Son. He would not agree with Him to come into the world and suffer such disgrace and extreme pain, promising Him this success, that if He so did, all who believed on Him would be saved by Him, and then not fulfill those promises.

• God has been very full and abundant in declaring the promises of this covenant to the church. The covenant was revealed unto Adam soon after the fall. God promised that the seed of the woman would bruise the serpent's head. Again, God renewed the covenant with Noah, and more fully and solemnly with Abraham, promising that in his seed all the families of the earth would be blessed, repeating it several times and giving him various assurances of it. Again God, in a very solemn manner, renewed this covenant with the children of Israel when He brought them out of Egypt by the hand of Moses, and gave them the ceremonial law to prefigure the glorious things that pertained to this covenant.

Again, God renews this covenant with David, and in him with His church, in the seventh chapter of the second book of Samuel. And God was often making new and clearer revelations of it by His prophets.

Thus God continued renewing this covenant with His church from the beginning of the world. He always spoke the same thing and continued to reveal the same covenant, which showed the sincerity of His promises and the immutability of His counsels relating to the redemption of men by Jesus Christ.

And He spoke the same thing in His providence from time to time. He renewed and confirmed this covenant by the language of His providence, especially in calling Abraham from his own country and separating the children of Israel to be a peculiar people to Him. The plain design of it was to make way for the introducing of Christ into the world and the promulgating of the gospel.

And at last, when Christ actually came, He revealed this covenant with more abundant clearness by Him—not in shadows and dark speeches, but with great plainness of speech, abundantly promising by Christ and His apostles that He who believes on the Son of God shall be saved. Now this gives the strongest ground of assurance of the truth of those promises, that God, who cannot lie, has not only promised, but has often renewed His promises from the beginning of the world.

• God has confirmed it with an oath. Thus God swore unto Abraham in Genesis 22:16–18: " 'By Myself have I sworn,' saith the Lord, 'that in blessing I will bless thee, and in multiplying I will multiply thy seed as the stars of the heaven, and as the sand which is upon the seashore; and thy seed shall possess the gate of his enemies. And in thy seed shall all the families of the earth be blessed.'" So again, God swore unto David in Psalm 89:3–4: "I have made a covenant with My chosen. I have sworn unto David My servant, 'Thy seed will I establish forever, and build up thy throne to all generations.' " And vs. 35–36: "Once have I sworn by My holiness that I will not lie unto David. His seed shall endure forever, and his throne as the sun before Me." And again in Psalm 110:4: "The Lord hath sworn, and will not repent, Thou art a priest forever after the order of Melchisedek."

Thus God, to give us the more abundant assurance, has not only promised, but sworn. Hebrews 6:17–18: "Wherein God, willing more abundantly to show unto the heirs of promise the immutability of His counsel, confirmed it by an oath, that by two immutable things, in which it was impossible for God to lie, we might have a strong consolation, who have fled for refuge to lay hold upon the hope set before us."

• Each of the three persons in the Trinity has distinctly

born witness to this covenant. There is nothing wanting with respect to witnesses needful in order to making it sure, if the persons of the Trinity may be allowed to be good witnesses. 1 John 5:7: "For there are three that bear record in heaven, the Father, the Word, and the Holy Ghost; and these three are one." Each of them distinctly has given an open and public testimony of it. The Word, the second Person, who is Jesus Christ, bore witness of it during the whole time of His public ministry. John 8:18: "I am one that bear witness of Myself, and the Father that sent Me beareth witness of Me."

The Father bore witness to this covenant by an audible voice from heaven at Christ's baptism, saying, "This is My beloved Son, in whom I am well-pleased" (Matthew 3:17), that is, well-pleased in Him as Mediator. And again at His transfiguration in Matthew 17:5: "While He yet spake, behold, a bright cloud overshadowed them: and behold a voice out of the cloud, which said, 'This is my beloved Son, in whom I am well-pleased; hear Him.'" And again when Christ was going to Jerusalem to be crucified, as He prayed that the Father would glorify His own name, that is, in the fulfillment of the covenant of redemption, "There came a voice from heaven, saying, 'I have both glorified it, and will glorify it again'" (John 12:28).

The Holy Ghost gave two remarkable testimonies: once by descending on Christ in the visible shape of a dove, and another time by His descent on the apostles at Pentecost, endowing them with power from on high, besides the testimony given by His inspiration of the prophets and apostles, and the inward testimony in the heart of every believer.

• This covenant is confirmed and made sure by its seals of. Here there are no witnesses, but seals.

First, God has sealed this covenant with His own blood. Christ preached the gospel while He lived here on earth, and at last sealed it with His blood. Christ died in attestation to the truth of His doctrine; though that was not all He died for, yet that was one thing. He knew that He would be put to death for preaching such doctrine, yet He continued to preach it. He would not have suffered death for testifying to that covenant if He had not known that the covenant was true. When Pilate asked Him at His trial whether He was the King of the Jews, He confessed it. 1 Timothy 6:13: "I give thee charge before Christ, who before Pontius Pilate witnessed a good confession." If Christians who die for professing the truth may be said to seal the truth with their blood, and are therefore called martyrs, that is, witnesses, much more may Christ's death be looked upon as a seal of His own doctrine. To prefigure this seal, Moses, at Mt. Sinai, when he promulgated the covenant, slew sacrifices and sprinkled the blood of the covenant on the people as a seal of the covenant, and called it "the blood of the covenant" (Exodus 24:8).

Second, there are the ordinary seals, or those sacraments that God has appointed as seals of the covenant. God, the more abundantly to confirm us in the sincerity of His design of saving of us through faith in Christ, has appointed certain outward signs that shall represent the blessings of that covenant to be administered in His name and repeated in the church to the end of the world so that we, remembering that He appointed those signs and that the significant actions are done in His name, might thereby have our faith strengthened in the belief that He will confer the blessings thereby signified of old—especially circumcision and the Passover, and since, Christ's baptism and the Lord's Supper.

•   Those things in the covenant of grace that are most

wonderful are already actually fulfilled, that is, that which God had promised that Christ would do and suffer for us. Those things are the most strange and incredible. 'Tis vastly more wonderful that God should send His Son into the world to do and suffer such things for us than that afterwards He should justify and save those who believe on Him. Romans 8:32: "He that spared not His own Son, but delivered Him up for us all, how shall He not also with Him freely give us all things?"

''Tis in this chiefly that the wonderfulness of the grace of this covenant consists. 'Tis a very wonderful thing indeed that God should give Christ to obey and die for us. And it is also wonderful mercy in God thus to choose out such and such and give them faith. But after Christ has died and the sinner has believed, it is no wonderful thing at all that God should be willing to justify and save him for Christ; for 'tis what Christ has bought at full price. He has merited it. He has paid as much as the price comes to. He has answered the demands of the law and the demands of justice for the believer's sins, and He has paid a grand price for this eternal life. There is no more grace in this than there was in the covenant of works, nor so much either; for Christ's righteousness properly merits the reward which Adam's perfect righteousness would not have done.

• We may be sure that they who believe in Christ shall be justified, because He who is their Surety and Representative has already been openly acquitted and justified. Christ was appointed by the Father to be our Surety and Representative, and He undertook to answer for us according to the appointment of the Father. So that He did, as it were, take our guilt upon Him. He stood as the guilty person. He was under the curse of the law. Since He became our Surety, the law stood against Him and not against us. But He has been justified and openly acquitted by His resurrection. God Himself opened the prison doors, and thereby declared that it was enough, that He was satisfied and demanded no more. 1 Timothy 3:16: "God manifest in the flesh, justified in the Spirit." Therefore the Apostle Peter writes in 1 Peter 1:3 that we are "begotten again to a living hope by the resurrection of Jesus Christ from the dead. And the Apostle Paul asks in Romans 8:34, "Who is he that condemneth? It is Christ that died, yea rather, that is risen again."

Christ was justified in the name of all who would believe, of all the elect. He was justified as their Head.

• We may be sure that the covenant of grace will be fulfilled to all believers, seeing that they have such an Intercessor at the right hand of God. Christ has gone into heaven with His own blood, there to appear for us; and we may be sure that He is disposed to plead our cause there because He has made us His own cause. Seeing that He has suffered so much for sinners, He doubtless will be concerned that His sufferings should succeed. But they will not succeed unless those who believe on Him are saved, for that is what He died for. And we need not doubt but that His intercessions will avail because He is a Person infinitely near and dear to God. He is God's own and only begotten Son, His eternal delight; and because He has so good a plea to make—the Father's own promise to Him in the covenant of redemption and to men in the gospel, and His having fulfilled the condition.

• The promises are sure, for our Mediator has received them already in our name. Christ, as He is not justified as a private person, but as our Head, so He is rewarded as the Head of the church. He has gone to receive a kingdom for believers, and He has received it. He has gone to prepare a place for them. When He had answered the law, God the Father did, as it were, give Him the reward into His own hands, to reserve it for those for whom He had bought it; and He has eternal glory naturally in His hands for all those whom the Father has given Him.

• We may be sure of the fulfillment of the covenant of grace, for God has given all things into the hands of the Mediator of the covenant, and has made Him Judge of the world. He has made Him Head over all things to the church. He has left the government of the world in His hands, so that now, doubtless, believers in Christ will be saved, for their Mediator Himself has the disposal of things that He might give eternal life to whom He will. John 17:2: "As Thou hast given Him power over all flesh, that He should give eternal life to as many as Thou hast given Him."

There is no danger, for the Mediator of the covenant Himself is appointed the Judge of the world. He who laid down His life and suffered such extreme things that they who believe might be saved, and who intercedes for believers in heaven, is Himself to be the Judge. He is to determine who is to be saved and who is to be damned. We may therefore be sure that He will bestow eternal life upon them for whom He bought it at the price of His own blood, and who believe in His righteousness.

Thus the covenant of grace is ordered in all things and sure.

APPLICATION

USE 1. Here we see one instance of the marvelous condescension of God to fallen man, that He has given us such abundant and so manifold confirmation of the covenant of grace. He has marvelously condescended to help our unbelief. 'Tis only through our unbelief and our sinful, depraved disposition of heart that we stand in need of such various confirmations of it. If God promised, if He gave His word, that would be enough; for it is impossible for God to lie, and heaven and earth shall pass away sooner than one jot or one tittle shall pass away from the law (Matthew 5:18). But we are so full of unbelief that God has condescended to give more abundant confirmation of the certainty of this covenant, so that we might have the more strong consolation. He has not only promised, but He has oftentimes and in various ways renewed His promises. And, not only so, but He has taken His oath to it once and again, and each of the three Persons in the Trinity have condescended distinctly to give their testimony, and God has appointed seals to be administered in His name continually. And that no doubt may remain, He has acquitted our Surety in an open manner, has exalted Him with His own right hand, and has given the blessing promised into His hands to reserve for us and bestow upon us in due season. Then He left the disposal of the whole matter with Him who died for us, and has appointed Him to be our Judge.

What could he have done more? How could he have made the covenant more sure? What circumstance is there wanting, or what circumstance could be added, to make it surer than it is? Well may the mercies of this covenant be called "the sure mercies of David," these mercies being already given into the hands of our Mediator and being left at His disposal. And He being appointed our Judge is the same as if they were already given into believers' own hands.

USE 2. Hence we learn the heinousness of the sin of unbelief, that refuses to receive God's testimony although He has been so abundant in it and has in so many ways confirmed it. It makes God a liar (1 John 5:10), and it makes Him the worst of liars. Unbelief charges God with lying, or at least suspects His truth in all those repeated promises that He has made since the beginning of the world. Unbelief says that His calling of Abraham, His separating the children of Israel from the rest of the world, His sending so many prophets, His sending Christ, and His sending forth the apostles to preach and convert the Gentile world, was only to delude mankind; and that each of the persons of the Trinity in their distinct testimonies lied, and that the seals of the covenant are given only to establish a lie.

Unbelief not only makes God a liar, but also a perjuror who has taken self-oath from time to time to deceive us with a vain hope.

And therefore it argues a great and strange distrust of God to disbelieve in this matter, after He has given such assurances of the fulfillment of His promise in revealing to us the eternal covenant of redemption, in already fulfilling those things that are most wonderful that pertain to the covenant of grace, that is, in sending His Son into the world, after He has given such open testimonies of his approbation of what Christ did and suffered as sufficient, after He has exalted Him to be the Intercessor for all believers, and appointed Him as the Judge of the world. It would provoke any man to see his neighbor so exceedingly distrustful of him, if he had taken such pains to give him assurance of his sincerity and fidelity.

USE 3. Let sinners awakened by this doctrine be encouraged to come to Christ and trust in Him for salvation. Seeing that the promise that all who so do shall be saved is so sure and firm, you may with the greatest safety venture yourself upon Him.

However sinful and vile you are, if your iniquities have grown up to heaven; if your sins stare you in the face and you are ever frightened at the sight of them; if it terrifies you to see what a wicked heart you have, and to think what a wicked life you have lived; if you are ready to think that surely God will not accept of such a filthy, loathsome creature as you are, or that Christ will not receive you—remember how sure the promises are. Certainly, however sinful you are, you need not be afraid to venture after such assurances.

Though you have affronted and provoked the majesty of heaven, and it seems to you that God is so angry with you that He never will forget your sins and that He never will upon any terms be reconciled to you, yet remember how sure the covenant is.

Though you see the law standing against you with all its terrors of threatenings and curses, yet consider how God in the covenant of redemption appointed Christ to be the Surety of all who believe, and how Christ undertook to take care to see the law answered for all who trust in Him. Then you need not be more concerned about that matter.

Though your case is never so singular, yet it is safe for you to trust in Christ. You won't find yourself or your case, which you suppose to be so singular, excepted in that sure covenant.

USE 4. Let this doctrine be improved to confirm the faith of the saints. Let it strengthen their consolation to see upon what a sure foundation they are built. The more you view your foundation, the more will you be sensible how strong it is. Zion is built exceedingly strong; the walls of it are strong, and her towers and bulwarks many. Psalm 48:12–13: "Walk about Zion, and go round about her; tell the towers thereof. Mark ye well her bulwarks." The covenant being so sure, you may have an assured confidence of the fulfillment of it.

First, the things promised are very wonderful. It appears as a very wonderful thing that ever God should bestow such great honor and happiness upon such a creature as man is. You may be ready to think sometimes that such things are too big for men, as David said when God made His covenant with him, "And is this the manner of man, O Lord God?" (2 Samuel 7:19). And yet we find that he fully entertained and believed it; it was all his salvation and all his desire.

It is yet more wonderful that such things should be bestowed on fallen man, a creature who has been so vile and sinful. But so it is. God has made an everlasting covenant, ordered in all things, and sure.

Second, although there are many difficulties in the way of the fulfillment of this covenant, yet if you have believed in Christ, you may be sure that it will be done. God has spoken it, and He will do it. If the corruption that remains in your own heart lays blocks in the way (it is often working and tempting you to backslide and to return again into Egypt), yet God is faithful who has promised; if He has begun a good work in you, He will perform it until the day of Jesus Christ (Philippians 1:6). If Satan casts all the blocks in the way that he can, if he is laboring to pervert your soul and to hinder your progress in holiness and to draw you off from your allegiance to Christ, yet none shall pluck you out of Christ's hands. Neither angels, nor principalities, nor powers shall not separate you from the love of God which is in Christ Jesus (Romans 8:38).

Third, you may rest in this, that the covenant will be fulfilled to you, though God may for a time hide His face from you. He may hide His face from you in a little wrath, but with everlasting kindness will He gather you (Isaiah 54:8). If you meet with great temporal trouble and are ready to fear that God is angry with you, yet if you trust in Christ, you may be sure that God will at last cause light to arise to you out of darkness.

If you meet with spiritual darkness, if God withdraws the comfortable influence of His Spirit for the present, yet if you are built upon the Rock, you need not fear but that God will return again to you.

Fourth, you need fear no ill, though you pass through the valley of the shadow of death. If you trust in Christ, the covenant is so ordered in all things and sure that you need not be afraid to leap into eternity; you shall be held up; you shall be kept safe.

The valley of death is a dark valley. It is full of terrifying appearances. It is a very solemn and awful thing to go into eternity, and to go and appear before God; but if you believe in Christ, if the covenant of grace is all your salvation, if that is the object of your dependence, you need not fear that it will ever fail you.

USE 5. This doctrine is for the consolation of believers. This doctrine teaches us the blessedness of those who believe, in that the promises that God has made to them are so exceedingly glorious.

God loves His people to the end. He will never leave them or forsake them. He will be their God and they will be His people. He will deliver them from all evil. He is their Refuge, their most high habitation. He is their defense. They shall dwell under secret places; therefore they shall never fall. Their place of defense shall be their munitions. He will subdue Satan under foot. God will tread on the lion and the adder. He will destroy the great leviathan, and give him to be meat to them. He will be to them a Father, and they will be His children. He will pity them all, and will be ready to help when they cry. He will hear their prayers. He will be a God close at hand and not a God afar off. He will provide for them. "The young lions do lack, and suffer hunger, but they that seek the Lord shall want no good thing." All things work together for good. Whoever is against us, He will be for us. Under calamities He will uphold by the right hand of His righteousness. He will be a shade on their right hand. He will be their sun and shield, their hidden manna. He will be their white stone and give them a new name.

He will be with them when passing through the valley of the shadow of death. The second death shall have no power. He will raise them up at the last day. Christ will confess their names. Their life shall be hidden with Christ. They shall see length of days forever and ever. They shall see God. Christ has promised them mansions of glory in His Father's house. He has gone to prepare a place for them and will come again for them. They shall see Him face to face; they shall be like Him and see Him as He is. They shall sit with Him on His throne. He will give them a crown of life, and they shall be made most blessed forever. They will drink of the rivers of pleasure, enter in through the gates into the city, and have a right to the tree of life.

Christ will greet them and lead them to living fountains of waters. They will hunger no more. All their tears will wiped away. They will be led into His banqueting house, where they shall eat and drink at His table in the kingdom. They will gather in the temple of God and go out no more. They will shine as the brightness of the firmament; they shall possess all things, for God will give them grace and glory, and no good thing will He withhold from them.

Such promises as these, and many others of the like nature, God has made. Well might it therefore be said, as in 2 Peter 1:4, that God has given them exceedingly great and precious promises. How blessed then are they who have believed, for there shall be a performance of all those things that have been told them by the Lord.

CHAPTER SEVEN

Some Men Shall Never Be Saved

❦

"Because all those men which have seen My glory and My miracles which I did in Egypt and in the wilderness, and have tempted Me now these ten times and have not hearkened to My voice, surely they shall not see the land which I sware unto their fathers; neither shall any of them that provoked Me see it."

NUMBERS 14:22–23

We have here in this chapter an account of the murmuring of the congregation at the report of the spies who had been sent to search out the land. They were not only discouraged, but the words put them into a dreadful fret against Moses and Aaron, and against God. And when Joshua and Caleb opposed them, and would have convinced them that their discouragement and murmuring

98

were causeless, they could not bear it but were about to stone them. Numbers 14:10: "But all the congregation bade stone them with stones." And upon this the glory of God appeared; it was time for Him now to appear. And in verses 11–12 we have an account of what God says upon this occasion: "And the LORD said unto Moses, 'How long will this people provoke Me? And how long will it be ere they believe Me for all the signs which I have shewed among them? I will smite them with the pestilence, and disinherit them, and will make of thee a greater nation and mightier than they.' "

In the words of our text we have part of what they said in reply to Moses. Upon this Moses, in a most humble and earnest manner, intercedes as he had been wont to do for the congregation. The words of the text are a part of what God says in reply to Moses' intercession. God is so far, as it were, overcome by Moses' intercession that He pardons them as a nation. Verse 20: "I have pardoned according to thy word." He conceded not to destroy the nation as he had threatened in verses 11-12. But as for that generation, those persons who had murmured and provoked Him, God would not pardon, as He declares in our text.

We may observe in the words:

1. What the thing is that is resolved upon: God here declares that all these men who murmured at the report of the spies would not see the land which he swore unto their fathers.

2. The fixedness and immutability of God's purpose and resolution declared: "Surely they shall not see the land." In the original it is "if they shall see the land." The expression is an oath. The expression is the same as the one referred to and repeated by the psalmist in Psalm 95:11: "to whom I sware in wrath." But it is "if they should enter into My rest" in the

Hebrew and in our singing psalms. The expression is abrupt; something else is understood beside what is expressed: "If they shall see the land then I am not God; then I don't live." That is what is signified, and that is expressed in verse 21: " 'As truly as I live, saith the Lord, 'all the earth shall be filled with the glory of the Lord,' " that is, "I will not allow the glory of My majesty to be thus condemned and trampled on." And again in verse 28: " 'As truly as I live, saith the Lord, 'as ye have spoken in Mine ears, so will I do unto you.' "

The expression shows God's wrath; they had so provoked God that His patience was at an end. He swore in His wrath. He is most peremptory and repeats it again and again in the verse before our text: "As truly as I live . . ." And then in our text: "If they shall see the land," again in verse 28: "As truly as I live, saith the Lord," again in verse 30: "Doubtless ye shall not come into the land concerning which I sware to make you dwell therein," and again in verse 35: "I the Lord have said it, and I will surely do it unto all this evil congregation."

God had threatened before, but now He resolves. He threatened when they made the golden calf: "Let me alone that I may consume them." But at Moses' intercession the Lord is said to repent of the evil; but now God swears and will not repent. After that sin God said to Moses, "Go lead the people into the place which I have sworn unto thee" (Exodus 32:34). But now He swears and will not repent. Now God bids them to turn back in verse 25: "Tomorrow turn you and get you into the wilderness by way of the Red Sea."

3. We may observe the reasons why God thus immutably resolves, and that is the number and repeatedness of their transgressions. First there is the aggravation of their provocation: "They have seen My glory and My miracles which I did in Egypt and in the wilderness." Second, this provocation was after so many others,

or the repeatedness of their transgressions: "They have tempted Me now these 10 times."

By taking notice of the history that Moses gives us, we may observe that this is the 10th public act of rebellion. The perverseness and rebellion of the congregation is mentioned from the time of their coming out of Egypt. The first was when they murmured at the Red Sea (Exodus 14:10–11). The second was their murmuring at Marah (Exodus 15:23–24). The third was their gathering and then murmuring at manna on the sabbath; for that is spoken of and reproved as a public act of rebellion (Exodus 16:27–28). God says upon that occasion, "How long refuse ye to keep My commandments and My laws?" The fourth instance was their murmuring in the wilderness of Sin (Exodus 16:1–2). The fifth instance was at Meribah (Exodus 17:4). The sixth was their making the golden calf (Exodus 32:1). The seventh took place at Taberah (Numbers 11:1). The eighth was their loathing of manna (Numbers 11:4). The ninth was Aaron's and Miriam's sedition, with whom doubtless many of the congregation joined (Numbers 12). And now the tenth is their murmuring at the relation of the spies.

DOCTRINE: There is such a thing as men's going on to provoke God by their sins till they have committed the last sin that God will bear with before He, as it were, takes up a resolution that they never shall be saved.

This rest that God swore the children of Israel would not enter into is typical of heavenly rest. God's thus dealing with the children of Israel in the wilderness, with respect to Canaan, is a representation of His dealing with some wicked men with respect to heaven and their eternal salvation. This is evident from the improvement which the psalmist and the Apostle Paul make of it to warn men not to do as they did lest God should deal with them, with respect to their salvation, as He did with those murmurers with respect to the promised land.

Thus the psalmist warns us in Psalm 95:8 not to harden our hearts as in the day of temptation in the wilderness. And he enforces his warning by telling us how that God dealt with them: "He swore in His wrath that they should not enter into His rest"—implying that if we do as they did we shall expose ourselves to the like treatment with respect to God's heavenly rest. For it was long after the children of Israel had obtained that temporal rest, as the apostle argues in Hebrews 3–4.

There the apostle expressly warns Christians to beware lest they provoke God to do with them with respect to heaven as He dealt with those men with respect to Canaan. You may observe this by the whole drift of these two chapters to the Hebrews, and particularly verse 11 of chapter 4: "Let us labor therefore to enter into that rest, lest any man fall after the same example of unbelief."

So it is evident that as God did with those wicked men of Israel at this time with respect to Canaan, so He sometimes does with wicked men with respect to their eternal salvation.

God is dreadfully provoked by men's continuing to go on in ways of wickedness, especially under clear light and while He is using means with them to reclaim them. And many so provoke Him that He, as it were, resolves not to let them enter into His rest; and His resolution may be dated from some particular transgression that sealed their damnation.

QUESTION. How may God be said to take up a resolution that a man never shall be saved?

ANSWER. To answer negatively, God can't properly be said to take up any resolution in time. That would argue mutability in

God. There is nothing new in God. Whatsoever God purposes He purposes from all eternity. He had determined when the children of Israel came out of Egypt, and even before, that generation should not see the land of Canaan. It was in God's decree then.

And when they made the golden calf, though God forgave that sin upon Moses' intercession, and said after that, "Go up and possess the land," yet God's decree was the same all along. Though the pillar of cloud and fire led them towards Canaan with it, God brought them to the borders of it.

Yet here God in our text is represented as resolving that, upon this transgression of their murmuring at the report of the spies, they shall not enter into the land.

Though God is unchangeable, yet He is represented after the manner of men as altering His purposes and taking up new purposes. So He is often said to repent, as in Genesis 6:6–7: "And it repented the Lord that He had made man on the earth; and it grieved Him at His heart. And the Lord said, 'I will destroy man' (there's His repentance). And the Lord said, 'I will destroy man whom I have created from off the face of the earth' " (there is His new resolution).

Genesis 8:21: "And the Lord smelled a sweet savor, and the Lord said in His heart, 'I will not curse the ground any more for men's sake." There God is represented as taking up a resolution not to curse the ground upon Noah's sacrifice. His saying in His heart is the same as the Hebrew way of saying that He resolved within Himself in our language. So God can't properly and in strictness be said to take up a resolution not to save man upon any sin of theirs.

But God acts as though He had taken up such a resolution, or He acts as men do when they have taken up a resolution against a thing, and here particularly with respect to those whom the doctrine speaks of, some of those who go on to provoke God by their sins.

1. God, from the time that they committed such a sin, finally withdraws from them and withholds the kindly influence of His Spirit. He absents Himself from them and refuses ever to give men saving repentance of their sins. He withholds from men those kindly influences of His Spirit that are necessary in order to their salvation.

None can be saved, according to God's immutable constitution, unless they experience such influences of the Spirit of God working grace in their hearts, causing a work of regeneration. But God is provoked to forever withhold this. He is so provoked that He resolves that His Holy Spirit never shall go and dwell in their hearts.

The apostle warns the Christian Hebrews not to commit fornication lest it should be with them as it was with Esau who, for a morsel of meat (for a moment's gratification of an appetite), sold his birthright, and who afterwards found no place for repentance (Hebrews 12:16–17).

2. From that time forward God refuses to save men though they seek salvation and do many things in order to obtain it. They design to be saved, but God disappoints them; they have a great desire to escape hell, but God will never deliver them; they design to set about the work of their souls at such and such a time, but God blasts their designs; they make attempts to forsake their sins and to set about the work of religion in good earnest, but God does not bless them in their attempt. He doesn't assist them to do as they attempt to do, and He doesn't prosper them in their attempts. They may do many things that they may be saved, but they aren't blessed in their endeavors. Judas had a mind to be saved; he did some thing in order to it.

Thus it was with the children of Israel: they made attempts to go up to Canaan after they had committed the sin of murmuring at the report of the spies, as you may see in verse 40 and following of our text: "And they rose up early in the morning [they seem to set about the work with considerable earnestness] and got them up into the top of the mountain, saying, 'Lo we be here, and will go up into the place which the Lord hath promised, for we have sinned.' " But Moses tells them in the next verse that their plan shall not prosper, that the Lord is not among them, and that they should be smitten before their enemies.

Yet they seemed to have a great mind to go, though before they were for returning to Egypt. And so they would go up, notwithstanding that the Ark of the Covenant of the Lord and Moses did not go with them, and the Amalekites and the Canaanites came down and smote them and discomfited them even unto Hormah.

Though they shed tears about their sins, yet God utterly refused to save them. When Moses brought the message from God, it is said that the people mourned greatly (v. 39). Often they were smitten by the Canaanites, and they returned and wept before the Lord; but the Lord would not hearken to their voice nor give ear unto them (Deuteronomy 1:44–45).

So the apostle warns Christians in the aforementioned place not to commit fornication lest it should be with them as with Esau, who found no place for repentance though he sought it carefully with tears.

3. God finally leaves them and gives them up to sin though they may have fears of damnation and great terrors of conscience. Though they have now and then great stings of conscience, yet they have no convictions; they may be now and then frighted, as though they beheld some frightful spectre. Judas had frightening convictions, yet they have no convictions that make them

forsake all their known sins. They do not set about in good earnest to use the means for their salvation.

They may design to set about seeking salvation, and project such a thing from time to time; yet sometimes Satan has power given him to hinder them in one way or another so that they never do it in good earnest. They may make attempts to break off their sins, yet when the temptation comes their lusts are stirred up and they are carried away again. So God gives them over to the power of their lusts; they are carried captive by them and become mere slaves to them. Conscience, from time to time, makes opposition, but conscience is worn down.

They may continue seeking and doing many things for a considerable time, but all the while they indulge some lust in a greater or lesser degree; they never wholly break off all their known sins. There was a concern and partial reformation in Judas; he had a mind to be saved.

And so God finally leaves men and gives them up to their sins. He never gives them such kindly influences and assistances of His Spirit as to cause them wholly to forsake their wickednesses. Thus God did by these murmurers in the wilderness. Psalm 81:11–12: "But My people would not hearken to My voice, and Israel would none of Me; so I gave them up to their own hearts' lust and they walked in their own counsels."

4. God refuses to hear the prayers of others for them. Though their godly friends, ministers, parents, or others pray for their conversion and salvation, God refuses to answer them. Moses earnestly interceded for this evil, rebellious congregation of Israel, and God heard him so far that He would not destroy the nation; but as for that evil generation, God would not hear him.

Thus, when God was resolved to destroy Jerusalem, He said in Jeremiah 7:16, "Therefore pray not then for this people; neither lift up cry nor prayer for them, neither make intercession to Me for I will not hear thee."

5. Ministers are sent to them to harden their hearts. Thus, when God was resolved upon the destruction of Judah and Jerusalem, He sent Isaiah upon this errand in Isaiah 6:10: "Make the heart of this people fat and make their ears heavy, and shut their eyes lest they should see with their eyes and hear with their ears and understand with their heart and convert and be healed."

The means of grace prove to be a savor of death with respect to them; their having continued under the means of grace is no argument that God has not resolved that they never shall be saved. That wicked, murmuring generation, whose carcasses fell in the wilderness, the manna still descended to them after God had sworn that they would not enter into His rest.

6. Sometimes God suddenly takes away men's lives after they have put an end to God's patience by some particular commission of sin. When they have been going on in wretchedness, they at last commit the last sin that God will bear, from whence He takes up a resolution that they shall be damned. And soon after God takes away their lives or sends them to hell so that they may not be kept out of hell any longer.

Ecclesiastes 7:17: "Be not over much wicked. Why shouldest thou die before thy time?" God is sometimes resolved to snatch men out of the world as being unfit to live, and He hastens their destruction in wrath. So it was with Judas. 'Tis God's manner sometimes thus to deal with wicked men, not only under the Old Testament, but also under the New. Ananias and Sapphira were struck dead for their sins. Herod was eaten with worms for his wickedness.

QUESTION. Why does God act in this manner?
ANSWER. He does so for the following reasons:

1. God does this to vindicate His own glory. God might glorify His sovereign and infinite grace in their conversion and pardon; but God is pleased to glorify His justice by His severity on some as well as by His mercy on others. And this is one way of His expressing His wrath, whereby He glorifies His justice. Thus God said to Moses when he interceded for Israel in the verse before our text, "As I live, all the earth shall be filled with the glory of the LORD."

Men who go on in sin, repeating their transgressions from time to time under light and against warning, dreadfully cast contempt upon God's majesty and trample on His authority. God sees it needful, for the vindication of the honor of His majesty and authority, to not bear with men, to do awfully with men who do thus.

2. God does this so that men may be afraid to go on in known sins. Lest God should do thus with them, those instances that we have in Scripture are written for our warning. And if men are sensible that this is God's method of dealing with so many wicked men who go on in their trespasses, it tends to make them afraid to go on; and when they are tempted to any sin, they are afraid to commit it lest it should be the last sin that God will bear with.

APPLICATION

USE OF WARNING. To those who are going on in sin, be warned by this. If you dare to go on in sin, you do not know how soon God may take up this resolution and swear in His wrath concerning you. Don't presume, you who have gone on in ways of wickedness hitherto; take heed that you proceed no further.

You who have been addicted to any particular way of wickedness, who have gone on in a way of indulgence of any particular lust, take heed that you are guilty of that wicked practice no more. You don't know but that the next time you are guilty of that wickedness will be the last time that God will bear with before He will take up such a resolution as that spoken of in the doctrine.

Don't venture for ten thousand worlds to indulge that lust again; if you do, you may, for all you know, do that which never can be undone again. It may, for all you know, prove to be the irreparable ruin of your soul. If you should venture to commit the sin again, consider how many sins you have committed already, and what aggravations they are attended with; what warnings you have had, what light you have gone against, and how dreadfully you have provoked the infinite Majesty of heaven!"

Consider how much you have provoked Him in that particular practice you have gone on in. And if you should, it is just if His patience is at an end. Would it be a strange thing if God's patience should be quite at an end if you are guilty but once more? If you should yet run the venture and commit the sin again, and the effect of it is that God should resolve that you should never obtain salvation, how doleful a thing would it be? You will, as it were, indeed be as dreadful as if you then should sink down into hell.

If God preserves your life it will be only that you may fill up the measure of your sins so that your damnation at last may be the more dreadful. Genesis 15:16: "But in the fourth generation they shall come hither again: for the iniquity of the Amorites is not yet full." Matthew 23:32: "Fill ye up then the measure of your fathers." 1 Thessalonians 2:16: "Forbidding us to speak to the Gentiles that they might be saved, to fill up their sins always: for the wrath is come upon them to the uttermost." And these will be more dreadful than if you should that minute be cast down into hell.

If you are afraid of hell, be afraid to presume to indulge your lust once more. You should be as afraid of committing one sin more as you would be afraid of hell; for you don't know but that hell is in its womb. You don't know but that you shall leap thereby into hell; you have ventured to the edges of the pit, and you don't know but that the next sin will set you to irrecoverably falling. You have been playing at the edges of the whirlpool, but it may be not so irrecoverably as to loosen the shore as yet; but if you go on to commit any more of that wicked practice, it may set you off so far into the draught of the whirlpool that you never can Recover—and then how miserable will your case be. It would be a thousand times better for you that you never had been born.

What confidence can you have that God will bear with your going on in willful wickedness, gainst so many solemn warnings as you have had? If you knew what a dreadful venture it is that wicked men run in perpetually committing their old wickedness, you would not venture upon it any longer for all the world. 'Tis a dreadful venture that wicked man run who go on in ways of known wickedness under the gospel. Yet there are so many who run such ventures. This is one reason why the greater part of those who die under the gospel go to hell.

Though it is so lamentable and doleful a thing for persons to be finally left by God to their eternal destruction, yet it is not any rare thing. There are doubtless many such persons of whom, with respect to them, God has resolved concerning the heavenly rest as He did concerning the children of Israel with respect to Canaan.

And here particularly be warned not to go on repeatedly committing those sins with those aggravations with which the children of Israel sinned in the wilderness:

First, beware of repeating sins against great light. Thus did the children of Israel. That evil generation had seen God's wonders and miracles which He had done in Egypt and in the wilderness; they had seen the great plagues that God had brought on the Egyptians, and how He had brought them out with a strong hand; they had seen God appearing in a wonderful manner on Mt. Sinai; they had heard the voice of God out of the midst of the fire; they had the law of God, His statutes and His judgments lately delivered to them by the hand of His servant Moses.

They had abundant means of to convince them of the truth of God's Word and of God's ability to bring them into the land that the spies had searched out; that train of miracles was sufficient to convince them that they had been brought forth, led along, and supported by a continual train of miracles. Yet they were ever murmuring and rebelling.

Beware, therefore, of repeating sins against great light and abundant means of conviction; beware of repeating sins against the dictates of the frequent instructions you have had, and against the convictions of your own consciences.

Second, beware of repeating sins against great mercies, as did the children of Israel. Those who are wicked in the Christian church and under the gospel sin against greater mercies; they sin against the dying love of Jesus Christ and gracious offers of peace and eternal salvation. Beware of abusing this redeeming mercy, and so beware of using the grace of God to embolden you in sin. Don't presume upon mercy.

Beware that you don't repeatedly sin against great personal mercies. Has God delivered you? Don't thus requite the Lord.

Third, beware of repeating known transgressions against great and repeated warnings as the children of Israel did. As they had often provoked, so they had often been reproved. When they made the golden calf, God then threatened to utterly destroy them. And though He did not do that, yet He plagued the people and commanded whoever was on the Lord's side to consecrate themselves. They were visited with terrible judgments for their murmuring at other times: the fire of the Lord burned among them at Taberah, and when they loathed manna. God smote them when the flesh of the quails was between their teeth. Beware, therefore, how you go on in sin against frequent warnings from God's Word and warnings in threatening dispensations, lest you provoke God.

I say to any who may be afraid that they have committed their last sin, the sin that has already made God take up such a resolution against them. To such I would say as Peter did to Simon Magus, earnestly seek repentance if perhaps you may find mercy. Acts 8:22: "Repent therefore of this thy wickedness, and pray to God if perhaps the thought of thine heart may be forgiven thee." The Ninevites were wise in crying mightily to God, "Who can tell if God will repent and turn away from His fierce anger that we perish not." And you see that they had success.

Here consider, first, you can't determine that God has so done. It is impossible that a person could know that he is finally left till life is at an end. If you have been left for a great while, that doesn't prove that you have been left finally, for God often absents Himself for a long time. He sometimes long hides His face and then appears at last. You have not been left finally, even if you have been under the power of lust, let your sins be never so great, even if you have sinned never so often against never so much light and mercies and warnings, unless you have committed the sin against the Holy Ghost.

God is sovereign in this matter. God may finally take up this resolution in some for less sins than against those who had committed never so much sin, nor continued so long. God's mercy is sufficient for you. Christ's blood is sufficient.

Second, if God stirs you up and enables you steadfastly and diligently to forsake all your sins, and to use all appointed means for your salvation; then there is matter of great encouragement in it. Let your sins have been what they will, the Word of God gives encouragement to such persons (Proverbs 2:1–5).

As you don't know what God has determined to do with you, be exhorted to resign yourself up into His hands. Have you gone on in sin? God is sovereign as to His resentments and treatment of you for it. He will do His pleasure with you. Own that you are in His hands, that you have forfeited all mercy, and that it would be just if He has sworn in His wrath that you should not enter into His rest.

Finally, seeing that you do not know what God has determined, do such as God directs you to do in His Word. Cast yourself down and yield yourself as God's prisoner, and resolve that if you perish you will perish at His feet.

CHAPTER EIGHT

A Heart to Do the Will of God

(Preached in November 1743)

Go thou near, and hear all that the LORD our God shall say;
and speak thou unto us all that the LORD our God shall speak
unto thee; and we will hear it and do it. And the LORD heard
the voice of your words, when ye spake unto me; and the LORD
said unto me, 'I have heard the voice of the words of this people,
which they have spoken unto thee. They have well said all that
they have spoken. Oh, that there were such a heart in them, that
they would fear Me, and keep all My commandments always,
that it might be well with them, and with their children forever!'"

DEUTERONOMY 5:27–29.

When the children of Israel had gotten through
the wilderness and were in the plains of Moab,
about to enter into the promised land, there

114

was a renewal of the covenant between God and the people. It was fitting that it should be so because now that old stiffnecked generation was dead. Moses was about to leave. Joshua was about to die, and therefore it was fitting that all things should be settled and established. So this was before Joshua's death, and God was about to do great things for that generation.

It is this renewal of the covenant that is the grand subject of this book, and therefore it is called Deuteronomy. To make way for and introduce this renovation, and to prepare the people for it, Moses rehearses the great acts of the Lord towards the people and their former covenant behavior towards God.

God in these words speaks two things. First He speaks of some things that were found in the children of Israel, and then of something that was found wanting in them. Several particulars may be observed concerning two things spoken of in them.

He speaks concerning some things that were found in the people, a purpose and profession of doing the will of God. Several things may be noted concerning these things: First, their purpose and profession was good. Second, the people were very forward in this purpose and profession. Third, those purposes and promises were made at an extraordinary time and on an extraordinary occasion. Fourth, they were made with great affection. These are the things that may be noted concerning what was found in the people.

But there is something else spoken of, that which was found wanting in them: a heart to really do what they proposed and promised. It is implied that it was wanting, and it proved to be so notwithstanding all their affection, forwardness, and zeal.

Observe two things concerning this:

1. That which was wanting was the great thing that God looked for and sought in them.

2. That this was the great thing which alone would avail them to their life and happiness.

DOCTRINE: Godliness consists not in a heart to purpose to do the will of God, but in a heart to do it.

The children of Israel had the former.

PROPOSITION 1. True godliness is a thing that has its seat originally in the heart. The word for "heart" oftentimes used in Scripture means the same as man's soul or his inward part, in opposition to what is external. But more commonly and more particularly by "heart" is meant the soul, with a more special relation to the faculty of the will, or with regard to its dispositions, affections, inclinations, and choices.

And thus godliness is a thing that has its seat originally in the heart, and not in any outward profession, show, or external behavior. Therefore God says in the text: "I have heard the voice of the words of this people, which they have spoken unto thee. They have well said all that they have spoken. Oh, that there were such a heart in them, that they would fear Me, and keep all My commandments always, that it might be well with them, and with their children forever."

There is a great proneness in mankind to place religion in those things that are external. But God is a spirit, and they who worship Him must worship Him in spirit and in truth. Man looks on the outward appearance, but God look on the heart. God says in Proverbs 23:26, "My son, give Me thine heart." It is said in Psalm 51:6, "Thou desirest truth in the inward parts."

God regards the truth in the inward parts.

We find some condemned and rejected in Scripture though they are found to have done that which was right, because it was not done with a perfect heart. Psalm 78:37: "That their heart was not right..."

But God ponders the heart and weighs the spirit. So often-times 'tis said that God searches the heart and tries the reign. And when God gives a man grace He is said to write His law on their hearts. Where God promises to bestow grace it is expressed thus, as in Ezekiel 11:19: "A new spirit will I...a new heart put... and I will take away the stony heart."

Godliness is the good treasure of the heart spoken of in Matthew 12:35. The ornament that is of great price in the sight of God is in the hidden man of the heart (1 Peter 3:4). Romans 2:28–29: "He is not a Jew that is one outwardly, but...."

Godliness has its origin in the heart rather than in speculation. As the heart is, so the man is. I say, godliness has its seat originally in the heart. It is not true that all that pertains to godliness has its seat there, but all true godliness has its seat originally in the heart, that is, it begins there; there must be the origin of all godly action. There it is in its foundation, and the streams flow out of the heart; and therefore it is compared to a spring in the heart in John 4:14.

PROPOSITION 2. Though godliness be a principle in the heart, yet 'tis a principle that has relation to godly practice. It is a conformity of heart to God's will which translates into a practice of God's will. It is not an inactive thing; nothing in heaven or earth is of a more active nature. It is life itself, spiritual life. The divine nature is pure act, not an unfruitful thing. Nothing in the universe has a greater tendency to bear fruit.

Godliness in the heart has a relationship to practice as much as a fountain has a relationship to streams, a root to the fruit, a foundation to a superstructure, or a luminary to light, as life has to breathing or the beating of the pulse, or any other vital acts.

A habit has a relationship to acts; it consists of thinking

and hearing. A habit of being anything has to the doing of it. Conversion, which is the work by which God's grace infused into the heart, has a relationship to act in practice. That is the end of conversion. Ephesians 2:10: "created in Christ Jesus unto to good works."

It is related to it in God's purpose. John 15:16: "ordained you that...." It is related in its nature. The nature of true godliness of heart is not to rest in itself. Sincerity is not locked up in the heart any more than it is the nature of a spring to produce stagnating dead water. If there is a fruitful principle in a good tree, it doesn't rest in the principle, but produces fruit.

Hence all godliness is in Scripture oftentimes expressed by doing the will of God, in obeying God, and in keeping His commandments. There is no one gracious and holy principle but what has a great relationship to holy practice, whether it be repentance, faith, or the like. Those principles that have no relationship to practice are as much in vain as a vine, apple tree, or fig tree is in vain without fruit.

PROPOSITION 3. The manner in which godliness in the heart is related is it doesn't consist only in a purpose to do God's will, but in that God gives a heart to do it. Here I would show, first, how or in what true godliness consists: not only in a heart to purpose to do God's will, but in a heart to do it. And, second, show the evidence of the proposition.

1. First, I would show how and in what sense true godliness consists, that it is a heart not only to purpose to do God's will, but a heart to do it. Negatively, it doesn't give a heart to do God's will perfectly, though that is indeed desired. Nor is it intended that the godly do many individual acts of obedience that they purpose to do. Godly men may fail in many particular instances to fulfill their purposes. Their resolution may fail

through the strength of temptation; so it doubtless was with the apostle. The saints are encompassed round with subtle, powerful, and indefatigable enemies.

But, affirmatively, what is intended is that the truly godly have that in their hearts that is sufficient to cause them to be in the way and to continue in the way of persevering, to be in the way of doing the whole will of God. The truly godly don't only intend to perform perfect obedience, but actually perform universal obedience. As the psalmist says, "I have sworn and I will perform it."

By universal obedience I mean that their manner is to strive to obey in the most difficult duties, in those that are most contrary to their particular inclinations and temporal interests. Proverbs 16:17: "The highway of the upright..." And this they continue in to the end, which is agreeable to the words of the text. They have a sufficiency of heart not only to bring them to intend and purpose thus to do, but actually to bring them to do it. Their choice is so fixed, their inclination is so strong, their sense of the greatness, importance, and excellency of divine things so great; their resolution is so steadfast that they are sufficient to actually carry them on through, bring them to and carry them through such a way of living.

These things are in such strength and fixedness in their hearts that they are sufficient to overcome the opposition. The godly have a heart to encounter the difficulties when it comes to the trial; they have a heart to forsake what stands in competition, a heart to continue notwithstanding the laboriousness of the work and the length of time.

2. I will now mention some things to show the truth of this. That they actually and perseveringly fulfill the whole will of God is often in Scripture mentioned as a characteristic of true saints. "He that heareth these sayings and doth them..." (Psalm

119 at the beginning). He who does righteousness is righteous, just as he who commits sin is wicked (see 1 John 5:18). Romans 2:7: "To them who by patient continuance bring forth fruit with patience..." Matthew 24:13: "He that endureth to the end the same shall be saved."

If the godly had only a heart to purpose to do the will, but did not have a heart to actually do as they purpose, they would still be slaves to sin. Herein appears the bondage of ungodly men. But the saints are not slaves. Romans 6:14: "Sin shall not have dominion over you." John 8:34: "He that committeth sin is the servant of sin." But as for true saints, the Son has made them free; they are brought into the liberty of the children of God (Romans 8:21). The law of God is to them a law of liberty and they have the spirit of adoption.

3. 'Tis often spoken of as the nature of true grace that it is victorious. God has promised that He will not bruise the and that out of the mouth of babes. The promises are made to them who overcome.

Herein appears the power of godliness. Christ gives those who are His the victory (1 Corinthians 15:57), and they are "more than conquerors."

Application

USE OF SELF-EXAMINATION. By this you may try yourselves whether you have true godliness or not. This is the proper trial and the greatest evidence the Scripture speaks of. John 14:21: "He that hath My commandments and keepeth them, he it is that loveth Me." John 15:14: "Then are ye My friends, if ye do whatsoever I command you." John 8:31: "If ye continue in My Word, then are ye My disciples indeed." 1 John 3:10: "Herein are the children of God manifest and the children of the devil: whosoever doeth not righteousness is not of God."

What expressions can be plainer? That is the meaning, and therefore these things that put it to the proof whether a man has such a heart or not are called by way of eminence "temptations or trials" all over the Scriptures. 'Tis true that godliness does not consist mainly in anything external, but has its seat in the heart, but it consists in such a heart as this. Inquire therefore whether you find that you have such a heart or not. Don't rest on what you found at such and such a time when you purposed that you were willing to serve God all the days of your life, in the sense that you had purpose and intention.

Many, when they feel this call, give themselves up to the service of God. They call this taking Christ for their King; they feel an affection that is sufficient to begat a purpose, as the children of Israel did, flowing affections to God and to Christ. They feel such a kind of love as they call holiness, in that it begets many good intentions.

But don't rest in this only. Many hypocrites find a heart to intend to do the will of God who do not have a heart to actually do it, and the reason of it lies very much in these two things:

1. They approve of religion and comply with it when they view it in general, but not when it comes to particulars. When hypocrites view religion in general they don't see the hardest things that belong to it. The hypocrite chiefly sees those things that approve themselves to all men. They strive to live a strict, righteous, temperate, humble, and charitable life that all men will approve of as being good and desirable.

Natural men may see a kind of beauty in it and so they may comply with it in their thoughts, in a general view of it. But the difficulty is when it comes to particulars.

Thus a man may comply with a life of temperance, considered

in a general view, but when it comes to a particular act of self-denial of a strong, importunate appetite, they are not so likely to be religious. This was manifestly the case with the man who said to Christ, "Lord, I will follow. Thee whithersoever Thou goest" (Luke 9:57). Hypocrites don't count the cost; they may comply with building the tower when thought of in general.

2. They approve of and comply with the practice of religion when viewed at a distance, but not when the difficulty is more in view and when the opposition is more felt. Men can think of different sufferings and self-denial without such an opposition of nature as would be is found in the view of something new to be undergone. A hypocrite is like a coward who, when he is at home in his corner, tells everyone what he will do in wartime.

Therefore here let your examination be strict, and answer impartially to your own conscience. How does your religion prove itself? You look back and you can remember the time when you had what you call a great discovery, a great sense, a time when you had great affections. But then that was not the chief time of trial. We read of some who hear the Word and receive it with joy, but in the time of trial following fall away. We read of some who believed on Christ, but Christ would not commit Himself to them (John 2:24). The reason was that He knew they did not have a heart to actually do the will of God.

So inquire whether or not, after all your affections and good intentions, you are like the man of whom Christ speaks in Matthew 21:30, who said, "I go, sir," and went not. The grand characteristic of counterfeit grace is that it is ineffectual; it doesn't bring any thing to pass, and so it appears to be void of the power of godliness. It is like a picture or image of a man.

False religion may have an effect in these two ways: First, to make men purpose to do the will of God; and, second, to make them sorrowful in not actually complying. But it is not effectual to bring men to actually do what they purpose. Counterfeit grace is not effectual because it is not substantial. These experiences of hypocrites are not substantial.

There is a certain solidity in the experiences and affections of the true saints, wherein they become effectual and are sufficient to carry them through trials. There is a solidity and weight whereby they have power with the man and govern him. They reach the bottom of the heart and have hold of his very nature; they influence all his faculties whereby he is fixed in the way of his duty. This difference between the experience of true saints and hypocrites seems to be intimated in Scripture by comparing the saints to wheat and the hypocrites to chaff.

We have such an expression in Hebrews 13:9 as the heart's being established with grace. And hence the trial of the heart is in Scripture called the weighing of it (Proverbs 16:2). The handwriting against Belshazzar was that he was weighed in the balance. There is something in the experiences and affections of true saints that render them of a practical nature.

USE OF EXHORTATION. Let this doctrine exhort you earnest to seek so that you may have such a heart as is spoken of in the doctrine, that you may have the great benefits of it. Consider the worthlessness of a heart that only purposes, but does not do. Of what significance was it to the children of Israel! How vain did it prove about 6 weeks or two months after, and it never did them any good; it was effectual only to their great condemnation.

Consider the great worth of such a heart, not only to purpose, but to do, as is signified in the text.

To help you gain such a heart, take these directions:

1. Seek a thorough conviction of the truths of the things of religion.

2. Seek that powerful principle of divine love. This has great power: it mortifies sin at the very root; it strikes at the life of it; it gives a hatred to sin itself, and not only to its consequences; it makes duty delightful and its yoke easy. Christ said that His commands were not grievous. Divine love gives new appetites and brings balance. If you have this principle, then you will have a heart to serve God forever, like the servant who had his ear bored (Exodus 21:6).

CHAPTER NINE

God Will Deal with Men According to Their Own Temper and Practice

"With the merciful man Thou wilt show Thyself merciful, and with the upright man Thou wilt show Thyself upright. With the pure Thou wilt show Thyself pure, and with the froward Thou wilt show Thyself unsavory."

2 SAMUEL 22:26–27

These words are part of a song of praise that David sang towards the latter end of his reign and life when he came to be in his old age. It was to praise God that he had rescued him in all his wars, and in all the dangers he had been involved in, that He had at length delivered him and appeared on his side against his enemies.

David had an abundance of enemies who sought his ruin in the course of his life. From his first being called from the sheep to come and stand before Saul till the latter part of his reign he had enemies to encounter. He was exceedingly persecuted by enemies before he came to the crown, and afterwards he had wars with all the nations round about him, besides the great troubles he met with from within his own dominion and even his own family.

But God was with him in all his troubles and dangers. He appeared on his side and never suffered his enemies to triumph over him. At last He gave him the victory over all; and David, in his old age, saw his throne and his kingdom in a well-established peace and quietness.

In this part of his song David is reflecting upon God's different dealings with him and with his enemies, and his righteousness and equity therein. He takes notice of how God had rewarded him according to his righteousness, and according to his cleanness in God's eyesight. This leads him to reflect on God's universal righteousness and equity in His dealings with men and His judging of them. He distributes to every one according to his own practice and prevailing disposition, as appeared in His different dealings with David and his enemies: "With the merciful Thou wilt show Thyself merciful."

DOCTRINE: God will deal with all men according to their own temper and practice.

This seems to be the design of the words of the text, to teach us this, and not only that God deals with men according to their own temper and practice in those particular instances here mentioned.

In speaking to this doctrine we shall first show in several

instances how God will deal with men according to their temper and practice towards Him, and, second, towards one another.

1. God deals with men according to their temper and practice towards Him. For instance, God loves those who love Him, and He hates none but those who continue to hate Him. Such is God's great condescension towards us worms that He assures us that if we truly and sincerely love Him, that love is mutual. Proverbs 8:17: "I love them that love Me."

Though we are so inferior and our love is so worthless, and we are not able, however great our love is to God, to profit or make Him the better for our love; though the love of men in the present state, the best love of the children of men is very imperfect, being mingled with the remains of sin; though they have formerly hated Him, and though there are still remains of that old principle of enmity—yet if there is any sincerity of love to God in the hearts of any of the children of men, they are the objects of the love of God. However mean they are, however unworthy or however great enemies they have been before. The love of those whose delight is in God, God takes delight and complacency in them; their prayers are acceptable to Him; their praises are as a sweet savor and an acceptable sacrifice to Him. They and all their good works that have any sincerity in them are precious to Him. Though God is so much above us, yet there is never is any difficulty in obtaining His love for those who love Him. He is ready to receive them into favor and to embrace them in the arms of His love.

On the other hand, there are none who are the objects of God's hatred but those who hate God. All such God hates and is an enemy to; they are enemies to Him. If God has a loathing and abhorrence of them, they loathe and abhor Him. Zechariah 11:8: "My soul loathed them and their soul abhorred Me."

Wicked men have an abhorrence of the holiness of God.

It is very distasteful to them. God casts the wicked out of His sight as those that are abominable to Him. Wicked men do, as it were, cast God out of their sight; they don't love to have Him in their sight; they avoid His presence; they avoid having anything to do with God in prayers and or in any other way as much as they can. They cast God behind their back (1 Kings 14 :9).

If God is angry with the wicked and destroys them, it is no more than they would do to Him if they had it in their power. God is not a being that they can reach, otherwise they would soon show their enmity against Him by doing Him all the injury that lay in their power. How did the wicked of the world do when God became man? They never left off till they had imbrued their hands in His blood.

God will honor those who honor Him and will condemn those who condemn Him. 1 Samuel 2:30: "Them that honor Me I will honor, but them that despise Me shall be lightly esteemed." There are some who have exalting thoughts of God; they esteem Him above all; they see and acknowledge His glorious and divine excellency and they truly honor Him in their hearts; they have a great veneration for His holy name, and they reverence Him as a Being of infinite greatness and majesty. Such as these are highly esteemed by God. One godly man is highly accounted of by God, esteemed more valuable and honorable than the whole world of ungodly men.

The wicked cast contempt upon God; they have mean thoughts of Him; they slight His majesty and authority. They cast contempt upon His commands; they despise His favor and make light of His threatenings and anger. He stands low in their regard and esteem; they prefer the world before Him; they set their money, their meat, drink, and almost all things above God. He has the lowest place in all their regard. But such as these are the objects of God's contempt. God despises them and has them in derision (Psalm 2:4: "He that sitteth in the heavens shall laugh. The Lord shall have them in derision." Psalm 59:7–8: "Behold, they belch out with their mouth; swords are in their lips, for who, say they, doth hear? But Thou, O Lord, shall laugh at them; Thou shalt have all the heathen in derision."

The righteous honor God in their lives. They show a preference to Him above all other things. They give honor to His law; they give honor to His Word, to His ordinances, to His day, to His name and to His image. They are grieved when He is dishonored and will at all times speak to His honor, and they will praise Him and give the glory to Him that is due to His name. They delight in ascribing sweetness to God and they'll appear against those who dishonor God.

Such as these God will honor. He'll honor them by receiving them into the number of His children, by making them heirs of His, heirs of a crown of life. Such as these shall be made kings and priests, and hereafter God will put great honor upon them by placing them at His own right hand in heavenly places, by giving them an honorable and glorious name, by crowning them with a crown of glory and clothing them with white robes.

God will do them honor at the day of judgment. They shall not only then be openly acquitted and rewarded, judged to a glorious reward and an everlasting glory, but they shall sit with God to judge the world; for the saints shall judge the world; they shall judge angels (1 Corinthians 6:2–3) .

But the wicked, who live to God's dishonor, who don't give God the glory that is His due, but show a contempt of God and religion, insomuch that many of them will even deride it and laugh at those who are religious, such as those God will put to great disgrace. Hereafter He will pour contempt upon them.

He will make them appear base and contemptible in the eyes of angels and men. Daniel 12:2: "And many of them that sleep in the dust shall awake, some to shame and everlasting contempt."

The wicked shall be, as it were, trodden under. God will put the wicked to such shame that He will, as it were, tread them under His feet. They shall be made God's footstool (Psalm 110:1). They shall be trodden down as the mire of the streets (Micah 7:10).

They who give themselves to God, He'll give Himself to them, and only those who refuse to give themselves to God shall fail to have Him for their portion. The truly righteous dedicate themselves to God; they give themselves up, body and soul, with all that they have. To such God gives Himself, with all that He is and has, to be their heritage. He gives Himself, with all His glory and perfection, so far as they are capable of enjoying them or receiving good by them. His power shall be theirs to deliver them from evil and to promote their welfare. His wisdom shall be theirs to guide and instruct them, and to contrive and order things for them. His holiness, His beauty, and His love shall be theirs to be seen and enjoyed by them.

But the wicked refuse to devote themselves to God, but claim an independent right to themselves; they say, "We are our own, and who is Lord over us?" They refuse to give themselves up to God's possession and government, and to be devoted to His service. To such as these God will never give Himself; they shall never come to the enjoyment of God; they shall have no portion or lot in anything that is in God. He will utterly leave and forsake them; they shall have no portion in His power to help them or deliver them from their enemies; they shall have no portion in His wisdom to guide them, but God will leave them to their own wisdom. They shall have no portion in His love, His care, or His good will. God will in no respect be theirs, but He will be entirely separate from them. And herein He does but deal with them as they deal with Him: they refuse to give themselves to Him and will allow Him no portion in them, and God refuses to give Himself to them or allow them any portion in Him. There are other gods that they devote themselves to, and that they choose for their portion, and God will leave them to their own choice that they have chosen. Judges 10:13–14: "Yet ye have forsaken Me and served other gods; wherefore I will deliver you no more. Go cry unto the gods whom ye have chosen. Let them deliver you in this time of your tribulation."

They who walk contrary to God's revealed will shall find that God will walk contrary to their will; and, on the contrary, they who comply with His will, He will comply with their desires. Wicked men set themselves in a way that is cross to the holy commands of God; they will not yield obedience to His revealed will. God will therefore act contrary to their inclinations. He will cross them in His providential dealings. They desire happiness, but they shall have misery; they desire ease and pleasure, but they shall have pains; they desire honor, but they shall have shame. They who are obstinate in a way of disobedience, God will set Himself against them as they do against Him. As they are stiff-necked and froward in a way of disobedience, so God will set Himself to cross the inclinations and appetites of their nature. Leviticus 26:28: "If ye will walk contrary to Me, then will I walk contrary to you also in fury."

But they who heartily comply with God's commands and walk with Him, He'll walk with them. He will order things so as shall be agreeable to them. God will perfectly and in everything comply with their desires; they shall have all the good, all the pleasure and happiness that their hearts can wish, yea. their desires shall be fully satisfied.

They who seek the advancement of God's kingdom in the

world, God will seek the advancement of their interest and welfare. But they who oppose it, He will oppose their welfare. God is above our reach, and we can't advance His welfare; but we may advance His kingdom and interests here in the world. Man may be the instrument of enlarging the kingdom of Christ by promoting the case of religion. By upholding and promoting the cause and interest of religion, he may be the instrument of bringing sinners off from their sins and turning men to righteousness. They who do thus with a true heart, who are at work for God and set themselves to do what they can for Him, He will set Himself to do for them. He will surely consult their best interest in all His providential dealings towards them; all things shall work together for their good; everything shall conspire to advance the happiness of such a man; even his enemies who most seek his hurt shall be under such a government and ordering of God that they shall be subservient to his good. And while they seek the advancement of God's kingdom in this world, God will seek a kingdom for them in another world. Luke 12:32: "Fear not, little flock, it is your Father's good pleasure to give you the kingdom."

They who frowardly contend with God about His dispensations, He will show Himself froward towards them, but will deal contrariwise with those who submit to His will. In this respect, "with the froward God will show Himself froward." There are some who are of a fretful, impatient spirit under adverse dispensations of providence; when they meet with losses, crosses, and disappointments from time to time, they are angry with providence, or are at least ready to vent themselves against God. They think they are singled out and that God deals hardly with them, that He has set them as His mark, and their hearts rise against providence; they find a great deal of fault. To be of such a spirit is the way to have God walk contrary to them and to cross them yet more and more. Proverbs 22:5: "Thorns and snares are in the way of the froward." This is the way to greatly provoke the Most High to anger and to set Himself forever to follow them with cursing and vexation.

Some are fretful and quarrel with God about His dealings with their souls; they object against the fairness and justice of God in His methods of dealing with mankind, with respect to their eternal estate. They reply against God; and though they are but the clay and God is the Potter, yet they are not afraid to say to Him, "Why hast Thou made me thus?" Their hearts rise in blasphemous thoughts against God because He doesn't hear their prayers because He holds them under the guilt of their sins, and in condemnation to eternal death because He doesn't regard their good works.

But this is the way to terribly enrage the fire of God's wrath, to provoke Him to withhold those mercies which they so presumptuously contend for, to make His sovereignty appear in their eternal destruction.

But they who are of a spirit of submission and resignation to the will of God, He will not show Himself froward with them; but however they may meet with some adverse things here in this world, yet if they conform their wills to the will of God, in a little time they shall see that God's will is conformed to theirs. They shall no more meet with anything that is cross or contrary to them; they shall have all things just as they would choose;. they'll have no desires of having anything otherwise.

They who exercise true repentance for their sin, God will, as it were, repent for them; when they mourn and are heartily grieved for their sins, God's heart will, as it were, be grieved for them. He will have compassion on them. His bowels will yearn towards them. As soon as ever the prodigal son came to himself and repented, his father saw him while he was yet a great way off and had compassion on him, and ran and fell on his neck and kissed him (Luke 15:20). When a sinner repents, God does, as it were, repent of the evil that He thought to do unto him. Deuteronomy 32:36: "The Lord shall judge His people and repent Himself for His servants, when He seeth that their power is gone." Psalm 106:44 –45: "Nevertheless He regarded their affliction when He heard their cry, and He remembered for them His covenant and repented according to the multitude of His tender mercies."

Those who humble themselves before God, God will, as it were, humble Himself for them. But they who are of a proud heart, God beholds them afar off. He beholds them with disdain. He will keep at a great distance from them; they must not expect that God will condescend to converse with them. Wherein they deal proudly, He is above them. God resists the proud, but they who are of a humble spirit, God will humble Himself to come and dwell with them. Though He dwells in the high and holy place, yet He, as it were, comes down to dwell with such as these. Isaiah 57:15: "For thus saith the high and lofty one that inhabiteth eternity, whose name is holy, 'I dwell in the high and holy place with him also that is of a contrite and humble spirit, to revive the spirit of the humble." Though God is so great, yet the psalmist informs us that God will not despise him who is of a broken and contrite heart (Psalm 51:17). Psalm 138:6: "Though the Lord be high, yet He hath respect to the lowly, but He beholdeth the proud afar off." Isaiah 66:1–2: Thus saith the LORD, 'The heaven is My throne, and the earth is My footstool. Where is the house that ye build unto Me? And where is the place of My rest? For all those things hath Mine hand made, and all those things have been,' saith the LORD. 'But to this man will I look, even to him that is poor and of a contrite spirit, and trembleth at My Word.' "

They who are most humble of heart are generally those who are favored with most of God's presence and communion. God delights in coming to such and manifesting Himself to them.

Those who are upright and pure towards God, He will be so towards them; that is, those who are real and steadfast in their adherence to Him, He will be so in His favor and friendship towards them. There are many whose adherence to God and friendship towards Him extends no further than to what is visible and outward. They seem to be God's friends; they are outwardly religious; they perform many outward duties, but they are not real friends, and God's dealings with them are agreeable: He rewards their outward religion and good works with outward blessings. He does them good outwardly, and they, it may be, think that therefore God loves them. But God is not indeed their friend. They do not perform their outward religion out of love for God, so neither does God bestow upon them outward blessings out of love for them. What they do is not for God's glory nor for their own good.

But they who are upright with God, He'll be upright with them; if they serve Him truly, in sincerity, and from love to Him, God will be faithful in ordering all things not only for their present good, but for their future and everlasting benefit. Whatsoever He does, whether He afflicts them or prospers them, it is out of love for them.

There are some who pretend friendship towards God who are not pure; they aren't universal in embracing His commandments. They yet harbor some lust. Their hearts aren't fixed and resolved, but are wavering. They are not to be depended on, but are treacherous to God and are not faithful in His covenant. With such as these God will not be pure. But however they may have mercy for the present, in enjoying the means of grace and having the common influences of God's

Spirit, and though they entertain great hopes of God's ever-lasting love, yet then God will at last forsake them and their hopes will utterly fail them. 1 Chronicles 28:9: "And thou, Solomon, my son, know thou the God of thy father and serve Him with a perfect heart and with a willing mind; for the Lord searcheth all hearts and understandeth all the imaginations of the thoughts. If thou seek Him, He will be found of thee. But if thou forsake Him He will cast thee off forever."

They who confess Christ, when God calls upon them He'll hear them; on the contrary, He'll refuse to hear their cries who refuse to hear His calls. God is in many ways calling upon us to forsake sin and turn to Him. He frequently repeats and renews His calls. He commands, counsels, urges, and even condescends to beseech the children of men. Those who hear Him, He will hear them when they call upon Him. Psalm 91:15: "He shall call upon Me and I will answer him. I will be with him in trouble; I will deliver Him and will honor him."

But they who won't hear when God calls, neither will He hear when they call. Proverbs 1:24: "Because I have called, and ye refused; I have stretched out my hand, and no man regarded; but ye have set at nought all My counsel, and would none of My reproof, I also will laugh at your calamity; I will mock when your fear cometh. When your fear cometh as desolation, and your destruction cometh as a whirlwind; when distress and anguish cometh upon you. Then shall they call upon Me, but I will not answer; they shall seek Me early, but they shall not find Me."

They who confess Christ before men, them will He confess before His Father. But they who are ashamed of Christ, of them will Christ be ashamed when He comes in His glory.

Those who esteem the name of Christ, by which they are called, to be their honor, and that however they may be condemned and despised by men for it, and who shall be ready in all trials to confess Christ and to glory in Him, such as these Christ will Confess and own to be His people another day, as He has promised in Luke 12:8.

But there are some who are ashamed of Christ and of Christianity. They dare not openly appear on the side of religion; they dare not let it be known that they have serious thoughts about religion, their souls, and another world, and that they are altered and have become religious. They disguise the matter for fear of being derided by their wicked companions—of such as these Christ will be ashamed hereafter. Mark 8:38: "Whosoever therefore shall be ashamed of Me and of My words in this adulterous and sinful generation, of him also shall the Son of Man be ashamed when He cometh in the glory of His Father with the holy angels."

Thus God deals with all men according to their own temper and practice towards Him.

2. I will now show how it is that God deals with men according to their own temper behavior towards one another, towards other men. God, who is our supreme Judge, has placed mankind in the world in such a state that they stand in need one of another. In many things they have a mutual dependence, and God beholds us from heaven and observes how we behave one towards another. He has given us rules in order to one another's welfare, and tells us that, according as we treat one another in an observance or neglect of those rules, so we must expect to be treated by Himself (Matthew 7:1). He observes what measure we give to our fellow creatures and He gives us the same. Matthew 7:2: "With what measure you mete, it shall be measured to you again."

We shall take notice of some instances:

First, God will be merciful to those who are merciful and liberal to those who are so to their fellow creatures. But those who are unmerciful to men shall not obtain mercy of God. Thus it is said in the text: "With the merciful Thou wilt show mercy."

The gospel is full of rules of mercy and compassion towards our fellow creatures under the calamities that they suffer. We are directed to look not only at our own things, but at the things of others: to love our neighbors as ourselves, to weep with them who weep. It is not enough to answer the rule to be merciful in word and in tongue, or to feel some slight motions of pity in our heart, but we must express our charity in deeds. We must be full of mercy and good fruits. And the rule is enforced by a promise of a like treatment from God, upon whose mercy and liberality we so exceedingly depend. We see that in many other places besides our text, such as Matthew 5:7: "Blessed are the merciful, for they shall obtain mercy."

Many are the promises of this nature that are especially made to mercy and liberality towards the poor. Psalm 41:1–3: "Blessed is he that considereth the poor; the LORD will deliver him in time of trouble. The LORD will preserve him, and keep him alive; and he shall be blessed upon the earth: and Thou wilt not deliver him unto the will of his enemies. The LORD will strengthen him upon the bed of languishing. Thou wilt make all his bed in his sickness."

They who have compassion upon their fellow creatures and deliver them in their trouble and want, God will deliver them in the times of their trouble. When Onesiphorus had compassion upon the apostle in his poverty and straits, the inspired apostle prayed for mercy of the Lord for him. 2 Timothy 1:16: "The Lord give mercy unto the house of Onesiphorus, for he oft refreshed me and was not ashamed of my chains."

They who are free to part with what they have for the good of their fellow creatures as they are called to it, God will reward them by being liberal and bountiful towards them. Ephesians 6:8: "Knowing that whatsoever good thing any man doth, the same shall he receive of the Lord." Isaiah 32:8: "The liberal deviseth liberal things, and by liberal things shall he stand." In Luke 6:38 Christ says to us, "Give and it shall be given unto you, good measure, pressed down, shaken together, and running over." If we are sparing in giving, it is because we are apt to be afraid lest we should wrong ourselves. If we are grudging when we give, avoiding occasions of charity and bounty, we must not expect to have such overflowing measure given to us, and God will deal with us accordingly. 2 Corinthians 9:6–8: "But this I say, he which soweth sparingly shall reap also sparingly; and he which soweth bountifully shall reap also bountifully. Every man according as he purposeth in his heart, so let him give, not grudgingly or of necessity, for God loveth a cheerfull giver. And God is able to make all grace to abound towards you."

They who are merciful and liberal, with a true spirit of Christian charity, shall be rewarded with mercy, eternal and saving mercies with God's mercy and bounty to their souls. And those who are only liberal and bountiful from a free, natural temper, or from a generous natural temper, or from education or the exercise of reason, shall be abundantly rewarded with temporal rewards.

But they who shut their bowels towards their fellow creatures and harden their hearts against them, keeping back what is necessary, seeking only their own good and not their neighbor's, those, we are taught, shall not find mercy from God. Proverbs 21:13: "Whoso stoppeth his ears at the cry of the poor, he also shall cry himself, but shall not be heard." And James 2:13: "He shall have judgment without mercy that showed no mercy."

Second, they who are of a spirit of forgiveness towards men shall be forgiven by God, but they who don't forgive men, neither will God forgive them. The rule of Christ requires of us that we be of a meek spirit towards our malicious neighbor, not a spiteful and vengeful one, and that we don't hate our neighbor for injuries, abuses, and affronts that we have received from them; that we be ready to forgive them whether they manifest any repentance or not. Though they continue still to malign and injure us, yet we are utterly forbidden to return any spirit of malice, revenge, hatred, or bitterness; we must, notwithstanding, forgive him so far as not so much as to even desire to seek revenge or wish him any ill; yea, so as, notwithstanding, to wish well to him and be ready to do him any kindness or to promote his welfare wherever we can.

They who do thus, and are indeed of such a spirit, may, from God's promise, expect the same from Him. The case is so with us towards God as that of our injurious adversaries is towards us. The injuries that we have been guilty of towards God have been abundant, and we never made Him any satisfaction, and are still daily injuriously treating Him by our sins. But we hope that God will, notwithstanding, forgive us, and we would be in a most deplorable condition if He should not. And this we shall obtain from God if we forgive one another. Luke 6:37: "Forgive and ye shall be forgiven." But if it is otherwise, we are not to expect it; if we are of a contrary spirit and practice, God will not forgive our sins.

This is one petition which Christ teaches us to insert in our prayer: "Forgive us our debts as we forgive our debtors" (Matthew 6:12), and He gives the reason for it in verses 14–15: "For if ye forgive men their trespasses, your heavenly Father will forgive you; but if ye forgive not men their trespasses, neither will your Father forgive you." Christ teaches us the same in a parable (Matthew 18:23–35).

Third, there are some who are very forward to judge and condemn others, to put bad constructions upon their behavior, to determine from what spirit, from what principle, and from what ends such and such actions are done. They love to put an ill face upon things; they delight to sit and talk against their brother and to dwell upon their ill qualifications and actions in their behavior. They who are of such a spirit and practice shall be judged by the Lord. Matthew 7:1–2: "Judge not that ye be not judged; for with what judgment ye judge, ye shall be judged."

When we see others' faults, it rather becomes us to reflect upon ourselves and to be humbled for what there is of the like nature there is or has been of the like nature in ourselves. We have all the same principle of corruption, and very often those who take most delight in talking against others are none of the freest from faults themselves. They are busy in observing the mote in their brother's eye, but there is a beam in their own; and therefore wherein they judge others they condemn themselves and shall not escape the judgment of God. He will judge them for the same faults that they are so forward to first judge others for. See Romans 2:3.

God often so orders it in His providence that such persons who are so apt to censure others don't escape being censured by the censurer as much by the censures of others. Such as are most in evil-speaking are the most spoken against. And besides this, seeing they are so careful to mark the faults of others, God will deal with them according to their own practice and will mark their faults.

APPLICATION

USE 1. This use may be of conviction to ungodly men to convince them of the righteousness of God in the punishments He inflicts upon them. The doctrine affords matter of abundant conviction that God deals with them according to their own temper and practice. God does but deal with them as they deal with Him.

Let wicked sinners who find fault with God's dealing with them, who object against the righteousness of the threatened punishment, consider that if God casts you off forever, if He destroys you in hell without showing you the least mercy, He'll only deal with you according to your own temper and practice towards Himself. Certainly it is just that God should do so. God may justly hate you forever. He may make you the everlasting object of His perfect detestation, for that is no more than you have done to Him. You have hated God; you were born full of a principle of hatred to Him and you have lived all your lifetime in hatred of Him. You have shown your hatred of God in some way or other ever since you were capable of knowing anything about Him. Everyday you have sinned against Him; you have done things that He loathes, and therefore it would be but just if God should manifest His hatred towards you by His dealings with you. You have shown your hatred towards God in deeds, and God may justly show His hatred of you in deeds against you, by pouring out His wrath upon you.

You have, as it were, cast God behind your back, and it would be but just if God should cast you out of His sight forever. If God destroys you in hell forever, it is no more than you would have done to Him if you had power and opportunity. It will be most just in God to put you to eternal shame and disgrace, for you have done what you could to dishonor Him. God may very justly have you in everlasting contempt and tread you under His feet as the mire of the streets; for you have trampled under foot the Son of God; you have cast contempt upon the great and glorious God; you have placed Him in the last and lowerst places; you have made light of God's favor and His anger.

How just would it be in God forever to refuse to give the enjoyment of Himself to you who refuse to devote yourselves unto Him. God has made you the offer that, if you would come to Him and give yourself up to Him to be His servant and His possession, if you would look upon yourself as God's and not your own, and all as belonging wholly to Him, that He would give Himself to you to be your Portion. But seeing that you have refused that, how just is it that He should refuse to give you any interest in Him and suffer you to have any portion in anything in Him, but should utterly leave you to those things that you have chosen and have devoted yourself to.

How just would it be with God that, seeing you have so long and so obstinately walked contrary to Him, He should walk contrary to you. You have gone contrary to God's revealed will; you have set yourself in a way that is cross to God's commands; you would not be conformed to God's nature and revelation—how just therefore would it be in God to cross your desire and inclinations. You have, in the whole course of your life, gone contrary to God's will; it would therefore be very just if God should, as long as He lives, in all things set Himself to cross and vex you. You haven't sought the advancement of God's kingdom in the world; therefore why is God obliged to seek your interest? You are desirous, it may be, that God should be careful and tender of your welfare, that He should regard and take notice when you suffer, that He would take pity on you and help you; you would have God watch over you to see that no evil befalls you, to defend you from Satan so that you may not be carried down to hell by him. But surely it would be very just if God should not; for you have not been careful and tender of God's interest in the world. You haven't been concerned when you have seen the interest of religion in a suffering condition; you haven't had pity on the kingdom of God when it has seemed to be in a suffering condition; yea, you have opposed the interest of religion in the world. You laid hands to help pull down the kingdom of God in the world; you have been guilty of encouraging sin and, by your example, of joining with the workers of iniquity; you have been carrying on the same design as Satan, the grand enemy of God. When God's ministers and people have labored to uphold and promote piety and godliness, you have worked on the other side.

Would it not be very just, therefore, if God should work against your happiness, and counterwork you in all your endeavors to promote it? Would it not be just if God should make your labors for the good of your souls to be all in vain, and to make your endeavors to seek deliverance from hell to be all in vain?

And you who have been guilty of frowardly contending with God about the dispensations of His providence towards you, who have been fretful and impatient under the afflictions that He has brought upon you, how just would it be with God if He showed Himself froward towards you, and should put thorns and snares in your way, and cross you more and more in His providence? Yea, would it not be just for Him to set Himself forever to follow you with cursing vexation and rebuke?

You who quarrel with God about His dealings with your souls, whosoever allow of heart risings against God's methods of dispensing His grace to the children of men, His giving it to some and denying it to others, His absolutely decreeing the future state of all man-kind, some to eternal life and others to eternal damnation; His denying you grace after pains and prayers made, and much pains taken for it; who are, in your thoughts, disputing against God's justice, calling God partial and unfair, hard and cruel, and the like—would it not be most just in God if He should darken counsel with words without knowledge? Would it not be very just in God if He should show Himself froward towards you and should, in His anger, forever deny you mercy? And seeing that you are so bold as to fight to quarrel with Him about salvation, would it not be just in God if He should leave you to yourself to see whether ever you could obtain it in your own way, or should make it known that He has power over you and is the absolute Disposer of you by destroying you without mercy?

It may be that you have made some pretences of religion, but have not been sincere and upright; you haven't served God with your whole heart. What you have done has not been out of true love to God; your religion has only been external. Would it not be very just with God therefore if all the reward that ever He bestows upon you should be in external things, and should forever refuse you soul mercies, spiritual and eternal mercies?

You have dealt falsely and treacherously with God, falsely in His covenant; you have not been universal in your obedience; you have obeyed when it suited your turn, and when it did not suit you then you turned aside to crooked ways; you have not been pure with God. Would it not be very just therefore if God should at last leave and forsake you as you have forsaken Him, and cast you off forever as you have cast Him off for the sake of profit or pleasure, or to escape some troubles or inconvenience?

Would it not be most just with God to refuse to hear your

prayers when you have so often refused to hear His calls? If you are afraid of damnation and cry never so earnestly to God for pardon of sin and an interest in Christ, and continue so doing never so long, yet if God refuses to hear you and is utterly regardless of your cries, seems to take no notice of what you say to Him, and denies you His grace, is it not very just with God to do so, seeing what you have done to Him? God has called to you from sabbath to sabbath for many years together, and you have refused; you did not regard His calls; they did not alter you. You still went on in sin as you used to do; you took no notice of what He said to you in any of His calls.

God would deal justly by you if He should refuse to hear your cries in your last sickness, when distress and anguish come upon you, and your soul is so dreadfully amazed with fear of eternal misery, seeing that you have refused to hear God when He called you in your health.

And if there are any here whose consciences arouse them for having been ashamed of Christ and of religion before their companions, how just would it be if Christ should be ashamed of you when He comes in the glory of His Father with His holy angels. Whenever, therefore, you find yourself disposed to find fault with God's dealings with you, consider how you have dealt with God, how you have behaved towards Him according to His adverse dispensations towards you.

You may see by these things how unreasonable the objections, cavils, and murmurings of sinners are against the justice of God, and what reason there is that all awakened sinners should fall down before God and acknowledge that they are in His hands, and that, let Him do whatsoever He will with them, it is just and right.

There is an infinite inequality between God and men. God is infinitely above them, and therefore, truly, if God deals with them no otherwise than according to their own behavior towards Him, it cannot be excepted against as being unjust.

The justice of God in punishing sinners appears also in His punishing sinners according to their own temper and behavior towards one another. How can that man complain of God as being hard towards him in that He shows him no mercy, though he himself shows no mercy to his fellow creature? He himself is unmerciful to others, and yet he complains that God is unmerciful to him. If he is recompensed in his own coin, certainly there is no just cause of complaint; if God gives him his own measure, certainly there is no just cause of complaint.

How can a man complain that God, who is infinitely above him, sees him in sorrowful and necessitous circumstances, and has no pity upon him, when he at the same time won't have pity upon one of his fellow men who needs his help and compassion?

How can he justly complain that God won't forgive him his ten thousand talents that he owes Him when he himself won't forgive his fellow servant a hundred pence, but takes him by the throat and bids him pay what he owes?

How can they expect any other than to be judged by a holy and righteous God who are very apt to judge, condemn, and speak evil of their neighbor.

Reflect therefore upon yourself and inquire whether you have not been guilty of doing these things towards your neighbor. And let your mouth be stopped if you find that it has been so. Let it stop your mouth from complaining of the righteousness of God, though you should have judgment without mercy, though God should refuse to pardon your sins, and though He should judge and condemn you as you have others.

USE 2. Let this use be of instruction, for hence we learn the great condescension and goodness of God to men; that though

He will deal with men according to their temper and practice towards Him, that though He is infinitely superior to us, yet He will love all who love Him and honor those who honor Him, and give Himself to those who give themselves to Him, that He will seek the advancement of their welfare who seek the advancement of the interest of religion in this world, that He will bestow a kingdom upon such as seek the advancement of His kingdom, that He will in everything fulfill their desires who fulfill His commands and hear their prayers who hear His calls, and will repent Himself for those who repent of their sins, and humble Himself to dwell with those who humble themselves before Him, and that He will be upright and pure with those who are pure towards Him, and that Christ will own and confess those before His Father who confess Him before men.

God is not at all obliged to us for performing these duties towards Him, yet He condescends to do the like towards us that we do towards Him. He rewards us by doing the same towards us, the same in kind but infinitely better in degree. He loves those who love Him, but He loves them in a more transcendent manner.

USE 3. Let this use be of exhortation. Let us be of such a temper and practice towards God and men. As we would have God's dealings with us be agreeable to ours with Him, then let us love Him, honor Him, give ourselves to Him, walk according to His commands, and seek God's kingdom. If we would not have God contend with us, then let us be upright and pure with Him and with our fellow creatures. Let us repent and be humble; let us hear Him when He cries out to us; let us confess Him before men; let us show mercy and forgiveness to others, and let us forsake evil speaking.

This doctrine lays out before us a plain way to have the

enjoyment of the benefits of God's favor and friendship, and to have Him be all that to us that we would have Him be, that whatsoever we would that God should do to us, let us do accordingly in our behavior towards Him and towards our fellow creatures.

CHAPTER TEN

The Ladder that God Has Set on the Earth for Man to Ascend to Happiness Reaches Even Unto Heaven

(Preached in March 1736)

*"And he dreamed and beheld a ladder set upon the earth,
and the top of it reached to heaven."*

GENESIS 28:12

It was now a time of affliction with Jacob. When he was at home with his parents, he was afraid for his life because Esau sought to kill him, and therefore was forced to flee. He was, as it were, banished from his own country and his father's house to go to Padan Aram, which was a country far distant from the place where his parents dwelt. He is now upon his journey, having lately had probably a melancholy parting from his parents.

What we have an account of here in the text seems to have been on the first night of his journey. When night came there was no place that he could turn into for lodging.

The inhabitants of the land were idolaters of the posterity of Canaan. Jacob, a stranger, therefore lodges in the open field. We are told that he lighted on a certain place and tarried there all night. To comfort him in his afflicted, melancholy circumstances, God appeared to him in a dream, of which we have an account in our text and the three following verses.

The vision that he had of the ladder is doubtless something typical of that which is spiritual, as indeed all divine visions are representations of spiritual things. This story seems to be a type that has respect to two things:

1. Jacob seems to represent Christ in this story. In Isaiah 49:3 Christ is called by the name of "Israel," one of the names of Jacob. Here in this vision Jacob sees heaven opened to him, and the angels of God ascending and descending upon him; and therein he represents Christ, as is confirmed by what Christ says in John 1:51, "You shall see heaven opened and the angels of God ascending and descending on the Son of Man." Christ plainly alludes to what is said here in this verse concerning Jacob.

2. Jacob's sleep here seems to represent the death of Christ. Sleep is the image of death; so as Jacob in his sleep has the gates of heaven opened and a ladder set on the earth whose top reached to heaven, so Christ by His death opened the gates of heaven that otherwise would have been eternally shut. So by His death Christ procured a union between earth and heaven that

otherwise would have remained forever separated. And that there should be a way from heaven to earth by way to heaven, He procured, as it were, a ladder by which there might be an ascent from this sinful, miserable world to heaven.

By His death Christ procured this way to heaven for His covenant people, His spiritual seed; and therefore the foot of Jacob's ladder was set on the land of Canaan, the land of Jacob's posterity, the land of his people. And Christ, by His death, procured a way in which His people might go up to heaven, and in which they might have the angels of God ascending and descending on them, as here Jacob sleeping sees the angels of God ascending and descending on the land of Canaan.

As God here appeared to Jacob when asleep as the covenant God of him and his posterity, promising to give Canaan to him and his seed, to multiply his seed as the dust of the earth, and that he should spread abroad to the east, west, north, and south; so through the death of Christ, God appears as His covenant God, the covenant God of Him and His seed, promising to give to His seed the heavenly Canaan, to multiply His seed as the dust of the earth, and to give Him the Gentiles for His seed who dwell on the earth, and promising to give His seed the heavenly Canaan.

Jacob seems also in this story to represent a believer, or the church, spiritual Israel, of whom Jacob or Israel is the father and the stone that was laid for his pillow that he slept or rested on represents Christ, who is from time to time compared to a stone, and is the rock or stone on which believers rest. That Christ is represented by this stone seems more evident because He anointed it, as in verse 18. Thereby Christ is represented as "the anointed," as the word "Christ" signifies. Another thing that confirms that this stone is a type of Christ is what Jacob sings of it in verse 22: "This stone that I have set up for a pillar shall be God's house," for Christ is the house of God in whom dwells all the fullness of the Godhead bodily, who was the Person that was signified by the temple or house of God. This is evident by what Christ says of His own body, "Destroy this temple and in three days I will build it up." The Lamb is said to be the temple of the new Jerusalem (Revelation 21:22).

It is still further evidence that this stone on which Jacob rested was a type of Christ by the use he put it to, for he set it up for a pillar, that is, for an altar. The oil that he poured on it was to consecrate it as an altar to God. This will appear more evident if we compare it with chapter 35:14, where we have an account that Jacob in the same place set up a pillar of stone. Probably it was the same stone and he poured a drink offering thereon and poured oil thereon. There it is evident that Jacob made use of it as an altar to offer a drink offering to God. Therefore there can be no dispute but that Christ, the great Altar on which all our spiritual offerings must be offered, was typified by it.

So Jacob's sleeping or resting on this stone is a type of faith by which believers rest on Christ. Christ invites the weary to come to Him and rest. While resting on this stone, Jacob has heaven's gate opened to him and a ladder reaching from him to God in heaven. So it is by faith in Christ whereby believers rest on Christ, and whereby they have heaven's gate opened to them and have a ladder or a way procured for them to ascend and come to God in heaven.

While resting on the stone, Jacob had God appearing to him as his covenant God. So it is through faith in Christ that God becomes the covenant God of His people. All this privilege was grounded to Jacob in Bethel, which word signifies "the house of God." This typifies to us that obtaining the promises of Christ is wont to be in God's church and in the improvement of the ordinances of God's house.

DOCTRINE: The ladder that God has set on the earth for man to ascend to happiness reaches even unto heaven.

In speaking to this doctrine I shall observe:

1. God has set a ladder on the earth for men to ascend upon to happiness.
2. Show what this ladder is.
3. Show that it reaches even unto heaven.
4. Show how God in and through Christ provides for our ascending to such a height.

1. God has set, as it were, a ladder on the earth for man to climb to happiness. Man has lost his primitive happiness. He was set at first in a great height of honor and dignity, at a high pitch of blessedness, but by transgression he has fallen from thence. He is sunk low in misery and now all mankind is naturally in a very doleful state and condition, fallen from God, bereft of all good, groveling on the ground, and unable to rise. In the state that we are in by the fall we are no more able to come out of our misery or reach happiness than we are able to rise up to the clouds or ascend to the stars.

Here we are fallen and here we would have forever lain in this low and miserable state had God made no provision for us. But God, who is infinite in mercy, has had pity on a fallen, miserable world; and seeing that man can't rise out of misery or to any happiness himself, God has sent, as it were, a ladder down on the earth for us to go up on so that we might climb up and get above the sin and misery of the world and arrive at happiness. God has provided a way by which we may escape the misery into which we have fallen and may come to be happy creatures, notwithstanding the fall.

There are two things we stand in need of: we need deliverance from that dreadful destruction that we have brought on ourselves, and we need positive supplies to make us happy. Man needs happiness; 'tis what the nature of man unavoidably thirsts after. But God has contrived a way for obtaining fait. He has sent down, as it were, a ladder by which we may climb up and get out of the misery in which the fallen world is involved, and by which we may climb up to happiness.

2. I come next to show what this ladder is. It is the way and method of salvation that God has provided in Jesus Christ. 'Tis by Christ alone that there comes to be such a ladder sent down on the earth for poor, sinful man to ascend on out of a state of misery to a state of blessedness. This was typified, as has been observed, in Jacob's vision, of which we have an account in the text and context. When Jacob was asleep, which is the image of death, he had heaven opened and the ladder sent down to represent that Christ, by His death, procures a way of salvation for His seed or posterity. So if we look on Jacob or Israel as representing the church, the spiritual Israel, he has this ladder set down before him while resting on the stone that was a type of Christ, so the church has a way to heaven in no other way than by resting by faith. "Neither is there salvation in any other, for there is none other name under heaven given among men whereby we must be saved" (Acts 4:12).

The ladder by which fallen men can climb to happiness is the covenant of grace. It is only by the glorious gospel of Jesus Christ. The promises, the ordinances, and the spiritual attainments of that gospel or that covenant are, as it were, the rungs of that ladder.

3. This ladder which God has set on the earth for man to

ascend to happiness on reaches even unto heaven. The ladder that Jacob saw that was seated on the earth did not end in the clouds, nor did it reach only to the starry heavens, but the top of it reached even to the highest heavens, the heaven of heavens, that is, the habitation of God. For we are told that God appeared at the further end of it. So the covenant of grace that is established in Jesus Christ is a ladder by which men may not only ascend way high, but by which they may ascend even to the third imperial heaven. The provision that is made so that men may obtain happiness in Jesus Christ is sufficient for his obtaining no less than heavenly glory.

But to be more particular here:

It is not only that by which we may ascend above the misery and destruction to which we are exposed by sin, but it is that which tends to positive happiness. This world is a world of misery; by nature we are, as it were, exposed to a flood or deluge of divine wrath. When Noah's flood was coming upon the world and the waters began to overspread the earth, the inhabitants of the world sought for something by which they might climb out of the reach of the waters so that they might not be overwhelmed. Many, without a doubt, when they found the waters coming into their houses went to the upper parts of their houses, even to the tops of them. Others may have climbed to the tops of high trees, and others may have gone up to the tops of mountains. But when they got to the top they could go no higher; but the waters followed them and came upon them, and however high they climbed the waters rose above them and overwhelmed them. When they got to the top they could go no higher; and when the waters followed them and came up to them they wanted a ladder or something on which they might ascend higher so as to keep above the waters and be out of their reach—but there was none for them, and so the waters got above their heads and they perished.

But this ladder that we are speaking of such that it is high enough to ascend above the deluge of God's wrath, and not only that, but it puts us quite out of its reach. And this is not all: it doesn't only serve just to keep the sinner above wrath; it doesn't only reach to the utmost height of all earthly things; it doesn't only reach to the top of earthly happiness and to the highest pinnacle of all earthly grandeur—but it leads to a positive happiness as the fruit of the favor and love of God.

The inhabitants of the world, as to their temporal circumstances, are greatly distinguished from others: some are inferior and of low degree; others are exalted to a great height of worldly honor, greatness, and worldly possessions. It is much with the inhabitants of the earth as it is with the face of the earth itself: it is very uneven; there are some plains and there other places that are low, valleys. There are little hills and there are mountains; there is a great deal of difference in their height: some are comparatively high and others are exceedingly low.

Earthly glory is compared in Scripture to high mountains (Isaiah 2:14). Now this ladder that we are speaking of doesn't only reach to the top of the highest mountains, but it reaches even unto heaven; it doesn't only reach to the top of the highest and most magnificent earthly palaces, but it reaches to the palace of the King of Kings; it doesn't only reach to the top of the highest earthly mountains, but it reaches even to the top of the heavenly Mt. Zion. It leads those who ascend upon it far above other earthly enjoyments, far above all earthly honor and glory, for it leads to heavenly glory, the happiness and the honor of heaven. It leads not to an earthly crown, but to a heavenly crown.

The highest of earthly things are low and base in comparison to the height of glory that this ladder leads to; they seem high to the children of men who see nothing higher. If men stand upon the ground and look upon earthly buildings, the tops of them seem to be at a great height. Especially when men stand below such mountains they appear of a vast height. But how low would all these appear if we could ascend into the visible heavens! Those high and magnificent buildings would soon disappear and those great mountains that make us gaze and wonder at their height would appear as little molehills.

Just so is the state and magnificence of wealth and the grandeur of princes and earthly potentates in comparison to that heavenly glory to which this ladder reaches. Not only the mountains would appear small if we were high in the heavens, but if we could ascend to the starry heavens the whole globe of the earth would doubtless appear as a little speck. So is all that the world contains; all its pleasures, all its honor, and all its riches are but as a mite of dust, a thing worthy of no regard in comparison to that glory and blessedness that is promised in the covenant of grace.

This ladder doesn't only reach to the highest and most excellent created things, but it leads to the most high God. We have just shown that this ladder reaches above the height of all earthly things, but there are other created things that are higher and more excellent than any earthly things; there are creatures that are more exalted and excellent in their nature than any in this world, the angels who are glorious and blessed creatures.

The provision that is made for us through Christ is not only that we may come to the enjoyment of the love and friendship of glorious angels, and blessed acquaintance and communion with them, but that we may be brought to God Himself, the Fountain of all good.

The angels in Scripture are compared to the stars in Job

38:7. This ladder that God has set on the earth for us to ascend to happiness on doesn't only reach to the top of the highest mountains, nor yet does it only reach to the stars, but it reaches to the throne of God itself, that is, far above all heavens, as in Ephesians 4:10. Jacob's ladder reached up to God Himself who, as we are told, appeared as standing at the top of it and appearing there as the covenant God of Christ and His seed. There is provision made through Christ for us to ascend to happiness; it leads to the glorious presence of God where those who ascend it shall dwell with God and see God and enjoy the most high God, who is infinitely above all creatures, even the highest angels.

This ladder leads those who ascend upon it not only to imperfect degrees of heavenly enjoyments, but to perfection of heavenly glory. Good things are attained by the saints on this side of heaven; some are eminent in this world in holiness. We read of many in the Scriptures who, while in this world, were very eminent for their acquaintance with God, for a holy life, and who were admitted to eminent privileges of communion or conversation with God. Some are favored at some particular times especially with very great discoveries of God's glory, and of the excellency of Christ, and their hearts are filled with as much joy as their natures can bear. But all those other attainments, though high, yet are imperfect. All spiritual attainments on this side of heaven are very imperfect. But this ladder doesn't only lead those who ascend upon it to imperfect degrees of spiritual enjoyments, but it brings them to perfect happiness, to perfect light.

Here in this world there is light mixed with darkness, but they who ascend that ladder will come to a world of perfect light without darkness; for it will bring them to God who is Light, and in whom there is no darkness at all (1 John 1:5).

Here in this world it will bring them to a knowledge of God that shall be without any darkness or obscurity. 1 Corinthians 13:12: "Now we see through a glass darkly, but then face to face."

This ladder will bring them to perfect holiness and conformity to God in freedom, from all remains of corruption. In this world there is bitterness mingled with all sweetness, but they who are in the way of life by Jesus Christ, it will bring them to the sweetness without any bitter brittle, to a pure river of the water of life. This river is as clear as crystal, a heavenly river of pleasure that is not defiled and that has no taint of any kind. There is joy without sorrow and pleasure without pain. There is fullness of joy, complete and perfect happiness. Psalm 16:11: "In Thy presence is fullness of joy."

The top of this ladder reaches above all the changes of the visible world. All things in the visible world are within the reach of corruption, even the most durable of them. Hence the body of man is subject to corruption for it is an earthly thing, and so man is a mortal creature and all earthly things are liable to corruption. Not only so, but the visible honors are corruptible honors; all earthly honors and happiness are liable to cease and come to an end. The best, the sweetest, and the greatest of earthly enjoyments corrupt and come to nothing as well as others; they all fade away. Commonly the sweetest fade the soonest.

And not only earthly things are liable to corruption, but corruption has yet a more extensive dominion: it extends its power to the visible heavens. Those heavens are corruptible heavens. The stars especially, some of them, are exceedingly high, but yet they aren't so high as to be out of the reach of corruption; those heavens shall all wax old as a garment; they shall corrupt and fade away and come to be dissolved.

But the top of this ladder that God has set on the earth for man to ascend to happiness on reaches above all corruptible, inconstant nature. It reaches up above where corruption has no reign and never could; it reaches above the utmost limits of corruption. There are no dominions where it cannot reach nor extend its power. This ladder reaches to a place where they shall be subject to no death, but shall have eternal life, where their light, their happiness, and their joy shall never fade, for they shall have an inheritance that is incorruptible and undefiled, that does not fade away (1 Peter 1:4). They shall come to an unfading crown; their glory shall remain when all these things shall be dissolved. They who ascend to this ladder shall come to a country that is immortal, where everything is incorruptible.

The top of this ladder that they ascend on reaches above all the changes of the visible world. They who ascend on it shall not only get above the corruption of the visible world, but they shall also get above the reach of all that could allow for any diminution or interruption. This world is full of change continually, and even the spiritual circumstances of the godly are exceedingly changeable in many respects. What different frames are the godly in at different times: sometimes in the light and sometimes in darkness; sometimes joyful and at other times cast down with sorrow. Sometimes the light doesn't always shines; 'tis sometimes day and sometimes night. Often the light is hidden with clouds.

But they who ascend on this ladder find that it will bring them to that glorious city where there is no night. Revelation 22:5: "And there was no night there, neither shall there ever be a cloud to hide any of the light of the sun of God's glory." In this world the saints oftentimes meet with sorrowful changes; they meet with great affliction; sometimes they are sorely persecuted. But they who ascend this ladder find that it will bring them there where there is no affliction or persecution.

The church here sometimes is afflicted and agitated with horrible storms and tempests. But the ladder which God has set on the earth will bring them far above the reach of stars, above the clouds and tempests where such things cannot molest them. They shall dwell in perfect and perpetual tranquility.

Not only is this earth that we live on full of changes, but the visible heavens are also. The sun, moon, and stars are continually changing. They perform their revolutions from day to day and from age to age. Sometimes one part of heaven and sometimes another part is liable to eclipses. But this ladder reaches far above all such changes to a world of immutable and eternal glory and blessedness.

4. I come now to show how God, in and through Christ, provides or makes way for our ascending to such a height, or how this ladder God has set on the earth reaches to heaven.

He to whom heaven belongs has united Himself to man from eternity by undertaking for man in the covenant of redemption. One of the Persons of the sacred trinity, the eternal Son of God has united Himself to man. Heaven belongs to Jesus Christ, for He is the Heir of all things. Heaven is His house. He is the Possessor of heaven and earth. Heaven is His house, His palace. He is the Owner of the house, for it was He who built it; for we are told in John 1:3 that without Him nothing was made that was made, and that God made the worlds by Him (Hebrews 1:2), not only this lowly world, but the heavenly world. And we are told in Colossians 1:16 that by Him all things were created that are in heaven and on earth, visible and invisible.

As Christ was the Builder of the house, so He is the Owner of the house, as the apostle argues in Hebrews 3:3–6. Christ is the King of Heaven. The kingdom of heaven belongs to Him. But He has been pleased to unite Himself to man. He did so in some sort from eternity in the covenant of redemption by undertaking to be man's Surety. Thus Christ speaks of Himself as united to man before the world was created. Proverbs 8:31: "Then was I by him as one brought up with him. And I was daily his delight, rejoicing always before him; rejoicing in the habitable parts of the earth, and my delights were with the sons of men."

In the fullness of time He united Himself to man by taking on Himself man's nature. He who is the owner of heaven and who dwells in heaven came down from heaven and was made flesh and dwelt among us. John 3:13: "No man hath ascended up to heaven but He that came down from heaven, even the son of man who is in heaven." That is, no man even ascended there in his own right but He; but He came down from heaven that all who are His might ascend there. Christ, who is the Owner and King of heaven, having thus united Himself to man, those to whom He is united cannot fail of ascending to heaven and being where He is.

By His death Christ has removed the great thing that separated heaven and earth, which is guilt. Before man fell there was a friendly communication between heaven and earth; but when man became a guilty creature the union was broken and a great separation was made. But Christ, by His death, has removed this for He has made a complete atonement for sin. So now those obstacles are removed out of the way, the gate of heaven is open, and the way is clear.

He has laid down a price for man, sufficient to purchase heaven, as high as heaven. It is as glorious and exalted as its happiness is, and though it is so much above all earthly glory, though it is eternal, yet Christ has paid the price for it, that is, equivalent to the worth of it. His righteousness is a jewel precious enough in the eyes of God to answer to this height of glory.

Since His resurrection He has gone into heaven and taken

possession of it in His people's name. He ascended into heaven in our nature; the man Christ Jesus has gone to heaven in our name as well as in our nature. He has gone as our Forerunner. He now has gone there, and there remains as a public Person, as the Head of believers. He has gone to heaven as the first-fruits (1 Corinthians 15:23).

Thus He has entered into heaven as the high priest of old entered into the holy of holies: not in his own name only, but in the name of the people. Christ has taken possession of heaven as the purchased possession so that He might reserve it for His saints and in due time bestow it upon them. Hebrews 6:19–20: "Which hope we have as an anchor of the soul, both sure and steadfast, and which entereth into that within the veil; whither the Forerunner is for us entered, even Jesus, made a High Priest forever after the order of Melchisedec."

5. Believers are united by faith to Him who has thus perished and is gone into heaven.

6. In regeneration Christ gives believers a heavenly principle. Men are by nature utterly unfit for heaven and incapable of it; they are wholly earthly; they have nothing in them that tends heavenward, but everything in them tends downward to the earth. But God in Christ in regeneration gives a new principle. He gives His Holy Spirit to dwell in them so that their souls thenceforth become the habitation or temple of a heavenly inhabitant. And by this Spirit heavenly dispositions, inclinations, and affections are wrought in them. The soul that before tended only to the earth has its earthiness mortified and there is thenceforward a tendency heavenward. There are earnest desires after heaven and heavenly objects and enjoyments. The principle that is infused is, as it were, a heavenly seed planted in the soul; it is a spark of fire from heaven there; it

is a beam of light, heaven's light, let into the soul that is, as it were, the daystar risen in the heart; but its tendency is to lead heavenward. It draws the soul that way and causes it to choose heaven for its portion, and stirs it up to seek a heavenly walk and conversation.

7. This principle is implanted by God, who makes it bring forth heavenly fruits in sanctification. Where this principle is infused, it shall always be maintained. Philippians 4:6: "He that has begun a good work in you shall complete it until the day of Christ Jesus."

God will never suffer this seed to be rooted out. He will never suffer this bright though small spark to be extinguished. Though sometimes it is buried in ashes, it shall be kept alive; yea, it shall increase and shine more and more; the seed shall take deeper and deeper root, and it shall be bountiful. The water that is given in regeneration shall be a living spring of water, a spring that is never dry, but springing up into everlasting life. The saints shall have their fruit unto holiness, and their end everlasting life (Romans 6:22).

8. Christ will come a second time from heaven to take the saints in both soul and body to heaven. Christ came down from heaven the first time to purchase heaven, but He will come the second time to bestow it. Hebrews 9:28: "So Christ was once offered to bear the sins of many; and unto them that look for Him shall He appear the second time without sin unto salvation." Christ went into heaven after His resurrection to prepare a place for His people; and He has promised them that He will come again to receive them to the place prepared. John 14:2–3: "I go to prepare a place for you. And if I go and prepare a place for you, I will come again, and receive you unto Myself; that where I am there ye may be also."

APPLICATION

USE OF SELF-EXAMINATION. Inquire whether or not one who is ascending towards heaven on this ladder. This ladder that I have been speaking of is the only way to happiness; there is no other way that God has provided by which men can ascend to or arrive at any happiness, or can ascend out of their misery. God has set down no other ladder on the earth for the sinful children of men to ascend on to escape the wrath to come.

There are other ways that men endeavor to rise to happiness on. 'Tis the strife of all the world to get happiness. Everyone strives in some manner: some climb on one thing and some on another; and the strife of men is very much who shall get the highest degree of happiness. Some men have ascents of their own by which they endeavor to arrive at happiness: some strive to rise to happiness by their great estates; some seek it by sensual pleasures; some seek it in the pinnacles of earthly honor and greatness. Many build towers and make ladders of their own by which they think to rise to heaven, even their own righteousness.

There is as general a strife to get up on high as there was in the time of Noah's flood, wherein some went to the tops of houses, some on the tops of trees, and some on high mountains; but their climbing will be as much in vain as theirs was in the time of Noah: not a none of them will be able to get where they aim at; but it will be with them as it was with the others. The wrath of God will overwhelm them. The flood of God's wrath is rising and it will soon overtop the height of their ascent and get above their heads. And all will perish but those who ascend on this ladder that God has set down on the earth.

But as for those who do ascend on it, we have heard to what a height of glory it will lead them. Therefore diligently inquire whether you are one who is ascending upon this ladder. And in order to aid you in that inquiry, ask yourself:

1. On whom do you depend for happiness? Do you depend on the Lord Jesus Christ alone? This ladder, as you have heard, is the way of salvation by Jesus Christ in the covenant of grace that God has established in Him. None therefore are in this way but those who have their dependence on Him.

Jacob had heaven opened to him; he had this ladder set down before him from heaven to earth while he rested on the stone of Bethel, that was a type of Christ. And so if ever you find this ladder, if you are ascending to heavenly happiness, you have been brought to rest on Jesus, that stone that God has laid in Zion.

What is the foundation of your trust and hope? On what basis do you take encouragement that God will have mercy on you and that you shall be happy? Is not the thought of what you have done and the lovely qualifications that you have obtained, your own goodness or loveliness of heart or life, the thing that is the secret ground of your encouragement and comfort? Or do you see that this is nothing, and that there is no dependence to be had on it?

Is the consideration of the greatness and sovereignty of mercy through a Saviour the only ground of your encouragement? Does your heart and soul seem to close with this way of salvation as a far more excellent way than by your own righteousness? Is that way of being saved through the merits of Christ and sovereign grace through Him only, making no account of your righteousness, sweet to your soul, a thousand times sweeter than being saved by your own righteousness? Do you abhor the thought of coming for acceptance in your own worthiness, because you see you are so far from having any worthiness?

Jacob rested and had sweet repose on the stone of Bethel. Does your soul take rest and acquiesce in the way of sovereign grace revealed in the gospel, seeing that there is no need of any other way, and that there can be no better way? And so, choosing this way and desiring no other, have you come to sit down under the shadow of this tree with contentment and rest of soul?

2. Have you in any measure gotten above the world? Is your heart in some good measure above earthly things? This way of salvation by Jesus Christ is upward; the ascent of this ladder is away from the earth towards heaven. Those who ascend this ladder do not stay upon the earth; they get off from it and get up above it. And the more they ascend, so much the further are they separated from the earth.

Are you one who has in your heart, in some measure, left the earth and ascended up above it, or do you yet stay down below, groveling upon the ground? Are you one who chooses your portion in this life, or do you see something above the world that is better than the world?

Is not your heart as knit to the world and earthly things as ever it was? Are not your appetites and inclinations as eager and violent as they used to be after the things of this world? Aren't you as much involved in earthly cares and anxieties as ever? Doesn't your heart stick as close to these things as it used to do? Is not your pretense of being better a mere pretense when, indeed, your heart sticks as close as ever to the world? Are you not as loath as ever to part with a little of the world for a pious life?

A godly man may have great remains of worldliness and earthly enjoyments for charitable uses. But when the world and your duty to God or Christ's honor and glory stand in competition, is it not your manner or practice to give the preference to worldly enjoyments? Don't you stick faster to the world than to God in such cases? Is it not your manner in such cases to excuse yourself from duty when it is cross to your worldly interests?

And so, by one means or the other, worldly men will cleave to the world. They won't forsake it. Because it is the character of a godly man that he must be ready to part with other things for God, he will labor to invent arguments to satisfy his case that such and such things are not his duty. Or, if he can't persuade himself of that, then he will plead that, though he is overcome by temptation, yet he doesn't allow himself in it.

When God and the world come into competition, he will be sure to stick to the world. If he can find excuses or arguments to satisfy his conscience or blind his eyes about his duty, he will; if not, he will strive to invent some other way to quiet himself. He is not a man who is wont, from time to time, to quit the world for God. He will find out some way or another to keep the world close by him. When it is thus with a man, it is a sign that he is not one who is ascending Jacob's ladder.

3. Do you find that the tendency of your heart is heavenward? The way that this ladder leads is upward toward heaven; the top of it reaches unto heaven, and therefore the tendency of all those who are ascending on it is heavenward.

Inquire therefore whether heaven is your chosen inheritance. Are heavenly enjoyments such as you have chosen? Have you had a sense of the sweetness of them so as to convince you that they are the highest good and so as to make you desire them above all things? Is your heart in heaven?

4. Do you make God your end? We have an account in the text that God appeared to Jacob as standing at the top of the ladder; therefore they who are ascending on that ladder are

ascending up to God; they make God their aim; their motion is Godward.

Is it so with you? Is God your aim in your life? Here I would not be understood as saying that it will prove you to be insincere if you aim at anything else, but consider it if you have any respect to your own interest. I would not be understood to say that you are insincere if you have acted in a great measure from self-love, but self-love is not all to the saints. The saints have a spirit in them to prefer God to themselves, and they are under the influence of a respect to God. It is God they seek and aim at; they aim at His glory and they aim at Him as their chief Good. They are influenced by a gracious respect to God, and that gracious respect to God has various ways of working. It is exercised in seeking the glory of God, and also in seeking to please Him. It seeks communion with Him, and seeks the enjoyment of God as the highest happiness.

This is what principally causes the saints to seek heaven, to enjoy God there. The God of heaven is the main object of their desire. Psalm 73:25: "Whom have I in heaven besides Thee, and on earth I desire none else."

This is what they climb the ladder for, and continue ascending all their lives: to get to God, who is at the top of the ladder. He stands at the top of it so that they may have their clear knowledge of Him, so that they may see Him, dwell with Him, praise and glorify Him, and enjoy Him forever.

5. Is it your sincere desire and earnest endeavor to get higher and higher, or are you content with past attainments? He who ascends a ladder gets higher and higher; he gets from one step to another, from one rung to another. The lower rungs that he first got upon he leaves behind, and his aim is still upwards to those rungs that are yet before him. He strives to get up to them, and he doesn't stop till he has gotten to the top of the

ladder. If you therefore are one who has looked upon yourself as converted and are content with that; if you don't find it to be the appetite and desire of your soul to get higher degrees of grace—it is a sign that you are not upon Jacobs ladder, nor are you in any way to get to heaven.

He who is converted has not completed his work. That labor of ascending the ladder yet remains. He has only gotten upon the first rung of the ladder. The labor of ascending the ladder yet remains and will continue till he has gotten to the top. Are you one who, since you have thought yourself to be converted, have done your work? Or, on the contrary, do you find a great work still to do and desire to do? Do find your mind engaged? Are you one who hungers and thirsts after righteousness, one who laments your present barrenness, and laments that you have made no more progress? Are you one who is everlastingly wishing and struggling to be more holy and to live better?

USE OF EXHORTATION. This exhortation is in three branches:

1. Take heed that you do not go about making ladders of your own to climb to heaven by. Don't go about to ascend on the ladder of your own righteousness. Men's imaginations are exceedingly vain about their own righteousness; they imagine it to be a ladder high and strong enough for them to ascend to heaven by. But this ladder will fail you; if you go about to ascend to heaven on it you will only rise far enough to fall.

You may entertain yourself with pleasing imaginations that you are in a fair way to get to heaven, but at last you will fall to your destruction and ruin. And the higher you seem to ascend, the more dreadful will be your fall at the end. Persons who ascend on that ladder, instead of getting to heaven by it, as they hope, they only rise to fall deeper into hell.

It is vain for men to think to build up anything whose top

may reach to heaven. Men who are building the tower of their own righteousness will find that their enterprise will issue like that of those who built the Tower of Babel. They said, of which we have an account in the chapter 11, "Let us build us a city and a tower, whose top may reach unto heaven." But they were confounded and scattered abroad in their enterprise and design.

2. Let these persons seek to find this ladder. If it reaches even unto heaven, and it leads to that by which you may ascend out of that dreadful misery that you are in by nature; and if it reaches not only to the utmost height of all earthly things, to the most excellent created objects, but to God Himself, and to that heavenly felicity that consists in the enjoyment of Him, and that not only in some imperfect degree, but in a perfect fullness, and that in a state that is above all corruption or any of the changes of the visible world—then surely it is well worth the while to very earnestly endeavor to find this ladder and to ascend upon it to happiness.

But here I would offer some things as motives:

MOTIVE 1. If you stay below in this world and don't ascend from it by this ladder you must perish with the world. This world is to perish; it is a world that is condemned by God. 1 Corinthians 11:32: "But when we are judged we are chastened of the Lord that we should not be condemned with the world." This world is a fallen, sinful world and is under the curse; and when Christ came into the world it was to save a number out of the world, to rescue them, as it were, out of a sinking ship. John 15:19: "Ye are not of the world, but I have chosen you out of the world." And John 17:6: "I have manifested Thy name to the men which Thou gavest Me out of the world."

Christ has denounced woe against this world. Matthew 18:7: "Woe to the world." And there will surely be a most fearful destruction come upon it. It is as devoted to destruction as the cities of Sodom and Gomorrah were.

Though the world is no more to be destroyed with a flood of waters, yet 'tis to be destroyed with a more dreadful destruction, even with a deluge of fire. It is a fire that never shall be quenched, and one that will bring torments that never will end. 2 Peter 3:5–7: "By the word of God the heavens were of old, and the earth standing out of the water and in the water; whereby the world that then was, being overflowed with water, perished. But the heavens and the earth, which are now, by the same word are kept in store, reserved unto fire against the day of judgment and perdition of ungodly men."

There is no other way to escape or get away from this accursed and condemned world, and so to get out of the reach of this destruction, but by this ladder spoken of in our text and doctrine. If we have not ascended this ladder when the fire of God's wrath begins to come on the world, we shall have no way to escape. When we see it coming like a flood, if we have nowhere to flee, if we go into dens and mountain caves, that will be in vain; for the fire will search us out. It shall set on fire the foundation of the mountains and burn to the lowest hell. It shall burn the earth to its very center and burn up the earth with its increase, as we read in Deuteronomy 32:22.

MOTIVE 2. If you can find this ladder, God will be your covenant God. We are told in our text that when Jacob saw this ladder, "Behold, the Lord stood above upon it and said, 'I am the Lord God of Abraham thy father, and the God of Isaac. And behold I am with thee and will keep thee in all places whether thou goest and will not leave thee until I have done that which I have spoken to thee of." And so will God appear as your covenant God if ever you find that way of life that God has provided in Jesus Christ.

MOTIVE 3. If ever you find this ladder, the angels will be ministering spirits to you. They will ascend and descend from God to you as they appeared in Jacob's vision. They will be sent forth with messages from God to you. We are told that they are all ministering spirits (Hebrews 1:14).

If you find this way of salvation that God has provided in Jesus Christ, the angels of God will be your angels. Matthew 18:10: "Take heed that ye offend not one of these little ones, for verily I say unto you that in heaven their angels do always behold the face of my Father which is in heaven."

God's angels will many times help you and protect you from unseen evils when you do not know it, and will do you many a good turn when you perceive nothing of them. It is said that "the angel of the Lord encampeth round about them that fear Him" (Psalm 34:7). They encamp round about them; they are an armed guard and oftentimes, without doubt, keep off evil spirits and help the saints against their assaults.

If you are found in this way of life, then the angels of God will have charge concerning you as long as you live. And when you come to die they shall surround your dying bed so that no evil spirit may come nigh, and will conduct your soul to eternal glory, as they did the beggar in Luke 16:22.

MOTIVE 4. Consider that there are but few who find this ladder. This is the same as with that narrow way that leads to life spoken of in Matthew 7:14, where Christ tells us that there are but few who find it. There are many who think they have found it, and think that they are ascending on it—but they are mistaken. They are many who hope to get to heaven who are mistaken. Many think they are on this ladder when it is only the ladder of their own righteousness they are ascending on. They are never likely to get to heaven, but in a little time will fall headlong into eternal destruction.

MOTIVE 5. This ladder may be come at by such sinful and unworthy creatures as you are; though you can't come at it of yourself, because you are dead in sin, yet 'tis not above the capacity of your natures, neither need your sin and unworthiness be a hindrance. For though the top of the ladder reaches to heaven, yet the foot of it is set on the earth so that those who dwell on the earth may come to it. It is offered so that the most vile and sinful creatures may come to it and may truly climb on it without presumption.

3. Let those who hope that they are on this ladder be exhorted not to stand still, but to ascend upon it. Labor continually to get higher. This ladder was made and set down on the earth for man to ascend upon, and not to stand still upon. One rung was made above another so that persons might get higher and higher; one rung was made so that persons might get from there to the next one and from there to the next rung.

Therefore, don't rest in what you have attained, but let it be your continual work every day to get from step to step, from one degree of grace to another.

The work of a Christian is to ascend; this is what he is to spend his life on, climbing this ladder. Let this therefore be your daily and continual work. Though it is hard work, though the weight of your body sways you down, though the ascent goes against the tendency of the flesh and the inclinations of your corrupt nature, yet it may encourage you to consider where the top of the ladder reaches. Consider that at the top of it is heaven's gate standing wide open, and that God stands above it, the Fountain of Blessedness. This may well stir you up to ascend with utmost diligence.

And though it is laborious, yet you will find that you are paid for your labor as you ascend; for the higher you rise, the more clear and full prospect you will have of the world of glory that is at the top of the ladder, and the more clear sight you will have of the God who stands above it.

At length you shall have a joyful arrival at that heavenly world of glory and be in the glorious presence of God, where you shall no more have any occasion for this laborious climbing. You shall rest forever from your labor and shall sit down forever in the kingdom of God; you shall be feasted with the fruits of the Tree of Life that grows in the midst of that glorious paradise and Christ Himself shall feed you.

Consider what you can do or which way you can turn for any help or support. You cannot bear the torment of hell, and that because it is so extreme and because it is everlasting. The thought of its being eternal will swallow you up. Isaiah 33:14: "The sinners in Zion are afraid; fearfulness hath surprised the hypocrites."

When pain and affliction are brought on the soul, the nature of the soul makes resistance, and labors to free and support itself. But as in Jeremiah 5:31: "What will you do in the end, and where will ye flee for help?"

Let this ladder lead you to the living fountain of virtues, where you shall have nothing else to do for all eternity but to drink of those rivers of pleasure that are at God's right hand forevermore.

CHAPTER ELEVEN

God, as the Giver and Judge of the Law, Deals with the Utmost Strictness

(Preached in July 1736)

"And Joshua said unto the people, 'Ye cannot serve the LORD, for He is a holy God; He is a jealous God; He will not forgive your transgressions nor your sins.' "

JOSHUA 24:19

In these two last chapters of this book we have Joshua's exhortation and counsel that he gave to the people before his death. We are told in the beginning of this chapter that Joshua gathered all the tribes of Israel together into Shechem and called for the elders of Israel, and for their heads and for their judges and their officers who presented themselves before God. And there Joshua rehearsed for them the wonderful things which God had done for Israel. Then, from verse 14 he applies all to enforce their duty to God upon them, earnestly exhorting and pressing them to live for the Lord and to serve Him in sincerity and truth, putting away all other gods from them to serve Him alone. In verse 15 he puts it upon them to choose whom they would serve, to give occasion to them to know their covenant with God to serve Him: "And if it seem evil unto you to serve the LORD, choose you this day whom ye will serve; whether the gods which your fathers served that were on the other side of the flood, or the gods of the Amorites, in whose land ye dwell; but as for me and my house, we will serve the LORD."

Upon this the people seem without hesitation to declare that they will serve the Lord, and seem to be very full and earnest in their resolution so to do, as in verses 16–18: " And the people answered and said, God forbid that we should forsake the LORD, to serve other gods. For the LORD our God, he it is that brought us up and our fathers out of the land of Egypt, from the house of bondage, and which did those great signs in our sight, and preserved us in all the way wherein we went, and among all the people through whom we passed. And the LORD drove out from before us all the people, even the Amorites which dwelt in the land. Therefore will we also serve the LORD; for He is our God."

This that they say is the occasion of the words of Joshua in the text. They are his reply to what they had said: "And Joshua said unto the people, 'Ye cannot serve the LORD, for He is a holy God; He is a jealous God; He will not forgive your transgressions nor your sins.' "

There are these several things that seem to be the occasion

of Joshua's making such a reply to them:

1. Joshua. was sensible that though they seemed so very fervent and earnest in their declaration, they did not sufficiently count the cost. Joshua seemed at this time to be under the miraculous inspiration of the Spirit of God whereby he knew what was in their hearts; and he was sensible that though they seemed so mighty forward for the present to declare that they would serve the Lord, and seemed to be so earnest in their resolution, that they were not yet sensible of the difficulties that were on the way; they did not sufficiently consider what it was to serve God. Sometimes those who for the present seem most earnest and resolute are indeed least prepared to go through difficulties. How earnest and resolute Peter seemed to be that he would never forsake his Master, and yet that very night he denied Him again and again.

People particularly seem to be insensible of how holy and strictly a walk it was that God required of them, and how universal their obedience must be in order to its being accepted as an acceptable service by so holy and just a God. They are insensible that God would not allow them to gratify any of their lusts, as to walk in any way of sin whatsoever, and that if they allowed themselves in any one wicked practice it would render all unacceptable to Him.

2. He was sensible that they took up this position with much self-confidence; and therefore Joshua, who was now about to lead the people to renew their covenant with God, was willing to let them know what was expected of them so that their covenant might be more explicit, that afterwards when they came to depart from this covenant, they might not say that they were not forewarned how great and difficult a thing it was to serve God aright, and how holy and strictly it was expected that they should behave themselves.

3. Joshua seems to have been sensible that the people took up this resolution with too much of a self-confident spirit, with too much of a confidence in their own strength, in their own ability to keep the law of God and to serve Him to His acceptance. They were insensible of the exceeding corruption that was in their hearts and how ready they wcre to go astray, to be overcome by temptations, how unstable their own hearts were, and what need they stood in of God's assistance to enable them to walk in His way.

They also did it with too much confidence in their own righteousness. They were not sensible, but thought that they could fulfill the law themselves, and could thereby perform the conditions of God's favor themselves. They did not consider how holy and just a God they had to do with, and how strict His law was and how exact God would be to His law in acting as a Judge.

When the people declared their resolution in the manner that they did, they showed a great ignorance of their own hearts. At the same time God saw their hearts to be otherwise than they thought them to be, like it was when the people publicly entered into covenant at Mt. Sinai. When the people heard the words of the Lord, when Moses rehearsed to them the words of the Lord, with great forwardness they made an answer with one accord: "All that the Lord hath spoken we will do" (Exodus 19:8). But see the account that Moses gives of what God said on that occasion in Deuteronomy 5:28: "And the Lord heard the voice of your words when ye spake unto me, and the Lord said unto me, 'I have heard the voice of the words of this people which they have spoken unto thee. They have well said all that they have spoken. Oh, that there were such an heart in them that they would fear Me and keep all My commandments always, that it might be well with them and their children forever." And how soon did they make the golden calf, notwithstanding.

In the words of the text we may observe:

1. That Joshua declares the people to be unable to serve God. And in this two things seem to be implied: First, that they were utterly unable in their own strength to perform an acceptable service to God; and, second, that they were utterly unable to fulfill the law or to do what the law required in order to be entitled by the law to God's favor.

2. The reason for this is given in two attributes of God: His holiness ("He is a holy God") and his jealousy of His holiness. His holiness would not allow Him to accept or to tolerate the least sin.

3. How His holiness and jealousy influenced in this affair to make evident what Joshua had said, that God would not pardon or forgive their sins, that is, that these attributes would not allow Him to accept a partial obedience so as to allow a man to go on in any way of sin. His holiness and jealousy would not allow Him to pardon one sin in a way of absolute mercy without that sin's being punished and satisfied for, and the law's being answered concerning it.

The meaning is not that God would on no account pardon sin, but the sense is the same as that in Exodus 34:7: "forgiving iniquity and transgression and sin, and that will by no means clear the guilty." In one clause it is said "forgiving iniquity and transgression and sin," yet in the next clause it is said "and will by no means clear the guilty." So that the meaning is not that God won't on any account pardon sin, but the meaning is that He won't let their sins pass without due testimonies of His displeasure and proper punishment. He won't let them pass as little things, not worthy to be taken notice of, as they did themselves and were too ready to think that God would do.

DOCTRINE: God, as the Giver and Judge of the law, deals with the utmost strictness.

In speaking to this doctrine I would, first, show that God deals with the utmost strictness as the Giver of the law and, second, as the Judge of it.

1. God deals with the utmost strictness as the Giver of the Law, and this appears by the strictness of the law. The strictness of the law appears in the precepts of the law and in the sanctions of the law. The strictness of the law in the precepts of the law appears in the evil it forbids and in the good that it requires.

The law of God is strict in the evil that it forbids as it forbids evil of all kinds, evil of all degrees, in all cases and at all times.

The law forbids evil of all kinds. It forbids gratifying any lust, doing any evil towards God, towards our neighbor, or towards ourselves. It forbids sins of thought, sins of actions, or sins of word. It forbids not only overt acts, but all notions of sin. The law forbids not only acts of sin, but habits of sin.

The law forbids evil of all degrees, whether it be degrees of evil in action, degrees of evil in sinful notion, degrees of evil in habit, or degrees of evil in sinful disposition.

The law forbids evil in all cases.

The law forbids evil at all times, not only in riper years but in youth. Many seem to think that God gives a liberty in youth. But the law forbids evil in childhood also. The law forbids evil not only on the sabbath day, not only when we are in the meetinghouse, but at times of work, when we are in discussions, or at home. Thus the strictness of the law appears in the evil it forbids.

The strictness of the law also appears in the good that it requires. The law doesn't only forbid all sinful acts and habits, but requires all holy acts and habits.

It doesn't only require holiness in every disposition and

action, but to the utmost capacity of our nature.

The law requires that every action be holy.

The strictness of the law appears in the sanctions of the law. By the law, all moral evil of every kind and degree is mortal and exposes the sinner to eternal death. The papists make a distinction between venial sin and mortal sin; they hold that some sins aren't mortal sins and they call them "venial sins." But herein they are very corrupt in their doctrine, for so strict is the law of God that it threatens eternal death for every breach of it, even the smallest. By the law, every sin is a damning sin; all moral evil exposes a man to the curse of God to all eternity. Romans 6:23: "The wages of sin is death." This is not only the wages of a wicked life or sinful course, but of our sin of any one thing that is a breach of the divine law, as appears from Galatians 3:10: "Cursed is every one that continueth not in all things which are written in the book of the law to do them." And James 2: 10: "He that offends in one point is guilty of all."

But to be more particular here, not only does the law threaten eternal destruction to a wicked practice or sinful course, but to any one sin in any one thing, whatsoever it is whereby a man verges from the rule or the precept of the divine law. The threatening of the law as it was given to Adam especially respected a single act of sin. Genesis 2:17: "In the day that thou eatest thou shalt surely die."

That particular sins distinctly expose to death is evident by the terrible manifestations which God has given of His displeasure against particular acts of sin. What terrible judgments were inflicted for that one sin of David's numbering the People. God offered either three years of famine or to flee three months before their enemies or three days pestilence. David chose the last one, and there died of Israel seventy thousand men (2 Samuel 24:15).

And yet God's mercies appeared to be exceedingly great in that this judgment was no worse. It was as David hoped when he chose to fall into the hands of God and not into the hands of man. The reason he gave for it was that God's mercies were great.

We read how that God in mercy repented of the evil and commanded the destroying angel to stay his hand when he stretched it out on Jerusalem to destroy it. And, after all this, sin must be atoned for by sacrifice. God commanded him to go and build an altar in the threshing — and there to offer sacrifices to atone for this sin. This showed that all these terrible judgments did not satisfy justice for the guilt of that sin nor at all take off the desert of death. That sacrifice must yet be slain for that sin or the demerit of eternal death would yet remain as much as ever.

See how terrible God's anger was for Achan's sin of taking the accursed thing. God was angry with the whole congregation, so much so that they could not stand before their enemies; and God tells Joshua in Joshua 7:12: "Therefore the children of Israel could not stand before their enemies, but turned their backs before their enemies because they were accursed." The whole congregation was spoken of as accursed because of this guilt, and it follows, "Neither will I be with you anymore except ye destroy the accursed thing from among you."

How terrible the judgment of Achan and his family was in verses 24–26: "And Joshua, and all Israel with him, took Achan the son of Zerah, and the silver, and the garment, and the wedge of gold, and his sons, and his daughters, and his oxen, and his asses, and his sheep, and his tent, and all that he had; and they brought them unto the valley of Achor. And Joshua said, 'Why hast thou troubled us? The LORD shall trouble thee this day.' And all Israel stoned him with stones, and burned them with fire, after they had stoned them with stones. And they raised over him a great heap of stones unto this day. So the LORD turned from the fierceness of his anger. Wherefore the name of that place was called 'The Valley of Achor' unto this day."

The fire with which these things were burned was a type of the eternal fire of God's wrath, signifying what that accursed thing sin deserved and should be punished with.

How dreadful the wrath of God was against the men of Bethshemesh for looking into the ark. He miraculously slew fifty thousand threescore and ten men (1 Samuel 6:19).

The law threatens eternal destruction not only for sins in deed, but for only one undue expression or word. Matthew 5:22: "Whosoever shall say unto his brother, 'Raca,' shall be in danger of the council; and whosoever shall say, 'Thou fool,' shall be in danger of hellfire.' " So Matthew 12:36–37: "For every idle word that men shall speak, they shall give account thereof in the day of judgment." These words show that one idle word exposes us to condemnation, for what is a man called to account for but only in order to a decision of the point, that is, whether they shall be justified or condemned. But the following words confirm it: "By thy words thou shall be justified and by thy words thou shall be condemned." So that one idle word exposes a man to be condemned at the day of judgment. But if it exposes him to condemnation, then it exposes him to eternal death, for there is no other punishment that a man will be condemned to there but eternal destruction. We read of no other sentence of condemnation to be pronounced at the day of judgment but that one found in Matthew 25: "Depart ye cursed into everlasting fire."

Every exercise of an evil inclination in the heart is husband with eternal destruction. Matthew 5:28: "Whosoever looketh upon a woman to lust after her in his heart hath committed adultery already." Thus death is threatened only for being angry without a cause (Matthew 5:22). Any exercise of an ill spirit towards an enemy, though it be only in the heart, is spoken of as a thing that exposes us to God's curse. Proverbs 24:17–18: "Rejoice not when thine enemy falleth, and let not thine heart be eased when he stumbleth. Lest the Lord see it and it displease Him, and He destroy the work of thine hands." Here it is spoken of as a thing that exposes to God's curse. Job mentions this as a wicked thing which, if he had been guilty of, would have merited the curse of God upon him. Job 31:29: "If I rejoiced at the destruction of him that hated me, or lifted up myself when evil found him."

Sins of omission are, in the law, threatened with eternal destruction. Thus Christ at the day of judgment will eternally condemn men to eternal burning for sins of omission. Matthew 25:41–43: "Then shall He say also unto them on the left hand, 'Depart from Me, ye cursed, into everlasting fire, prepared for the devil and his angels; for I was an hungry and ye gave Me no meat, I was thirsty and ye gave Me no drink, I was a stranger and ye took Me not in; naked and ye clothed Me not, sick and in prison and ye visited Me not."

Only a tendency to any soul omission in the inclination or thought is a damnable sin by the law, as appears from Deuteronomy 15:9: "Beware that there be not a thought in (or, as it is in the original "of a word") in thy wicked heart, saying, 'The seventh year, the year of release, is at hand'; and thine eye be evil against thy poor brother, and thou givest him nought; and he cry unto the LORD against thee, and it be sin unto thee."

This is one of the precepts written in the Book of the Law, of which it is said, "Cursed is everyone that continueth not in all things written therein."

An evil disposition or temper of word, though it is only negatively evil, is spoken of as damnable. 1 Corinthians 16:22: "if any man love not the Lord Jesus Christ, let him be anathema."

Sins of ignorance, by the law, expose to eternal damnation. This is evident because God appointed sacrifices of slain beasts to be offered for sins of ignorance, as you may see throughout Deuteronomy 4. This is plain evidence that these sins deserved eternal damnation, for when the beast. was slain in sacrifice it signified that it was slain in the name of him for whose sin it was offered, and signified that he deserved to be slain. And when the sacrificed beast was burned in the fire, that fire was a type of the fire of God's wrath and signified that this deserved the fire of God's wrath. Offering the sacrifices of slain beasts for sins of ignorance plainly allows that sins of ignorance deserve God's eternal wrath because all these sacrifices were types of the sacrifice of Christ; they signified that persons, by sins of ignorance, stood in need of the death and sufferings of Christ to make atonement for them. But if they did not deserve eternal death, they could not stand in need of the death of Christ and His suffering in the fire of God's wrath to make atonement for them.

This is with evident by God's awful dealing with Uzzah, only for his mistake when he put forth his hand to hold the ark when the oxen shook it (2 Samuel 6:6–7). He meant well, but he was struck dead for it. He ought to have taken more care to have acquainted himself with what the law of God was, and then he would not have been exposed to such mistakes.

When God inflicts temporal death on a man for any sin, it truly signifies that sin deserves eternal death; for temporal death is spoken of by Christ as signifying eternal destruction in Luke 13. Speaking of those whose blood Pilate mingled with their sacrifices, and those on whom the tower of Siloam fell, He said, "Except ye repent ye shall all likewise perish." Christ didn't mean that they should be slain with the same sort of temporal death for their sin, but that as they perished and suffered death temporally, so would they perish and suffer death eternally if they did not repent.

In the instance of God's slaying Abimelech, it is also evident that sins of ignorance deserve the penalty of the law. In Genesis 20, God said to Abimelech that he had ignorantly taken Sarah. "Behold, thou art but a dead man; for the woman which thou hast taken is a man's wife." This certainly implies that he deserved death; and yet in verse 6 God says to him, "Yea, I know that thou didst this in the integrity of thine heart." And Abimelech says to Abraham in verse 9, "What hast thou done to us, and what have I offended that thou hast brought on me and on my kingdom a great sin?" He not only calls it a great sin, but signifies that it would have brought guilt on him and on his kingdom.

Only the expressions of a corrupt or depraved judgment are mortal sins and expose to eternal damnation, according to the law.

First, when this depravity of the judgment appears in corrupt error and is embraced. Thus, how greatly did Simon the sorcerer expose himself unto eternal perdition by entertaining an unworthy thought or judgment in his heart that was very unworthy of and dishonorable to God. He thought that he could purchase from the apostles with money the power of conferring the Holy Ghost on whomsoever he pleased. "Thy money perish with thee," said Peter in Acts 8:20, "because thou hast thought that the gift of God may be purchased with money." And he exhorts him to repent of his wickedness: "if perhaps the thought of thine heart may be forgiven thee," intimating the difficulty that was in the way of his obtaining pardon. This also intimates that even if he sought it never so earnestly, there was but a "perhaps" in the case as to his obtaining it.

We have another remarkable instance in the case of the prophet, of whom we have and account of in 1 Kings 13. God had charged him that when he came to Bethel he should eat no bread nor drink water in that place. But an old prophet invited him to turn back and to eat bread, pretending that an angel had spoken to him by the Word of the Lord, saying, "Bring him back with thee into thine house that he may eat bread and drink water." And so the prophet went with him, really believing that he spoke truly and that God had reversed His former command.

If it had indeed been so that God had given these new informations to this old prophet, which he pretended, it would have been his duty to have gone back. He thought it to be true, but herein he showed his great corruption and sinfulness in believing and judging as he did, that he made the word of man sufficient to counterveil the Word of God. But the prophet knew that God had commanded him to not to eat bread there and that God had given contrary orders to the old prophet that he did not know; he only had the prophet's word for it, and so he thought he obeyed God in doing as the old prophet said. Yet God sent a lion who slew him as he was returning from the old prophet's house.

Second, when the expression of this depravity of the judgment is only negative in not believing divine truth, it is mortal sin according to the law, and exposes to eternal damnation. Such was the sin of the children of Israel. in the wilderness in not believing the promises which God made of Canaan, and they were punished for it by being refused entrance into Canaan and by being destroyed in the wilderness. Deuteronomy 1:32–36: "Yet in this thing ye did not believe the Lord your God who went in the way before you to search you out a place to pitch your tent in, in fire by night, to show you by what way you should go, and in a cloud by day. And the LORD heard the voice of your words and was wroth and sware, saying, 'Surely there shall not one of these men of this evil generation see that good land save Caleb the son of Jephunneh; he shall see it, and to him will I give the land that he hath trodden upon, and to his children, because he hath wholly followed the LORD.' "

Psalm 78:21–22: "Therefore the Lord heard this and was wroth; so a fire was kindled against Jacob, and anger also came up against Israel because they believed not in God and trusted not in His salvation." And verses 32– 33: "For all this they sinned still and believed not His wondrous works; therefore their days did He consume in vanity and their years in trouble."

Merely being ignorant of divine things is a sin that, by the law, exposes to eternal damnation. Romans 3:17: "And the way of peace they have not known." The apostle quotes this from the Old Testament, that all men are under sin and so stand in need of a Savior, as may be seen by the foregoing and following verses. Then in Psalm 95:10–11: "Forty years long was I grieved with that generation, and I said, 'This people do err in their heart and have not known My ways, unto whom I swore in My wrath that they should not enter into My rest." Their being a people that erred in their hearts and who did not know God's ways excited His wrath and provoked Him to swear that they should not enter into His rest, which shows that this deserved damnation by the law.

Again, Isaiah 27:11: "It is a people of no understanding; therefore He that made them will not have mercy on them, and He that formed them will show them no favor." This is spoken of as the punishment of their ignorance or their having no understanding, that is, that He who made them would show them no mercy."

Again, 2 Thessalonians 1:7–8: "...when the Lord Jesus shall be revealed from heaven with His mighty angels, in flaming fire taking vengeance on them that know not God, and that obey not the gospel of our Lord Jesus Christ." The sons of Eli are called sons of Belial because they did not know the Lord (1 Samuel 2:12). Thus God deals with the utmost strictness as the Giver of the law.

2. I proceed now to show that God also deals with the greatest strictness as the Judge of the law, and that in taking thorough care to see it fully and exactly executed. The business of a judge is to see that the law is duly executed. God is the not only the Lawgiver of men, but their supreme Judge. And as He was strict in giving the precepts and sanctions of the law, so He will be no less strict in executing it. He will see to it that His strictness in this regard appears in two things:

First, it will appear in God's care to see the law fully executed and exactly executed, as the there is nothing in the law but God will have fulfilled. Matthew 5:18: "Till heaven and earth pass, one jot or one tittle shall in no wise pass from the law till all be fulfilled." What God has said in His law is not vain words, but "He will magnify the law and make it honorable" (Isaiah 42:21).

The execution of the law appears in three things:
• God will take care that the sins of everyone shall be punished; not one guilty person shall be acquitted. God will deal with the sins of all alike; all shall be punished. It is not with the divine law as it often is with human laws; human laws commonly take place with respect to the more mean sort of men, but great men oftentimes escape. Human laws have sometimes been compared to spider's webs that hold

the little flies: great men break through and escape. But the sins of great men must have their punishment as well as those of little men. When God comes to sit as Judge, none are so great as to be above the exact reach of divine justice; nor are any so smooth as to be below His notice.

• Another thing implied is that God will take care that all their sins shall be punished, not only that the sins of everyone shall be punished, but that all the sins of each should be punished. Not one sin shall escape the Judge of the law, but the penalty of the law shall be executed. Let the sins be never so many and never so great, they shall all receive a just recompense of reward; for God does, as it were, keep a book of remembrance. Their iniquities are marked before all or are laid up with Him and sealed up among His treasures.

• God's strictness will be seen in executing the full penalty of the Law for each sin. The least sin, even of idle words or thoughts, as much as amounts to everlasting destruction.

Second, God's care thus to execute the law will be thorough. Herein we speak after the manner of men, but these things are implied in it: God is fully disposed thus to execute the law. He fully approves of the threatening of the law and won't repent that He threatened so severely. He is immutably resolved to do it. It is impossible to alter God's mind with respect to this matter. He will see His law executed. 'Tis easier to move mountains, yea, to renounce heaven and earth, than to alter God's mind with respect to this matter. God has proposed it and He won't alter His decree. He has said it and He will do it (Isaiah 46:11). Infinite power is engaged to do it. This is a power that it is impossible to resist, and infinite wisdom that is impossible to circumvent.

There will be no hiding in caves and dens; it will be in vain to try to escape; it will be in vain to try to get out of God's hands. Amos 9:1: "He that fleeth of them shall not flee away, and he that escapeth of them shall not be delivered." To resist or fight against God will be in vain; to cry to Him or beg mercy of Him he will be inaccessible. To look to others for help will be in vain (Proverbs 1:24).

God's strictness in executing the law appears remarkably in two things: in the eternal damnation of the ungodly, in part before the damnation of the soul in a state of separation, and more fully in the total destruction of the whole man.

After the day of judgment, the execution of the law will take place without any abasement; there will be no pity, no regard to piteous cries, no relentings for the extreme case they are in. Those who have sinned most numerously and aggravatedly shall have their fire hot in proportion; and the extremity of the misery will be no restraint when the heart sinks in despair.

With regard to the sins of the elect in the sufferings of Christ, here the strictness of God appears much more remarkably. The infinite dignity of the Person of Christ, His nearness to the Father, and the Father's infinitely dear love for Him don't restrain Him from fully executing the law. This appears more in the greatness of His sufferings. The inflexibleness of God's justice here more abundantly appears. His immutability appears in His sticking close to the law.

There are reasons why God deals with so great a strictness as the Lawgiver and Judge of the law. And I shall give the same reasons that are given in the text:

First, it is because God is so holy a God. He is an infinitely holy Being. Infinite holiness is His very essence. And it is because He is so holy that it is impossible that when He gives a law to men that His law should be any other than exceedingly strict. 'Tis impossible upon this account that His law should allow of any unholiness; 'tis impossible but that He should forbid all unholiness . And as God is infinitely holy, so 'tis necessary that He should infinitely hate all unholiness or that He should not have an infinite enmity against it. And here it is that all sin is threatened in His law with eternal death, which is an infinite punishment; for if God's enmity against sin is infinitely great, it is fitting that the manifestations and testimonies of this enmity should be proportionably great in the punishment of sin.

God as a Judge will be strict in executing the law and will not acquit the wicked or clear the guilty. The same holiness that caused Him to threaten will cause Him to execute His threatening. God executes the threatenings of the law because He is an infinitely just and righteous Judge; but God's justice is included in His holiness.

God will be strict to execute His law because His truth obliges Him to it. In the threatening of the law God has posted His word that He will punish sin with eternal death, and He is not a man that He should lie. "Hath He said, and shall He not do it? Hath He spoken, and shall it not come to pass?" (Numbers 23:19). But God's truth is also included in His holiness. God cannot lie because He is an infinitely holy God.

As a jealous God, He is jealous of His own honor and glory. And hence He will deal with such strictness as the Giver and Judge of the law. 'Tis hence that God has threatened all sin with so dreadful a punishment as eternal death, because that sin is against the honor of His majesty. Their sin is committed against God; it strikes at the honor of God and endeavors to dishonor Him; it is rebellion against the rightful authority of God and has its foundation in a contempt of God. God's jealousy for the honor of His own infinite authority and infinite majesty influences Him so severely to threaten sin, and will influence Him to execute His threatenings for all sin. God's jealousy is often given as a reason for God's strictness in punishing sin. God is so jealous for His own honor and glory that He values it more than He does the welfare of the creature; and therefore He will glorify Himself though it is in the creature's destruction.

The jealousy of God is often given as a reason for His strictness in punishing sin. So it is in the Second Commandment: "I the Lord thy God am a jealous God, visiting the iniquity of the fathers upon the children...." Deuteronomy 4:23–24: "Take heed unto yourselves lest ye forget the covenant of the Lord your God which He made with you, and make you a graven image in the likeness of anything which the Lord thy God hath forbidden. For the Lord thy God is a consuming fire, even a jealous God." And Deuteronomy 6:15: "For the Lord thy God is a jealous God among you, lest the anger of the Lord thy God be kindled against thee and destroy thee from off the face of the earth." Nahum 1:2: "God is jealous, and the Lord revengeth; the Lord revengeth and is furious; the Lord will take vengeance on His adversaries, and He reserveth wrath for His enemies."

APPLICATION

How strict our lives ought to be. If we have to do with so strict a Lawgiver and Judge, certainly we need to behave ourselves with the greatest possible strictness. The strict law that He has given us He has given for the rule of our life; and though we are set at liberty by Christ from the threatenings of the law, yet we are still under the law as a rule of life and we must consider that judgment will proceed according to law. God will see that the law is fulfilled. How strictly then should we behave ourselves who are to stand before so strict a Judge, whose eyes are as a flame of fire and who sees our secret actions and even our thoughts, and sees in our hearts and will render to everyone according to the deeds done in the body, whether good or bad.

How careful ought we to be, notwithstanding, not to commit the least sin, not even so much as in thought, seeing that every sin is a damning sin. And though Christ has suffered so that we may escape the punishment, we ought not to be less strict for that. The manifestation of God's strictness in the suffering of Christ for our sins ought to have as much influence upon us as if we ourselves must suffer.

How ought we to watch over ourselves, resist with all diligence, set a watch on things, guard the door of life, and pray that the words of our mouths would be acceptable in His sight.

This doctrine may show us the glory of the way of salvation by Jesus Christ in two respects:

First, it shows the glorious wisdom of it, that there should be a way contrived wherein God may deal with such exceeding strictness as Judge of the law and yet pardon all the sin and save sinners. Romans 3:26: "That God may be just and yet the Justifier of him that believeth in Jesus." What glorious wisdom, that there should be such a way contrived wherein God may be so strict in punishing all the sin that ever may have committed and yet deliver those who have committed sin from all punishment; that He may be thus strict in executing the threatening of the law and yet set at liberty them who have broken the law; that God may save the sinner from all misery, yea, and bring them to greater happiness than if they had never sinned at all and yet manifest His strictness in punishing the sin. What a marvelous wisdom this discovers in Him who has contrived the way of salvation by Jesus Christ! How glorious is this wisdom! How much it is above the wisdom of men or angels.

Second, it shows the gloriousness of the grace of God in our redemption because it is such grace as doesn't interfere with the holiness and justice of God. If the grace of God, such as is manifested in our redemption, consisted in forgiving sin in a way of absolute mercy, without any sins being punished at all, this would have been inconsistent with the strictness of God as a Lawgiver and a Judge. Then the mercy of God would have been unbecoming the majesty of God and inconsistent with the holiness of God, and so would not have been a glorious mercy. That mercy would not have been a glorious mercy that was not a holy mercy; it would have diminished the glory of God's majesty. But now in this way, the salvation of the sinner is done in holy mercy. The holiness of God most remarkably appears in giving Christ to die. God's appointing Christ to die for sinners above all other means manifests the mercy of God. There is no other act that so magnifies God's holiness and majesty.

CHAPTER TWELVE

God's Wisdom in His Stated Method of Bestowing Grace

*"An altar of earth thou shalt make unto Me, and shalt
sacrifice thereon thy burnt offerings, and thy peace offerings,
thy sheep, and thine oxen: in all places where I record My
name I will come unto thee, and I will bless them."*

EXODUS 20:24

God is now speaking to Moses out of the thick
darkness from Mt. Sinai. We read in the foregoing chapter of the first coming of the children of
Israel to this mountain after their coming out of Egypt, how
Moses went up to God to the mount, and how God ordered the
attendance of the congregation at the foot of the mountain to
see the tokens of His presence and majesty, to hear Him speak
to them, and to receive the law at His mount.

And so God came down in a very awful and terrible manner upon the mountain and spoke in the hearing of all the congregation. He spoke the Ten Commandments to them with a very loud and mighty voice; this was attended with Mt. Sinai's being altogether in smoke, with the appearance of devouring fire, and with terrible thunders and lightning. The mountain and the ground around it quaked exceedingly and the sound of a trumpet was exceedingly loud—besides the awful majesty of the voice of God which spoke to them—so that all the people who were in the camp trembled and were exceedingly frightened. It was more than they could bear to hear God thus speaking to them. They therefore said to Moses, as in the nineteenth verse, "Speak thou with us, and we will hear; but let not God speak with us lest we die." Upon this, the people stood afar off, and Moses drew near to the thick darkness where he was to hear God speak to him, so that he might speak to the people and carry God's message to them.

When Moses drew near, God told him His mind concerning His worship, in what way He would be worshipped by the people, and first forewarned them of making other gods or worshipping Him by images. Verse 23, "Ye shall not make with Me gods of silver, neither shall ye make unto Me gods of gold."

And in the verse of our text, God gives a commandment concerning the place and manner of His own worship as to the altar: "An altar of earth shalt thou make unto Me, and shalt sacrifice thereon thy burnt offerings, and thy peace offerings, thy sheep, and thine oxen." Not that an altar of hewn stone was not as good in itself as one of earth or whole stone, but God is sovereign, and appoints for His own worship what way He pleases. Though another way may seem as good or better to us, yet we can expect to find His acceptance only in his own way.

And so, second, as to the place: "In all places where I record My name I will come unto thee, and I will bless thee." Not that one place was any better than another in itself, or that there is any particular virtue in one place more than another, but because it was God's pleasure so to appoint.

In the words observe, first, a benefit proposed and offered to God's people, that in that place God would meet with them and would bless them. His meeting with them means His accepting them, His manifesting Himself to them, and giving them tokens of His friendly and gracious presence among them. His blessing them means His bestowing on them all good things which they stand in need of, His doing the part of a God to them.

Observe, second, how it is to be sought and obtained: in the place where God shall record His name, that is, in the place that He shall appoint for His people for their public worship and where He will give the outward tokens of His presence, such as answering from the mercy seat, and the like.

DOCTRINE: If we would be in the way of God's grace and blessing, we must wait upon Him in His own way and in the use of His appointed means.

1. Here we shall show that it is God's manner to bestow His grace and blessing in a way of the use of certain appointed means, and give the reasons for it.
2. Show what those means are.
3. Show that His grace and blessing are to be expected in no other way but the use of them.

1. It is God's manner to bestow His grace and blessing in a way of the use of appointed means. God is the sovereign Disposer of His own favor and blessing. He may bestow it on whom He pleases and in what way He pleases. None of us can challenge any right to God's grace. We have to a great degree deserved

the contrary from Him. He might in our first state of innocence bestow His favors and bounties in what way He pleased. He might appoint what conditions He would, as He was absolute Lord over us.

Much more now, since we have sinned and His justice has infinite demands upon us, it is wonderful, unspeakable grace that He is willing to be gracious to us in any way. But if He is, it is His prerogative to say in what way He will do so, whether in the use of means or without them. And it has pleased God to bestow His mercy in the use of certain means, and He has told us what means.

God has not only appointed a way of salvation for us by Jesus Christ, by what He has done and suffered, but He has appointed something to be done by us as a way wherein we are to seek the benefit of what our Savior has done for us.

God doesn't let mankind alone, everyone to go his own way, without any sort of directions from Him how to behave and act. He chooses not, in some extraordinary, miraculous way, to immediately snatch one and another out of their misery and bestow salvation upon them without any directions given by Him how to seek salvation, or anything at all done by them any way in order to obtain it. But God chooses to bestow His mercy in a way of appointed means. And we shall mention some of the reasons why God does this.

But we would first take notice, negatively, that God doesn't bestow His grace and blessing in a way of the use of certain appointed means because He could not as easily bestow it immediately without the use of any means. The means that are used don't make the salvation less wholly from God. Men, by using means, don't help God; they don't do part of it themselves. It is no less the work of God's power or the gift of His grace for the means that are used.

The means have no power in themselves to reach the end, nor are they the way to those glorious blessings offered, by any proper efficiency or any virtue in themselves. Nor are those blessings any less absolutely from God for them, any more than there was any proper virtue in Moses' rod to divide the Red Sea and do all those miracles in Egypt; or in the sound of rams' horns to make the walls of Jericho fall flat to the ground; or in the clay that Christ made to open the eyes of the blind man; or in the hem of His garment to cure the woman of her issue of blood; or in handkerchiefs and aprons carried from Paul's body to cure sick people and cast out devils.

But for the positive reasons, first, it is agreeable to God's wisdom to govern the moral world as He does the natural world, in a stated method. God has no need of any means in order to govern the natural world and bring to pass the events of common providence, such as growing grass, corn, or trees, the propagating and nourishing of animals and sustaining the body of man. God nevertheless accomplishes these by stated means, according to a certain method, which we call the law of nature. And God sees it agreeable to His wisdom so to do. 'Tis an abundantly more beautiful way of ordering things to thus accomplish things according to a regular method, a constant succession of causes and effects, and mutual dependence of one event upon another that God has fixed, than to have them done all as miracles are done, without any such regularity or natural dependence.

So likewise, God orders the affairs of grace in a more beautiful way, that bestows His grace in a stated method in a way of appointed means, than if it were given immediately to one and another without any means or any stated manner or method. And as there is a natural connection in natural things between the means and the end, so God has been pleased to constitute an arbitrary connection between the means and the end in the moral and spiritual world. Thus God in His ordinary works does, as it were, set a rule for Himself so that there may be proportion and regularity in His works.

Second, 'tis most agreeable to the state of mankind in this world. God observes a harmony between one work of His and another; and as God has placed us here in the natural world where we are governed by stated means and the laws of nature in things that respect the outward man, so God saw fit that while we are here, our spiritual affairs should be ordered in an appointed way, and our spiritual good obtained in the use of appointed means. This way is much more agreeable to the state of God's church here in the natural world than if all things were done as miracles are, without any stated means.

God saw fit that, seeing we are here in the body, we should have grace in the use of outward means; that as we receive natural knowledge by our outward senses, so we should receive His grace by seeing and hearing, and the like. And therefore God has appointed outward ordinances to be the vehicles of His grace. The other world, and not this one, is the world where God will communicate Himself visibly and immediately without any such vehicle.

It is more agreeable to the state of the church in this world on another account. It is God's design that His people here should live by faith and not by sight, whereas, if God bestowed grace upon men in a miraculous manner when they never used any means, then there would not be that exercise of faith that there is now in believing that God is the Author of all grace. God now works secretly upon men's hearts. His power is inward and not seen by the world, and oftentimes not by him who is the subject of it except by faith.

But if men should be taken in a moment, in their full

career in sin, in gross ignorance and darkness and heathenism, without the preaching or hearing of the gospel, reading the Word, or any outward instruction, without using any means themselves or any means with them; if all who had the grace of God bestowed on them should at once be taken, instructed, made to believe, and be under the government of the doctrines of the gospel—then it would cease to be a matter of faith that these things were not from ourselves.

It was not God's design that miracles should always be continued in the world. Miracles are only for introducing the true religion into the world, to accompany the revelation and first promulgating of the Word of God by them to whom it was revealed by inspiration, to confirm to the world that it was a divine revelation. But now, when the true religion has long since introduced and the canon of the Scripture completed, the use of miracles in the church ceases.

Third, if God did not bestow His grace in a way of the use of appointed means, there would not be that opportunity for the manifestation of God's wisdom in ordering the affairs of His church and accomplishing the designs of His grace in the world, either in accomplishing the design of His grace in particular persons or in His church in general. God shows a great deal of wisdom oftentimes in so ordering things in His providence so as to bring great sinners to the saving knowledge of Christ by bringing them to such means, to see or hear such things whereby they are awakened, in directing them to avoid the rocks of temptation, in leading them along through all difficulties and temptations till they come to Christ; and so after conversion in preserving them and guiding them.

And so it is with the church in general, in propagating the gospel and giving it victory. But there would be no gospel if God did not bestow His grace in a way of appointed means; in so ordering things as to destroy and confound His enemies; to destroy Antichrist; to make Satan and his enemies a means of their own ruin, which could not be if there was no means; in working things about so as to fulfill His glorious prophesies and promises to His church.

If things were all done miraculously and without means, there would be indeed a manifestation of infinite power, but not such a manifestation of infinitely wise contrivance. This way shows more of infinite wisdom and contrivance. To create a tree with ripe fruit already on it, though it shows the same power, yet is not so great a manifestation of contrivance as producing it from the seed gradually to such a state by the influences of the sun and rain in a constant method.

God showed a wonderful wisdom in His gradual revelation of the gospel in the world. First, He revealed it darkly in types. He revealed it first to the Jews and then rejected them and revealed it to the Gentiles; afterwards He called the Jews again, and with them brought in the fullness of the Gentiles. This wisdom was so wonderful that it made the apostle cry out in Romans 11:33–36, "Oh, the depth of the riches both of the wisdom and knowledge of God! How unsearchable are His judgments, and His ways past finding out! For who hath known the mind of the Lord? Or who hath been His counselor? Or who hath first given to Him and it shall be recompensed unto Him again? For of Him, and through Him, and to Him are all things, to whom be glory forever. Amen."

Fourth, if grace was bestowed without the use of appointed means, there would be no opportunity for the exercise of many moral virtues and Christian graces. Moral virtues are exercised in unconverted men. They show prudence in care for their souls. They show diligence in seeking salvation, as well as constancy and resolution.

The converted must also show diligence in seeking God, in striving to grow in grace. Hence they show constancy in the use of means. God uses means in charitable endeavors for the good of souls, in endeavors for the advancement of Christ's kingdom. Particularly do ministers show diligence in studying, in exhorting and warning. And both ministers and magistrates use means in seeking the good of the church in the world. Learned men do so by their preaching and writing.

Fifth, if it were otherwise, it would open a door for all manner of confusion and wickedness among unconverted men. The appointed means for the bestowal of grace are a mighty restraint upon wicked men; 'tis a principal thing whereby God restrains the wickedness of men.

If there were no appointed means, then the most wicked in the world would be in as likely a way to obtain salvation as any.

If there were no means, there would be no such thing as the Word of God, no revelation of God, no revelation of heaven and hell—and what a doleful place would this world be in then!

Sixth, the diligent use of means prepares the heart for God's grace and makes it better entertained.

Seventh, and last, it renders those who miss salvation the more inexcusable.

2. We shall just take notice what the appointed means of grace are. And we shall include not only the means of obtaining grace, but the means of persevering and growing in grace. They may be mainly reduced to these headings:

The first means is reading and hearing the Word of God. Search the Scriptures (John 5:39). Faith comes by hearing (Romans 10:17). The Word of God is a principal means, yet how much men fail in reading Scripture.

The second means is consideration. We should think on death, eternity, judgment, God, creation, and the like. We should think on our ways and consider our latter end. God expects that we should exercise our reason and our powers as men in order to having His grace.

The third means is prayer in its various kinds. Ephesians 6:18: "Praying with all prayers." There is secret prayer (Matthew 6:6) as well as family prayer. Both these are recommended by Christ's own example and the common practice of saints in Scripture. And then there is public prayer. God expects that we should come to Him for grace, call upon Him for it, and thankfully acknowledge what we have received.

The fourth means is attending on the sacraments, baptism and the Lord's Supper. God uses all manner of means with us. He speaks to us not only by his Word, but by sensible figures and representations of spiritual things.

The fifth means is to carefully and conscientiously avoid all moral evils and do all moral duties. We must avoid moral evils of thoughts, words, and deeds. Whatever ordinances are attended, if men go on in a way of wickedness, in indulging any lust whatsoever, it will be to no purpose. The prayers of such persons, and their attendance on sacraments, is but mockery, and is not accepted by God.

Living soberly, doing justly, and observing the gospel rules of charity, forgiveness, temperance, meekness, and the like are as much as any other the means of God's appointment for seeking conversion, and more insisted on by God. And they are a very main and principal means for growth in grace.

3. Last, we can expect to obtain God's grace and blessing in no other way but this. To seek it in any other way is to cast reflection upon God's wisdom and authority, and to set up our own wisdom in opposition to His. It is a reflection upon His sovereign grace, as though salvation and spiritual and eternal life were not His to give in whatever way He pleased, but we

could obtain it on our own way or by our own strength.

God, by appointing these to be the means of grace, as much as says that He'll bestow His grace ordinarily in this way and no other. Not that He never bestows it in another way. He has not bound Himself, but has only given us directions and told us in what way it is our duty and our interest to seek His grace in, and this is the only rule for our expectations. And therefore we can't expect to obtain grace except through the use of God's appointed means.

We can't expect to obtain grace if we only desire it and are idle, and use no means at all; or use some, and slothfully or knowingly neglect others.

We can't expect to obtain grace if the means we use are not those appointed. Therefore, they are most unhappy who embrace false religions: Quakers, who neglect ordinances; papists, who add a multitude of their own and corrupt God's ordinances. When persons become superstitious and think to obtain heaven by some extraordinary thing not appointed, they are not on the way there.

APPLICATION

1. How greatly privileged they are who know and enjoy the appointed means of grace. They know the way whereby they may find God, the way that He is wont to meet with men and to bless them.

How great a part of the world are utterly ignorant of this way, who do not have God's Word to tell them what the means of grace are. They haven't that Word to read and hear, and to present to them subjects for their consideration and meditation. They do not know how to call upon God, nor indeed what god to call upon. They do not have the sacraments that God has appointed. And indeed, their understandings are so darkened that they have obscured the light, and in considerable measure obliterated the law of nature.

Many who enjoy some means of grace have exceedingly corrupted them with human alterations, additions, and detractions.

Happy is that people who enjoy the means of grace as God has given them, who have them all and have them pure, just as He has instituted them.

Happy is that people who have the Word of God, and make that the only rule to direct them in this affair of seeking the grace and favor of God.

2. Hence we learn how much it is persons' prudence to continue steadfastly in the use of all the means of grace.

The appointed means of grace—notwithstanding that they are the only way that men have any reason to expect to meet with God or obtain his favor in—are very much neglected even by those who know them. And indeed, there are but few who will be persuaded to a thorough use and improvement of them.

Many neglect them because they are contrary to their lusts and sinful inclinations. They can't bear to tie themselves to such strict rules, and so to abridge themselves of that sweet license in sin which they have been wont to give themselves.

Many neglect them through sloth and an indisposedness to such diligence and striving as is requisite to a universal use of the means of grace. And therefore there are some who would feign be saved who are but partial in their use of means: they attend some ordinances and not others; they are careful as to some moral duties, but not others; they will pray to God sometimes, but not others; they are careful of external actions, but not their thoughts.

And there are others who are ready to be discouraged in

the use of the means of grace, thinking them to be vain things. They imagine they have hitherto served no benefit, and they think they aren't likely to.

But by the doctrine stated earlier we learn that they act with far greater prudence who thoroughly attend the means of grace, and do so constantly and perseveringly without discouragement; hearkening to no temptations as though it was a vain thing, not ceasing because they have used them so long and haven't yet met with God in them. This is the declared way wherein God has told us He will be found; and if ever they find Him, they can expect to find Him in no other way.

3. Hence we learn how far persons may take encouragement from their own use of the means of grace.

All the encouragement that a person may take from their own diligence and constancy in the use of those means is not self-righteousness, because God has revealed that this is the ordinary way wherein He meets with men and blesses them. Persons who have God's Word for their foundation are in a far more likely way to obtain salvation in their using means than if they used none, and in their diligent use than if they were slothful and partial, and so may take encouragement from their own endeavors.

Indeed, for sinners to take encouragement, as though God were under any obligation to them for their use of means either naturally or by promise is self-righteousness. But the godly who faithfully and with a true heart use means may assuredly expect success from God's promise, that in that way they shall grow in grace.

CHAPTER THIRTEEN

The Way to Obtain the Blessing of God Is to Resolve Not to Let God Go Unless He Blesses Us

"And he said, 'Let me go, for the day breaketh.' And he said, 'I will not let thee go except thou bless me.' And he said unto him, 'What is thy name?' And he said, 'Jacob.' And he said, 'Thy name shall be called no more Jacob, but Israel; for as a prince hast thou power with God and with men, and hast prevailed.' And Jacob asked him, and said, 'Tell me, I pray thee, thy name.' And he said, 'Wherefore is it that thou dost ask after my name?' And he blessed him there."

GENESIS 32: 26–29

W e have here that remarkable account of Jacob's wrestling with God. It was at a time when Jacob was expecting to meet his brother Esau, who was now coming out with four hundred armed men upon a hostile design against him. Jacob had divided his company, and put them into that order in which he would have them meet Esau, and sent them away over the ford Jabbok. But he himself stayed behind alone. Probably it was that he might have the better opportunity to pour out his supplications to God and seek His favor and mercy at this juncture when they were so eminently threatened with destruction from Esau and his company.

While he was there alone in the night there came one in a human form and with a human body. It seems to have been the Son of God, the second Person in the Trinity, who appeared to him. The Son of God who had undertaken to be man's Mediator and Representative, his Surety, and who was to take on Himself the human nature, was wont frequently under the Old Testament to appear in human shape. Occasionally He assumed a human body, as He did before His proper incarnation, or as He did when He ate and drank with Abraham in the plains of Mamre, and as He did now when He wrestled with Jacob. Whenever God appeared under the Old Testament it is probable that it was the second Person of the Godhead. This is evident by what Christ says in John 1:18: "No man hath seen God at any time; the only begotten Son who is in the bosom of the Father, He hath declared Him." We have an account that this is He who came to Jacob and wrestled with him the remainder of the night.

It seems that Jacob did not know that it was God till the last. But he doubtless immediately perceived that He was some very extraordinary person, eminent in wisdom and holiness, by His appearance, though it was in the night, and also by His conversation Jacob perceived that He was some very extraordinary person, and not a mere man. Jacob thought

Him to be an angel, for Jacob had not been altogether unused to such a thing as angels appearing to him. He had a vision of angels at Bethel, and the angels of God met him again at Mahanaim before this.

Jacob not only wrestled with Him in a figurative sense, as the saints may be said to wrestle with God in prayer, but he wrestled with Him literally, though he did not know then that it was God. I will not presume to determine how Jacob came to wrestle with Him, what the occasion was of Jacob's wrestling with Him, or how they came to be engaged in such exercise, but I will venture to inform you what appears to me to be probable: The man who came to Jacob, or who appeared to him as a man, had been in a most free, condescending, and friendly manner conversing with Jacob. He appeared to Jacob, in His conversation with him, so holy, wise, excellent, and amiable a person, and had conversed with him in so condescending and friendly a manner that Jacob was greatly delighted with His company. And upon His making as though He would go away, Jacob could not bear it, being very loath to part with Him; so he laid hold of Him so that he might have more of His company. Hence followed a wrestle between them. The divine person appeared as though He would get away, and Jacob strove mightily to hold Him back.

Jacob was emboldened to such freedom by the extraordinary meekness, goodness, and friendliness of his conversation with Him. And so they wrestled till the break of day. The divine person then appeared more resolute to depart and said to Jacob, "Let me go, for the day breaketh." Jacob replied, "I will not let thee go except thou bless me." Jacob was resolved upon this that if He would depart, and he could have no more of His company, yet he would, if possible, obtain His blessing before He went. That extraordinary excellency, wisdom, and holiness that appeared in Him made him value His blessing.

But still Jacob did not know that it was God. But when upon this the person asked Jacob what his name was, and when He told Jacob that his name would no longer be Jacob, but Israel, "for as a prince hast thou power and hast prevailed with God," upon His saying, "Thou hast power with God and hast prevailed," Jacob began to suspect that it was God. And upon that he prayed Him to tell him his name.

God did not tell him His name, but asked, "Wherefore is it that thou dost inquire after My name." But before He departed He blessed Jacob according to his desire. Then Jacob was sensible that it was God and was, as it were, astonished what a conversation he had with God Himself. And therefore it is said that Jacob called the name of the place "Peniel, for I have seen God face to face and my life is preserved."

It was a most wonderful transaction, a marvelous manifestation of the infinite grace and condescension of God to His people, and seems to have been ordered to typify and represent the wonderful power and prevalence of the faithful and fervent prayers of the saints with God.

DOCTRINE: The way to obtain the blessing of God is to resolve not to let God go unless He blesses us.

Under this doctrine I would first explain what is implied in this duty here expressed by not letting go of God, and, second, show that this is the way to obtain the blessing of God.

1. I would explain the duty here expressed by not letting God go until He blesses us. And by showing what it is not, it will sufficiently appear what it is.

First, it is not a demanding the blessing of God as a mere debt, with a disposition to contend with Him if He doesn't bestow it. To not let God go in the sense of the doctrine does not mean to let Him go as a creditor who won't forgive his debtor may be said to let him go, but if he doesn't pay him will contend with him or go to law against him. That is what he in the parable did who took his creditor by the throat, saying, "Pay me what you owe."

There are some who won't let God go in the sense that they express themselves thus in their prayers: "Thy blessing is my due. I have merited it by what I have done. I have behaved myself so well and have taken such pains for a blessing that it will be very unreasonable to deny me one. Thou hast bestowed a blessing upon others who did a great deal more to deserve Thy curse than ever I did, and who never took half so much pains for a blessing. And if Thou deniest it to me it will be very unfair. I cannot see the reasonableness of it. I won't let Thee go. I'll hold Thee to Thy obligation. And therefore, if I am denied, I shall look upon myself as having been wronged, and will have just cause to complain and to call Thee hard and cruel."

They won't say so to God, but if they should express themselves so they would express the very disposition and thoughts of their hearts.

But not letting God go in this sense is far enough from being the way to obtain the blessing of God that it is the way to obtain His curse, to stir up His fearful indignation, and to be pursued with His wrath.

Second, the duty expressed in the doctrine is not merely an importuning God in words for a blessing without seeking it in deeds at the same time. If persons pray to God often for a blessing, doing it with a seeming earnestness and in suitable expressions, and content themselves with that but don't at the same time use other proper means to obtain a blessing, they neglect those things attending those institutions which God has appointed as means for obtaining a blessing, and in which He directs them to wait for it. Or if they pray and seem to beg for God's blessing, but at the same time indulge their lusts and live in some known sin, these are not those intended in the doctrine who won't let God go unless He blesses them. Nor are they in the way to obtain a blessing for they show themselves not to be in earnest when they ask God to give them one, and act as if they were earnestly desirous of it. Their practice contradicts their words and shows that, let them say what they will, they are not very desirous of obtaining the blessing they ask God for.

Such persons' seeming importuning God for a blessing is nothing but a mere mockery. They speak as though they had a mind that God should bless them, but they act as though they would provoke God to deny them a blessing and to follow them with a curse.

The duty spoken of in the doctrine is not a being constant in seeking and persevering, in seeking a blessing in a cold, remiss, and unresolved manner. There are some who are seeking the blessing after a sort, and who seem to be pretty constant at it; they keep doing something and so, it may be, they continue as long as they live. But they are not like Jacob who wouldn't let God go unless He blessed him; nor are they in a likely way to obtain God's blessing. A person may ask God every day, twice a day, and as long as he lives for His blessing, and yet not be Jacob's follower, not be one of them who won't let God go in the sense spoken of in the doctrine.

They who would imitate Jacob must do something to answer his wrestling. There must be an earnest spirit for a blessing. Jacob was exceedingly loath to let God go; he could not bear the thought of parting with Him, which was the occasion of his wrestling with God.

So those who do the duty mentioned in the doctrine have a

great and very earnest desire for a blessing. They can't bear to think to go without it; they are engaged in their spirits to obtain a blessing; they are resolved in their spirits that if it is possible by anything they can do. As long as they can obtain a blessing they will obtain it. They are so engaged that they seek a blessing with all their might; they are vigorous in it and lay out their strength. Jacob doubtless laid out all his strength in wrestling with the Angel of the Lord.

The duty spoken of in the doctrine is opposite to being remiss and dull in seeking whether it is for want of earnest desires of a blessing or from a discouragement. He who will not let God go unless He blesses him is sensible of his necessity of a blessing and the great worth of it. He is also encouraged with hopes that it won't be altogether a vain thing to seek a blessing from God. And if God seems to deny him, that doesn't for the present so discourage and dishearten him, but he will still be very earnest for it. When a man seeks a benefit from another and is denied, if he thinks that asking and pleading is in vain, he'll leave off or will ask, but will have no heart to be earnest with him.

But he who won't let God go unless He blesses him encourages himself by thinking that it may be that God will bestow a blessing, though He has not done so yet. Who can tell but he will turn and repent and leave a blessing behind him, as in the Joel 2:12–14?

'Tis not being earnest for a blessing in an inconstant way. Some, by turns, seem to be very earnest and much engaged in their spirits for a blessing; but it doesn't hold; they are unsteady in it. While seemingly very earnest, they are cold and remiss; and, it may be, they are as earnest for the world as they were before for a blessing. At one time they are all for salvation, and another time they are for their pleasures and diversions, and have their minds taken up about the vanities of youth. These are not some of those who won't let God go unless He blesses them.

'Tis not being both earnest and constant for a limited or set time. If a man takes up a resolution with himself, "I'll seek so long for a blessing, and during that time I'll make a business of it and do all that I can. If a obtain a blessing in that time, well; if not, I'll leave off for the present and won't trouble myself about it and bereave myself of the comforts of my life any longer—or at least won't determine that I will seek any longer." These are not some who do the duty mentioned in the doctrine.

They who resolve that they will seek God for a blessing for a year, or for two or three years; if their resolve is for any limited time short of the limits of their lives, they can't be said to resolve that they won't let God go unless He blesses them. Patient waiting upon God for His blessing in that way of seeking it which His Word directs us to is one thing implied in not letting God go unless He blesses us.

Last, 'tis not asking the blessing of God and, at the same time, expecting it from ourselves. There is such a thing, and it is common among men that they will beg that God would bestow the blessing upon them, and seem to be importunate, but at the same expect to have it of themselves. They hope to get by their own strength; they beg God to give them His grace, but they are hoping to make themselves holy, to work up their own hearts to a gracious frame, to a disposition to love God and trust in Jesus Christ. But they who won't let God go unless He blesses them don't only make a show, as though they expected a blessing of Him or partly of Him; but they are sensible that it must be He who must bestow the blessing upon them. They are sensible that they can never get it of themselves, and that no other can bestow it upon them but God only.

2. Not to let God go unless He blesses is the way for us to obtain the blessing. This is the way that God has taught us to seek a blessing in; 'tis the way that Christ has taught. Christ compares it to wearing a person out with continual importunity, who is unwilling of himself. He encourages us to follow God with incessant prayers for a blessing by representing to us how men who are very backward and unwilling of themselves to do what another seeks of them yet may be tired out and overcome with unceasing importunity. In the parable of the unjust judge and the importunate widow in the beginning of Luke 18, there was a widow who besought a judge who neither feared God nor regarded man to avenge her of her adversary. Now she being a poor widow, the judge thought he should get nothing by it and so he refused. But she followed him with her importunity so that he was tired out and did what she asked to get rid of her. From this example of an unjust judge, Christ encourages us not to let Him alone, He who is far from being unjust or unmerciful, till He blesses us.

Christ teaches us the same thing again in Luke 11, beginning at verse 5, in the parable of the man who went to his friend's house at midnight for bread for his guest. The man was loath to get out of bed to give him what he asked for and refused at first; but he continued his importunity till his friend saw the trouble would be greater than getting up, so he arose and gave him what he desired.

There is again great encouragement to take this method from the instance of the woman of Canaan, who did by Christ much as Jacob did. We have an account of this in Matthew 15, beginning with verse 21. The woman came and begged Christ to have mercy on her daughter. She told Him how much she needed His pity, being grievously tormented with a devil. At first Christ gave her no answer at all, but she continued still;

then He gave here a repulse, and such a repulse that she must have been very resolute indeed not to have been repelled by it. This did not discourage her, however, but only made her the more importunate, and thus she obtained the blessing she sought. The experience of God's people throughout the world will confirm that this is the way to obtain a blessing.

I will say a few words respecting the reasons for it and so hasten to the application.

'Tis not that God needs it to make Him willing to bestow the blessing, or that the will of God is properly prevailed with and overcome by men's importunity. God did not need Jacob's wrestling with Him in order to make him willing to bless him. God was willing before and came to him with the design to bless him. God is willing to bless His people, and that is the reason that He stirs them up to wrestle with Him for a blessing.

And when God seems to delay and to give repulses while they are seeking, 'tis not that He is unwilling. 'Tis not because He is backward, for He is all the while exceedingly ready. God delights to bestow His blessings as much and more than men delight to have them; and therefore they don't tire Him out—though the effect is much the same as it is with men when they are tired out with importunity, and so it is represented by it in Christ's parables.

But there are four reasons we shall give why God will bestow His blessing in this way:

1. 'Tis very suitable and becoming that before men have the blessing they should in this way show their sense of their need of it and the value of it. 'Tis very suitable that before God bestows His blessing, persons should be sensible that they need it. And 'tis by their importunity and earnest seeking of it that they express their not letting God go unless He bestows it. Thus

they show their sense of their need of it.

'Tis very suitable that before God bestows His blessing persons should be sensible of the great value of the blessing, and the advantage it will be to them. They also show a sense of this by their not letting God go unless He bestows it.

2. By denying persons the blessing for a while when they seek one, God tends to lead persons to reflect on their unworthiness of the blessing. They have that seeming denial to put them upon thinking what they have done to provoke God to withhold a blessing from them. While Christ seemed to deny the woman of Canaan what she sought, she was put in mind of her unworthiness. "It is not meet to take the children's bread and cast it unto dogs," said Christ. This leads them to seek it in a more humble manner.

3. 'Tis suitable that before God bestows the blessing upon a person that he should in this way acknowledge Him to be the Author of the blessing. This is earnestly seeking it of God. To not let Him go till He bestows it is a becoming acknowledgment that God is the Fountain of blessing, and that no other can bestow it but He. This earnestness and resolve in seeking it of God shows a person to be in earnest in such an acknowledgment.

4. The person, by such a seeking of the blessing, is prepared for it; he is put into a suitable disposition to receive it, to entertain it joyfully and thankfully, and to make much of it when it is obtained and to give God the glory of it.

Application

USE OF DIRECTION. This doctrine may be of direction to those who would have the blessing what method to take in order to obtain it. There are many who have some mind to have the blessing, but yet how few obtained it. Most men do to all eternity lie under the wrath and curse of God.

The greatest blessing that is ever bestowed is that which God bestows on men when they are converted. This may be called the blessing. Many seek this blessing, but few obtain. We may conclude the reason is that they don't seek this blessing in the method that we have spoken of. 'Tis not because the blessing is not a thing that is attainable; all of us have a happy and blessed opportunity to obtain it if we will but take this method.

Here I would particularly apply myself to two sorts of persons:

I would first apply myself to those who have for a long time been doing something for a blessing and have had no success. You may be ready to wonder that God hasn't blessed you who have been seeking of so long. But haven't you reason to reflect upon yourself and consider whether or not you have ever taken this method? Have you wrestled and resolved that you would not let God go unless He blessed you. You say that you have been seeking a long time; but has your heart been verily engaged all this while for a blessing? No one can do determine that it has or has not been so in any steady way for one half the time. You think, it may be, that you have done a great deal, have taken what pains you could, and don't see how you could have done any more. But if God should give you a truly earnest, engaged spirit, you'd soon see how you could do more.

By the little opportunity I have had to observe souls in such matters, I think that I may judge that once God gives persons a truly engaged spirit to wrestle and resolve that they will not let God go unless He blesses them, ordinarily they don't hold on in that way, but let go a little while before they obtain the blessing.

You are ready, it may be, to be discouraged and think it in vain for you to seek any longer; you have sought so long and haven't obtained. But you have no reason to be discouraged from anything that you have found as of yet; you have no reason to think it will be in vain for you to seek from anything you have found as of yet, for you never have made trial yet of the right way of seeking, whether it will be in vain or not. You never have made trial of this way that you have heard on in the text and doctrine. It is not time for you to talk of being discouraged till you have made trial.

If you mean that you have reason to be discouraged with the way that you have been seeking in hitherto, that very likely may be true; it may be high time for you to be discouraged with that and to draw the conclusion that it is likely to be in vain to seek any longer in such a slack, dull, remiss, irresolute manner as you have done, and that it is high time for you to begin in a new method.

It may be that you attribute your want of success to God; you say that God won't hear you; you fear that God has given you up. But it is quite wrong to lay it on God, but 'tis all the while to be laid on yourself, to your own coldness, sloth, and unresolvedness. God is ready enough to bestow the blessing upon you if you would but seek it with suitable earnestness and resolution. 'Tis no wonder at all that God doesn't hear you and give you the blessing for you for the way that you have sought it hitherto.

Here I would propose three things to you more particularly:

1. Haven't you found that when at any time you have been stirred up and thought you would be more earnest than ever your resolutions have been but short-lived? You have been doing something a long time for the blessing, and very probably, at one time or another, when you have heard sermons upon some

particular subjects or have seen awful providences, you have for the present been stirred up and thought that you would turn over a new leaf, that you would for time come to seek more earnestly than ever, and make more of a business of seeking than ever you had done? But haven't you found that in a little time all this has vanished away, and you have been no more earnest than you used to be; for all this while you have never come to comply in both the resolution and deed not to let God go unless He blesses you? And so, if you haven't a care, you may keep along in such a way till you die; you may take up good resolutions from time to time, but you will soon lose them, and never come to be thoroughly engaged as long as you live.

2. Haven't you reason to think that the world has been one great cause of hindering the success of your seeking a blessing? You have sought your salvation and the grace of God for a long time, but have also been encumbered about many things. Have not the cares of the world very much taken up your mind and possessed your thoughts? When you have received awakening impressions by the Word or providences, have not the cares of the world soon crowded out the thoughts of them? Has not talking and thinking of worldly concerns been what has in a good measure kept down your concern about your soul all this while, and prevented your so striving and wrestling for a blessing as is needful?

Is it not therefore needful that you should disengage your heart of worldly cares more, so that you may be more entirely devoted? Is it not therefore needful that you should watch yourself more carefully so that the world isn't your undoing, and so that your heart may more entirely be taken up about the concerns of your souls?

3. Do you not find that there arise more difficulties in this affair of seeking your salvation as you grow older? Don't you find that

your heart grows harder? Don't you find that you are not so apt to have impressions made upon your mind by anything you hear in the Word, or by awful providences, as once you were? Do you not find that you can hear and see dreadful things now, and be less worried and affected than formerly? Don't you find that the older you grow, the less apt you are to be moved by anything? And don't you find it more difficult to engage your thoughts on the things of religion, and more difficult to have an engaged spirit in prayer? Are you not more apt to be disengaged than once you were?

If it is so with you, surely this is intimation enough that it is high time for you to awaken out of sleep, to alter your hand, and now to more begin to make thorough work of seeking salvation.

I would, second, direct myself to those who are but newly setting out in seeking a blessing, if any such are here present. From what you have heard, see that you set out in a right method; take that method that you are directed to in the doctrine. You should be well-directed now at your first setting out. A person who is setting out on a journey should take care that he sets out on a right road at his beginning; otherwise he may travel all day in vain and get nothing in the end but to be lost and bewildered, and, it may be, perish in the woods in the night. Therefore see to it that you seek in such a manner as you have now been told of, for this is the very way to obtain a blessing.

Here I will briefly forewarn you of some things you will be in danger of:

You will be in danger of looking upon yourself as being more in earnest than you are. You will be in danger of judging by the affectionateness of your prayers, the tears you shed, and the like. Those who are very young are commonly very full of such kind of affection when under some awakenings; and yet it may be not be so seriously resolved as some others who have so deep a sense of their danger and misery; a lesser thing would turn 'em aside than some who aren't half so affectionate. The most affectionate persons aren't always the steadiest. Tears are very deceitful things, and are much less to be regarded than some other things. If you think that you are more engaged than you really are, it will be a great disadvantage to you; for then you will think you are more likely to obtain than you are. You won't likely be sensible how much you need to be more earnest, and will rest as you are and won't endeavor to be more earnest because you'll think you are earnest enough already. Then you won't be aware how easily a little thing would divert you; and, not being sensible of your danger, you won't be as wary as otherwise you would be.

You will be in danger of flattering yourself in your beginning, and then afterwards running into discouragement. 'Tis common for persons, when they first set out in seeking salvation, to flatter themselves that they shall soon get through. And then, when they keep on a while and don't find it as they expected, they run to the other extreme and are discouraged.

It may be now in the heat of your affection you think that you are resolved that you will seek till you die, though it should be fifty years. But it may be that you have a secret hope and expectation at the same time that it won't be above one year before you shall be converted. And when you come to be disappointed of your expectation, you won't hold your resolution of seeking as long as you live, and never would have made such a promise to yourself of seeking so long. What makes you so free to promise such things is that you never expect to have the occasion to perform them.

You will be in danger of having carelessness steal in upon

you insensibly. You will be in danger of losing convictions by degrees. You will probably lose them so gradually that, after you have begun to lose them, you flatter yourself that you haven't lost your convictions, but are as much concerned as ever in general.

You will be like persons in a consumption, or under some other lingering distemper: the distemper steals in on them insensibly. And the patient flatters himself that he doesn't grow worse; and sometimes he hopes that he grows better. So often they'll flatter themselves till they see their strength and life is almost gone and death approaches.

CHAPTER FOURTEEN

Christian Charity: The Duty of Charity to the Poor Explained and Enforced

If there be among you a poor man of one of thy brethren within any of thy gates in thy land which the Lord thy God giveth thee, thou shalt not harden thine heart, nor shut thine hand from thy poor brother: but thou shalt open thine hand wide unto him, and shalt surely lend him sufficient for his need, in that which he wanteth. Beware that there be not a thought in thy wicked heart, saying, The seventh year, the year of release, is at hand; and thine eye be evil against thy poor brother, and thou givest him nought; and he cry unto the Lord against thee, and it be sin unto thee. Thou shalt surely give him, and thine heart shall not be grieved when thou givest unto him: because that for this thing the Lord thy God shall bless thee in all thy works, and in all that thou puttest thine hand unto. For the poor shall never cease out of the land: therefore I command thee, saying Thou shalt open thine hand wide unto thy brother, to thy poor, and to thy needy, in thy land."

DEUTERONOMY 15:7-11.

The Words Explained

'Tis the most absolute and indispensable duty of a people of God to give bountifully and willingly for the supply of the wants of the needy.

The duty here enjoined is giving to the poor. "If there be among you a poor man of one of thy brethren, thou shalt not harden thine heart, nor shut thine hand from thy poor brother... Thou shalt surely give him." Here, by "thy poor brother" is to be understood the same as in other places is meant by "neighbor." It is explained in Leviticus 25:35 to mean not only those of their own nation, but even strangers and sojourners. "And if thy brother be waxen poor, and fallen in decay with thee, then thou shalt relieve him; yea, though he be a stranger or a sojourner." The Pharisees indeed interpreted it to signify only one of their own nation. But Christ condemns this interpretation in Luke 10:29, and teaches, in contradiction to their opinion, that the rules of charity in the law of Moses are to be extended to the Samaritans, who were not of their nation, and between whom and the Jews there was the most bitter enmity, and who were a people very troublesome to the Jews.

God gives us direction how we are to give in such a case: bountifully and willingly. We should give bountifully and sufficiently for the supply of the poor's need. Deuteronomy 15:7–8: "Thou shalt not shut up thine hand from thy poor brother; but thou shalt open thine hand wide unto him, and lend him sufficient for his need, in that which he wanteth." And again in verse 11: "Thou shalt open thine hand wide unto thy brother, to thy poor, and to thy needy, in thy land." Again, we should give willingly and without grudging. Deuteronomy 15:7: "Thou shalt not harden thine heart from thy poor brother," And verse 10: "And thine heart shall not be grieved when thou givest him."

We may also observe how peremptorily this duty is here enjoined, and how much it is insisted upon. It is repeated over and over again, and enjoined in the strongest terms. Deuteronomy 15:7: "Thou shalt not harden thine heart, nor shut thine hand from thy poor brother." Verse 8: "But thou shalt open thine hand wide unto him." Verses 10–11: "Thou shalt surely give him. I command thee, saying, Thou shalt open thine hand wide unto thy brother, to thy poor, and to thy needy."

Moreover, God strictly warns against objections. Deuteronomy 15:9: "Beware that there be not a thought in thy wicked heart, saying, The seventh year, the year of release, is at hand; and thine eye be evil against thy poor brother, and thou givest him nought, and he cry unto the Lord against thee, and it be sin unto thee." The matter concerning the seventh year, or year of release, was this: God had given Israel a law that every seventh year should be a year of release, so that if any man had lent anything to any of his poor neighbors, if the latter had not been able to repay it before that year, the former should release it and should not exact it of his neighbor, but give it to him. Therefore God warns the children of Israel against making this an objection to helping their poor neighbors, that the year of release was near at hand, and it was not likely that they would be able to refund it again before that time, and then they should lose it wholly because then they would be obliged to release it. God foresaw that the wickedness of their hearts would be very ready to make such an objection. But He very strictly warns them against it, that they should not be more backward to supply the wants of the needy for that, but should be willing to give to him. "Lend, expecting nothing again."

Men are exceedingly apt to make objections against such duties, which God speaks of here as a manifestation of the wickedness of their hearts: "Beware that there be not a thought in thy wicked heart." The warning is very strict. God not only says, "Beware that you do not actually refuse to give to him," but, "Beware that you have not one objecting thought against it, arising from a backwardness to liberality." God warns against the beginnings of uncharitableness in the heart, and against whatever tends to a forbearance to give. "And thou give him nought, and he cry unto the Lord against thee, and it be sin unto thee." God warns them from the guilt which they would be liable to bring upon themselves hereby.

We may observe here several enforcements of this duty. There is a reason for this duty implied in God's calling him who is needy our brother: "Thou shalt not shut thine hand from thy poor brother." Deuteronomy 15:9: "Beware that thine eye be not evil against thy poor brother." Verse 11: "Thou shalt open thine hand wide to thy brother." We are to look upon ourselves as related to all mankind, but especially to those who are of the visible people of God. We are to look upon them as brethren and treat them accordingly. We shall be base indeed if we are not willing to help a brother in want.

Another enforcement of this duty is the promise of God that for this thing He will bless us in all our works, and in all that we put our hands to, a promise that we shall not lose but gain by it (Deuteronomy 15:10). Another is that we shall never lack proper objects of our charity and bounty. Verse 11: "For the poor shall never cease out of thy land." This God said to the Jewish church, and the like Christ said to the Christian church in Matthew 26:11: "The poor ye have always with you." This is to cut off an excuse that uncharitable persons would be ready to make for not giving, that they could find nobody to give to or that they saw none who needed. God cuts off such an excuse by telling us that He would so order it in His providence that His people everywhere, and in all ages, shall have occasion for the exercise of that virtue.

From this account the doctrine is obvious.

DOCTRINE: It is the absolute and indispensable duty of the people of God to give bountifully and willingly to supply the wants of the needy.

More particularly, it is the duty of the people of God to give bountifully for the aforesaid purpose. It is commanded once and again in the text, "Thou shalt open thine hand wide unto thy poor brother." Merely to give something is not sufficient. It does not answer the rule, nor does it come up to the holy command of God. But we must open our hand wide. What we give, considering our neighbor's wants and our ability, should be such as may be called a liberal gift. What is meant in the text by opening the hand wide, with respect to those who are able, is explained in Deuteronomy 15:8: "Thou shalt open thine hand wide unto him, and shalt surely lend him sufficient for his want, in that which he needeth." By lending here, as is evident by the two following verses, and as we have just now shown, is not only meant lending to receive again; for the word "lend" in Scripture is sometimes used for giving. Luke 6:35: "Do good and lend, hoping for nothing again."

We are commanded, therefore, to give our poor neighbor what is sufficient for his need. There ought to be none allowed to live in pinching want among a visible people of God who are able, unless in case of idleness, or prodigality, or some such case which the Word of God excepts. It is said that the children of Israel should lend to the poor, and in the year of release should release what they had lent, save when there should be no poor among them. It is rendered in the margin, "to the end there be no poor among you." That is, you should so supply the wants of the needy that there may be none among you in pinching want. This translation seems the more likely to be the true one, because God says in Deuteronomy 15:11 that there shall be no such time when there shall be no poor who shall be proper objects of charity. When persons give very sparingly, it is no manifestation of charity, but of a contrary spirit. 2 Corinthians 9:5: "Therefore I thought it necessary to exhort the brethren, that they would go before unto you, and make up beforehand your bounty, whereof ye had notice before, that the same might be ready, as a matter of bounty, and not as of covetousness."

It is the duty of the visible people of God to give for the supply of the needy freely and without grudging. It does not at all answer the rule in the sight of God if it is done with an inward grudging, or if the heart is grieved, and it inwardly hurts the man to give what he gives. "Thou shalt surely give," says God, "and thine heart shall not be grieved." God looks at the heart, and the hand is not accepted without it. 2 Corinthians 9:7: "Every man, according as he hath purposed in his heart, so let him give, not grudgingly, or of necessity; for God loveth a cheerful giver."

This is a duty to which God's people are under a very strict obligation. It is not merely a commendable thing for a man to be kind and bountiful to the poor, but it is our bound duty, as much a duty as it is to pray, to attend public worship, or anything else whatsoever. And the neglect of it brings great guilt upon any person.

The obligation of Christians to perform the duty of charity to the poor

This duty is absolutely commanded, and is much insisted on, in the Word of God. Where have we any command in the Bible laid down in stronger terms, and in a more peremptory urgent

manner, than the command of giving to the poor? We have
the same law in a positive manner laid down in Leviticus 25:35:
"And if thy brother be waxen poor, and fallen in decay with thee,
then thou shalt relieve him; yea, though he be a stranger or a
sojourner, that he may live with thee." And at the conclusion of
verse 38, God enforces it with saying, "I am the Lord thy God."

It is mentioned in Scripture not only as a duty, but as a great
duty. Indeed, it is generally acknowledged to be a duty to be
kind to the needy. But it does not seem to be looked upon as
a duty of great importance by many. However, it is mentioned
in Scripture as one of the greater and more essential duties of
religion. Micah 6:8: "He hath showed thee, O man, what is good;
and what doth the Lord thy God require of thee but to do justly,
to love mercy, and to walk humbly with thy God?" Here, to love
mercy is mentioned as one of the three great things that are
the sum of all religion. So it is mentioned by the Apostle James
as one of the two things wherein pure and undefiled religion
consists. James 1:27: "Pure religion, and undefiled, before God
and the Father, is this, to visit the fatherless and widows in their
affliction, and to keep himself unspotted from the world."

Christ tells us that it is one of the weightier matters of the
law. Matthew 23:23: "Ye have omitted the weightier matters of
the law, judgment, mercy, and faith." The Scriptures again and
again teach us that it is a more weighty and essential thing than
the attendance on the outward ordinances of worship (Hosea
6:6). "I desired mercy, and not sacrifice" (Matthew 9:13 and
12:7). I know of scarcely any duty which is so much insisted
on, so pressed and urged upon us, in both the Old and New
Testaments, as this duty of charity to the poor.

The reason for the thing strongly obliges us to it. It is not
only very positively and frequently insisted on by God, but
it most reasonable in itself. And so, on this account, there is

reason why God should much insist upon it.

It is most reasonable considering the general state and nature of mankind. This is such as renders it most reasonable that we should love our neighbor as ourselves; for men are made in the image of our God, and on this account are worthy of our love. Besides, we are all nearly allied one to another by nature. We have all the same nature, like faculties, like dispositions, like desires of good, like needs, like aversion to misery, and are made of one blood. And we are made to subsist by society and union one with another. Mankind in this respect are as the members of the natural body: one cannot subsist alone without a union with and the help of the rest.

Now this state of mankind shows how reasonable and suitable it is that men should love their neighbors, and that we should not look everyone at his own things, but every man also at the things of others (Philippians 2:4). A selfish spirit is very unsuitable to the nature and state of mankind. He who is all for himself, and cares none for his neighbors, deserves to be cut off from the benefit of human society, and to be turned out among wild beasts to subsist by himself as well as he can. A private, miserly spirit is more suitable for wolves and beasts of prey than for human beings.

To love our neighbor as ourselves is the sum of the moral law respecting our fellow creatures. And to help them, and to contribute to their relief, is the most natural expression of this love. It is vain to pretend to a spirit of love for our neighbors when it is grievous to us to part with anything for their help when they are under calamity. They who love only in word and in tongue, and not in deed, have no love in truth. Any profession without it is a vain pretense. To refuse to give to the needy is unreasonable because we therein do to others contrary to what we would have others to do to us in like circumstances. We are very sensible of our own calamities. And when we suffer we are ready enough to think that our state requires the compassion and help of others; we are ready enough to think it hard, if others will not deny themselves in order to help us when in straits.

It is especially reasonable considering our circumstances under such a dispensation of grace as that of the gospel. Consider how much God has done for us, how greatly He has loved us, what He has given us, when we were so unworthy, and when He could have no addition to His happiness by us. Consider that silver, gold, and earthly crowns were, in His esteem, but mean things to give us, and He has therefore given us His own Son. Christ loved and pitied us when we were poor, and He laid himself out to help. He even shed His own blood for us without grudging. He did not think much to deny Himself, and to be at great cost for us vile wretches in order to make us rich, and to clothe us with kingly robes when we were naked; to feast us at His own table with dainties infinitely costly when we were starving; to advance us from the dunghill and set us among princes, to make us to inherit the throne of His glory, and so to give us the enjoyment of the greatest wealth and plenty to all eternity. This is agreeable to 2 Corinthians 8:9: "For ye know the grace of our Lord Jesus Christ, that though He was rich, yet for your sakes He became poor, that ye through His poverty might be rich." Considering all these things, what a poor business will it be that those who hope to share these benefits yet cannot give something for the relief of a poor neighbor without grudging! How can it grieve them to part with a small matter to help a fellow servant in calamity when Christ did not grudge to shed His own blood for them!

How unsuitable is it for us who live only by kindness to be unkind! What would have become of us if Christ had been so saving of His blood, and loath to bestow it, as many men are of their money or goods? Or if He had been as ready to excuse Himself from dying for us as men commonly are to excuse themselves from charity to their neighbor? If Christ would have made objections of such things as men commonly object to performing deeds of charity to their neighbor, He would have found enough of them.

Besides, Christ, by His redemption, has brought us into a more near relations one to another. He has made us children of God, children in the same family. We are all brethren, having God for our common Father; which is much more than to be brethren in any other family. He has made us all one body. Therefore we ought to be united, serve one another's good, and bear one another's burdens, as is the case with the members of the same natural body. If one of the members suffer, all the other members bear the burden with it (1 Corinthians 12:26). If one member is diseased or wounded, the other members of the body will minister to it and help it. So surely it should be in the body of Christ. Galatians 6:2: "Bear ye one another's burdens, and so fulfill the law of Christ."

Apply these things to yourselves, and inquire whether you do not lie under guilt on account of the neglect of this duty in withholding that charity which God requires of you towards the needy? You have often been put upon examining whether you do not live in some way displeasing to God. Perhaps at such times it never came into your minds whether you do not lie under guilt on this account. But this neglect certainly brings guilt upon the soul in the sight of God, as is evident by our text. "Beware that thine eye be not evil against thy poor brother, and thou givest him nought, and he cry unto the Lord against thee, and it be sin unto thee" (Deuteronomy 15:9). This is often mentioned as one of the sins of Judah and Jerusalem, for which God was about to bring such terrible judgments upon them.

And it was one of the sins of Sodom, for which that city was destroyed, that she did not give to supply the poor and needy. Ezekiel 16:49: "This was the iniquity of thy sister Sodom, pride, fullness of bread, and abundance of idleness in her, and in her daughters; neither did she strengthen the hand of the poor and needy."

And have we not reason to fear that much guilt lies upon this land on this very account? We have a high conceit of ourselves for religion. But do not many other countries shame us? Do not the papists shame us in this respect? So far as I can understand the tenor of the Christian religion, and the rules of the Word of God, the same are in no measure in this respect answered by the general practice of most people in this land. There are many who make a high profession of religion. But do not many of them need to be informed by the apostle James what true religion is?

Let everyone examine himself, whether he does not lie under guilt in this matter. Have you not forborne to give when you have seen your brother in want? Have you not forborne to deny yourselves a little for his relief? Or, when you have given, have you not done it begrudgingly? And has it not inwardly hurt and grieved you? You have looked upon what you have given as lost. So that what you have given has been, as the apostle expresses it, a matter of covetousness rather than of bounty. Have not occasions of giving been unwelcome to you? Have you not been uneasy under them? Have you not felt a considerable backwardness to give? Have you not, from a grudging, backward spirit, been apt to raise objections against giving and to excuse yourselves? Such things as these bring guilt upon the soul, and often bring down the curse of God upon the persons in whom these things are found, as we may show more fully hereafter.

An exhortation to the duty of charity to the poor

We are professors of Christianity; we pretend to be the followers of Jesus, and to make the gospel our rule. We have the Bible in our houses. Let us not behave ourselves in this particular as if we had never seen the Bible, as if we were ignorant of Christianity and knew not what kind of religion it is. What will it signify to pretend to be Christians and, at the same time, to live in the neglect of those rules of Christianity which are mainly insisted on in it? But there are several things which I would here propose to your consideration.

• Consider that what you have is not your own; you have only a subordinate right. Your goods are only lent to you by God to be improved by you in such ways as He directs. You yourselves are not your own. 1 Corinthians 6:20: "Ye are not your own, for ye are bought with a price." Your body and your spirit are God's. And if you yourselves are not your own, then neither are your possessions your own. Many of you have by covenant given up yourselves and all you have to God. You have disowned and renounced any right in yourselves or in anything that you have, and have given God all the absolute right. And if you are true Christians, you have done it from the heart.

Your money and your goods are not your own. They are only committed to you as stewards to be used for Him who committed them to you. 1 Peter 4:9–10: "Use hospitality one to another, as good stewards of the manifold grace of God." A steward has no business with his master's goods, to use them any otherwise than for the benefit of his master and his family, or according to his master's direction. He has no business to use them, as if he were the proprietor of them. He has nothing to do with them, only as he is to use them for his master. He is to give everyone of his master's family their portion of meat in due season.

But if, instead of that, he hoards up his master's goods for himself, and withholds them from those of the household, so that some of the family are pinched for want of food and clothing, he is therein guilty of robbing his master and embezzling his substance. And would any householder endure such a steward? If he discovered him in such a practice, would he not take his goods out of his hands, and commit them to the care of some other steward, who would give everyone in his family his portion of meat in due season? Remember that all of us must give account of our stewardship, and how we have disposed of those goods which our Master has put into our hands. And if, when our Master comes to reckon with us, it is found that we have denied some of his family their proper provision, while we have hoarded up for ourselves, as if we had been the proprietors of our Master's goods, what account shall we give of this?

• God tells us that He shall look upon what is done in charity to our neighbors in want as done unto Him, and what is denied unto them as denied unto Him. Proverbs 19:17: "He that hath pity on the poor lendeth to the Lord." God has been pleased to make our needy neighbors His receivers. He in His infinite mercy has so interested Himself in their case that He looks upon what is given in charity to them as given to Himself. And when we deny them what their circumstances require of us, He looks upon it that we therein rob Him of his right.

Christ teaches us that we are to look upon our fellow Christians in this case as Himself, and that our giving or withholding from them shall be taken as if we so behaved ourselves towards Him. In Matthew 25:40 Christ says to the righteous on His right hand, who had supplied the wants of the needy, "In that ye have done it to one of the least of these My brethren, ye have done it unto Me." In like manner, in verse 45 He says to the wicked who had not shown mercy to the poor, "Inasmuch as ye did it not unto one of the least of these, ye did it not to Me." Now what stronger enforcement of this duty can be conceived, or is possible, than that Jesus Christ looks upon our kind and bountiful, or unkind and uncharitable, treatment of our needy neighbors as such a treatment of Himself?

If Christ Himself were upon earth, and dwelt among us in a frail body as He once did, and were in calamitous and needy circumstances, would we not be willing to supply Him? Would we be apt to excuse ourselves from helping Him? Would we not be willing to supply Him so that He might live free from distressing poverty? And if we did otherwise, would we not bring great guilt upon ourselves? Might not our conduct justly be very highly resented by God? Christ was once here in a frail body, stood in need of charity, and was maintained by it. Luke 8:2–3: "And certain women which had been healed of evil spirits and infirmities, Mary, called Magdalene, out of whom went seven devils, and Joanna the wife of Chuza, Herod's steward, and Susanna, and many others, which ministered unto him of their substance." So He still, in many of His members, needs the charity of others.

• Consider that there is an absolute necessity of our complying with the difficult duties of religion. To give to the poor in the manner and measure that the gospel prescribes is a difficult duty in that it is very contrary to corrupt nature, to that covetousness and selfishness of which there is so much in the wicked heart of man. Man is naturally governed only by a principle of self-love. And it is a difficult thing to corrupt nature for men to deny themselves of their present interest, trusting in God to make it up to them hereafter. But how often has Christ told us the necessity of doing the difficult duties of religion if we will be His disciples, that we must sell all, take up our cross daily, deny ourselves, and renounce our worldly profits and interests. And if this duty seem hard and difficult to you, do not let that be an objection with you against doing it. For you have taken up quite a wrong notion of things if you expect to go to heaven without performing difficult duties, if you expect any other than to find the way to life a narrow way.

• The Scripture teaches us that this very particular duty is necessary, First, the Scripture teaches that God will deal with us as we deal with our fellow creatures in this particular, and that with what measure we mete to others in this respect God will measure to us again. This the Scripture asserts both ways. It asserts that if we are of a merciful spirit, God will be merciful to us. Matthew 5:7: "Blessed are the merciful, for they shall obtain mercy." Psalm 18:25: "With the merciful Thou wilt show Thyself merciful." On the other hand, it tells us that if we are not merciful, God will not be merciful to us; and that all our pretenses to faith and a work of conversion will not avail us to obtain mercy unless we are merciful to them who are in want. James 2:13–16: "For he shall have judgment without mercy that hath showed no mercy. What doth it profit, my brethren, though a man say he hath faith, and have not works? Can faith save him? If a brother or sister be naked, and destitute of daily food; and one of you say unto them, 'Depart in peace, be you warmed, and filled'; notwithstanding ye give them not those things which are needful to the body; what doth it profit?"

Second, this very thing is often mentioned in Scripture as an essential part of the character of a godly man. Psalm 37:21: "The righteous showeth mercy, and giveth." And verse 26: "He is ever merciful and lendeth." Psalm 112:5: "A good man showeth favor, and lendeth." Verse 9: "He hath dispersed and given to the poor." Proverbs 14:31: "He that honoreth God hath mercy on the poor." In Proverbs 21:26 and Isaiah 57:1, a righteous man and a merciful man are used as synonymous terms: "The righteous perisheth, and merciful men are taken away."

It is mentioned in the New Testament as a thing so essential that the contrary cannot consist with a sincere love to God. 1 John 3:17–19: "But whoso hath this world's goods, and seeth his brother have need, and shutteth up his bowels of compassion from him, how dwelleth the love of God in him? My little children, let us not love in word, neither in tongue, but in deed and in truth. And hereby we know that we are of the truth, and shall assure our hearts before Him." So the Apostle Paul, when he writes to the Corinthians, and proposes their contributing for the supply of the poor saints, tells them that he does it for a trial of their sincerity. 2 Corinthians 8:8: "I speak to prove the sincerity of your love."

Christ teaches that judgment will be passed at the great day according to men's works in this respect. This is taught us by Christ in the most particular account of the proceedings of that day that we have in the whole Bible. See Matthew 25:34. It is evident that Christ thus represented the proceedings and determinations of this great day as turning upon this one point on purpose, and on design to lead us into this notion, and to fix it in us, that a charitable spirit and practice towards our brethren is necessary to salvation.

• Consider what abundant encouragement the Word of God gives, that you shall not be losers by your charity and bounty to them who are in want. As there is scarcely any duty prescribed in the Word of God which is so much insisted on as this, so there is scarcely any to which there are so many promises of reward made. This virtue especially has the promises of this life and that one which is to come. If we believe the Scriptures, when a man charitably gives to his neighbor in want, the giver has the greatest advantage by it, even greater than the receiver. Acts 20:35: "I have showed you all things, how that so laboring ye ought to support the weak, and to remember the words of the Lord Jesus, how He said, 'It is more blessed to give than to receive.' " He who gives bountifully is a happier man than he who receives bountifully. Proverbs 14:21: "He that hath mercy on the poor, happy is he."

Many persons are ready to look upon what is bestowed for charitable uses as lost. But we ought not to look upon it as lost because it benefits those whom we ought to love as ourselves. And not only so, but it is not lost to us if we give any credit to the Scriptures. See the advice that Solomon gives in Ecclessiastes 11:1: "Cast thy bread upon the waters, for thou shalt find it after many days." By casting our bread upon the waters, Solomon means giving it to the poor, as appears by the next words, "Give a portion to seven, and also to eight." Waters are sometimes put for people and multitudes.

What strange advice would this seem to many, to cast their bread upon the waters, which would seem to them like throwing it away! What more direct method to lose our bread than to go and throw it into the sea? But the wise man tells us, "No, it is not lost; you shall find it again after many days. It is not sunk, but you commit it to Providence." You commit it to the winds and waves. However it will come about to you, and you shall find it again after many days. Though it should be many days first, yet you shall find it at last, at a time when you most need it. He who gives to the poor lends to the Lord. And God is not one of those who will not pay again what is lent to Him. If you lend anything to God, you commit it into faithful hands. Proverbs 19:17: "He that hath pity on the poor lendeth to the Lord, and that which he hath given will He pay him again." God will not only pay you again, but He will pay you with great increase. Luke 6:38: "Give, and it shall be given you," that is, in "good measure, pressed down, and shaken together, and running over."

Men do not account that lost that is let out to use. But what is bestowed in charity is lent to the Lord, and He repays with great increase. Isaiah 32:8: "The liberal deviseth liberal things, and by liberal things shall he stand." Here I would particularly observe:

If you give with a spirit of true charity, you shall be rewarded in what is infinitely more valuable than what you give, even eternal riches in heaven. Matthew 10:42: "Whosoever shall give to drink unto one of these little ones, a cup of cold water only, in the name of a disciple; verily I say unto you, he shall in no wise lose his reward."

Giving to our needy brethren is in Scripture called laying up treasure in heaven in bags that do not get old. Luke 12:33: "Sell what ye have and give alms, provide for yourselves bags that wax not old, a treasure in the heavens that faileth not, where no thief approacheth, nor moth corrupteth." When men have laid up their money in their chests, they do not suppose that they have thrown it away. But, on the contrary, that it is laid up safely. Much less is treasure thrown away when it is laid up in heaven. What is laid up there is much safer than what is laid up in chests or cabinets.

You cannot lay up treasure on earth but it is liable to be stolen, or otherwise to fail. But there no thief approaches nor moth corrupts. It is committed to God's care, and He will keep it safely for you. And when you die, you shall receive it with infinite increase. Instead of a part of your earthly substance thus bestowed, you shall receive heavenly riches, on which you may live in the greatest fullness, honor, and happiness to all eternity, and never be in want of anything. After feeding with some of your bread those who cannot recompense you, you shall be rewarded at the resurrection and eat bread in the kingdom of

God. Luke 14:13–16: "When thou makest a feast, call the poor, the maimed, the lame, and the blind; and thou shalt be blessed for they cannot recompense thee; for thou shalt be recompensed at the resurrection of the just. And when one of them that sat at meat with Him heard these things, he said unto Him, 'Blessed is he that shall eat bread in the kingdom of God.' "

If you give to the needy though but in the exercise of moral virtue, you will be in the way greatly to gain by it in your temporal interest. They who give in the exercise of a gracious charity are in the way to be gainers both here and hereafter; and those who give in the exercise of a moral bounty and liberality have many temporal promises made to them. We learn from the Word of God that they are in the way to be prospered in their outward affairs. Ordinarily such do not lose by it, but such a blessing attends their concerns that they are paid doubly for it. Proverbs 11:24–25: "There is that scattereth, and yet increaseth; there is that withholdeth more than is meet, but it tendeth to poverty. The liberal soul shall be made fat: and he that watereth shall be watered also himself." Proverbs 28:27: "He that giveth to the poor shall not lack."

When men give to the needy, they sow seed for a crop. When men sow their seed, they seem to throw it away. Yet they do not look upon it as thrown away because, though they do not expect the same again, yet they expect much more as the fruit of it. And if it is not certain that they shall have a crop, yet they are willing to run the venture of it; for that is the ordinary way wherein men obtain increase. So it is when persons give to the poor. Though the promises of gaining thereby in our outward circumstances perhaps are not absolute, yet it is as much the ordinary consequence of it as increase is of sowing seed. Giving to the poor is in this respect compared to sowing seed in Ecclessiastes 11:6: "In the morning sow thy seed, and in the evening withhold not thine hand; for thou knowest not whether shall prosper, either this or that, or whether they both shall be alike good." By withholding the hand, the wise man means not giving to the poor (see verse 1–2). It intimates that giving to the poor is as likely a way to obtain prosperity and increase as sowing seed in a field.

The husbandman does not look upon his seed as lost, but is glad that he has opportunity to sow it. It does not grieve that he has land to be sown, but he rejoices in it. For the like reason we should not be grieved that we find needy people to bestow our charity upon. For this is as much an opportunity to obtain increase as the other.

Some may think this is strange doctrine; and it is to be feared that not many will so far believe it as to give to the poor with as much cheerfulness as they sow their ground. However, it is the very doctrine of the Word of God. 2 Corinthians 9:6–8: "But this I say, he which soweth sparingly shall reap also sparingly; and he which soweth bountifully shall reap also bountifully. Every man, according as he purposeth in his heart, so let him give; not grudgingly or of necessity, for God loveth a cheerful giver. And God is able to make all grace abound towards you; that ye always having all sufficiency in all things, may abound to every good work."

It is easy with God to make up to men what they give in charity. Many but little consider how their prosperity or ill success in their outward affairs depends upon Providence. There are a thousand turns of Providence to which their affairs are liable, whereby God may either add to their outward substance or diminish from it a great deal more than they are ordinarily called to give to their neighbors. How easy is it with God to diminish what they possess by sickness in their families, by drought, frost, mildew, or vermin; by unfortunate accidents, by entanglements in their affairs, or disappointments in their business! And how easy is it with God to increase their substance by suitable seasons, or by health and strength; by giving them fair opportunities for promoting their interest in their dealings with men; by conducting them in His providence so that they attain their designs; and by innumerable other ways which might be mentioned! How often is it that only one act of providence in a man's affairs either adds to his estate or diminishes from it more than he would need to give to the poor in a whole year.

God has told us that this is the way to have His blessing attending our affairs. Thus Deuteronomy 15:10: "Thou shalt surely give him, and thine heart shall not be grieved when thou givest unto him; because that for this thing the Lord thy God shall bless thee in all thy works, and all that thou puttest thine hand unto." Proverbs 22:9: "He that hath a bountiful eye shall be blessed." It is a remarkable evidence how little many men realize the things of religion, whatever they pretend; how little they realize that the Scripture is the Word of God, or, if it is, that He speaks true; that, notwithstanding all the promises made in the Scripture to bounty to the poor, yet they are so backward to this duty, and are so afraid to trust God with a little of their estates. Observation may confirm the same thing which the Word of God teaches on this heading. God, in His providence, generally smiles upon and prospers those men who are of a liberal, charitable, bountiful spirit.

• God has threatened to follow with His curse those who are uncharitable to the poor. Proverbs 28:27: "He that giveth to the poor shall not lack; but he that hideth his eyes shall have many a curse." It says "he that hideth his eyes" because this is the way of uncharitable men. They hide their eyes from seeing the wants of their neighbor. A charitable person, whose heart disposes him to bounty and liberality, will be quick-sighted to discern the needs of others. They will not be at any difficulty to find out who is in want. They will see objects enough of their charity, let them go where they will.

But, on the contrary, he who is of a miserly spirit, so that it goes against the grain to give anything, will be always at a loss for objects of his charity. Such men excuse themselves with this, that they find no one to give to. They hide their eyes and will not see their neighbor's wants. If a particular object is presented, they will not very readily see his circumstances. They are a long while in being convinced that he is an object of charity. They hide their eyes. And it is not an easy thing to make them sensible of the necessities and distresses of their neighbor, or at least to convince them that his necessities are such that they ought to give him any great matter.

Other men who are of a bountiful spirit can very easily see the objects of charity. But the uncharitable are very unapt both to see the proper objects of charity and to see their obligations to this duty. The reason is that they are of that sort spoken of here by the wise man: they hide their eyes. Men will readily see where they are willing to see. But where they hate to see, they will hide their eyes.

God says that such as hides his eyes in this case shall have many a curse. Such a one is in the way to be cursed in soul and body, in both his spiritual and temporal affairs. We have shown already how those who are charitable to the poor are in the way of being blessed. There are so many promises of the divine blessing that we may look upon it as much the way to be blessed in our outward concerns as sowing seed in a field is the way to have increase. And to be close and uncharitable is as much the way to be followed with a curse as to be charitable is the way to be followed with a blessing. To withhold more than is meet tends as much to poverty as scattering tends to increase

(Proverbs 11:24). Therefore, if you withhold more than is meet, you will cross your own disposition and will frustrate your own end. What you seek by withholding from your neighbor is your own temporal interest and outward estate. But if you believe the Scriptures to be the Word of God, you must believe that you cannot take a more direct course to lose to be crossed and cursed in your temporal interest than this of withholding from your indigent neighbor.

• Consider that you do not know what calamitous and necessitous circumstances you or your children may be in. Perhaps you are ready to bless yourselves in your hearts, as though there were no danger of you being brought into calamitous and distressing circumstances. There is at present no prospect of it; and you hope you shall be able to provide well for your children. But you little consider what a shifting, changing, uncertain world you live in, and how often it has so happened that men have been reduced from the greatest prosperity to the greatest adversity, and how often the children of the rich have been reduced to pinching want.

Agreeable to this is the advice that the wise man gives us in Ecclessiastes 11:1–2: "Cast thy bread upon the waters; for thou shalt find it after many days. Give a portion to seven, and also to eight; for thou knowest not what evil shall be upon earth." You do not know what calamitous circumstances you may be in yourself in this changeable, uncertain world. You do not know what circumstances you or your children may be brought into by captivity, or other unthought-of providences. Providence governs all things. Perhaps you may trust your own wisdom to continue your prosperity. But you cannot alter what God determines and orders in providence, as in the words immediately following the forementioned text in Ecclesiastes: "If the clouds be full of rain, they empty themselves upon the earth; and if the tree fall toward the south, or toward the north; in the place where the tree falleth, there it shall be." You cannot alter the determinations of Providence. You may trust your own wisdom for future prosperity. But if God has ordained adversity it shall come. As the clouds when full of rain empty themselves upon the earth, so what is in the womb of Providence shall surely come to pass. And as Providence casts the tree, whether towards the south or towards the north, whether for prosperity or adversity, there it shall be, for all that you can do to alter it. Agreeably the wise man observes in Ecclessiastes 7:13: "Consider the work of God; for who can make that straight which He hath made crooked?"

The consideration that you do not know what calamity and necessity you or your children may be in tends very powerfully to enforce this duty in several ways.

First this may put you upon considering how your hearts would be effected if it should so be. If it should happen that you or some of your children should be brought into such circumstances as those of your neighbors, how grievous would it be to you! Now perhaps you say of this and the other poor neighbor that they can do well enough. If they are pinched a little, they can live. Thus you can make light of their difficulties. But if Providence should so order it that you or your children should be brought into the same circumstances, would you make light of them then? Would you not use another sort of language about it? Would you not think that your case was such as needed the kindness of your neighbors? Would you not think that they ought to be ready to help you? And would you not take it harshly if you saw a contrary spirit in them, and saw that they made light of your difficulties?

If one of your children should be brought to poverty, how would your hearts be affected in such a case? If you should hear that some persons had taken pity on your child and had been very bountiful to him or her, would you not think that they did well? Would you be at all apt to accuse them of folly or profuseness, that they should give so much to it?

Second, if ever there should be such a time, your kindness to others now will be but laying up against such a time. If you yourselves should be brought into calamity and necessity, then would you find what you have given in charity to others lying ready in store for you. "Cast thy bread upon the waters, and thou shalt find it after many days," said the wise man. But when shall we find it? He tells us in the next verse: "Give a portion to seven, and also to eight; for thou knowest now what evil shall be upon the earth." Then is the time when you shall find it, when the day of evil comes. You shall again find your bread which you have cast upon the waters when you shall want it most, and stand in greatest necessity of it. God will keep it for you against such a time. When other bread shall fail, then God will bring to you the bread which you formerly cast upon the waters so that you shall not famish. He who gives to the poor shall not lack.

Giving to the needy is like laying up against winter, or against a time of calamity. It is the best way of laying up for yourselves and for your children. Children in a time of need very often find their fathers' bread, that bread which their fathers had cast upon the waters. Psalm 37:25: "I have been young and now am old, yet have I not seen the righteous forsaken, nor his seed begging bread." Why? What is the reason for it? It follows in the next verse: "He is ever merciful and lendeth, and his seed is blessed."

Whether the time will ever come or not that we or our children shall be in distressing want of bread, yet doubtless evil will be on the earth. We shall have our times of calamity wherein we shall stand in great need of God's pity and help, if not of that of our fellow creatures. And God has promised that at such a time he who hath been of a charitable spirit and practice shall find help. Psalm 41:1–4: "Blessed is he that considereth the poor; the Lord will deliver him in time of trouble. The Lord will preserve him and keep him alive, and he shall be blessed upon the earth; and thou wilt not deliver him unto the will of his enemies. The Lord will strengthen him upon the bed of languishing; thou wilt make all his bed in his sickness." Such as have been merciful and liberal to others in their distress, God will not forget it, but will so order it that they shall have help when they are in distress. Yea, their children shall reap the fruit of it in the day of trouble.

Third, God has threatened that if ever uncharitable persons come to be in calamity and distress, they shall be left helpless. Proverbs 21:13: "Whoso stoppeth his ears at the cry of the poor, he shall cry himself and not be heard."

Objections that are sometimes made to the exercise of charity answered

I proceed now to answer some objections which are some-times made against this duty.

OBJECTION 1. I am in a natural condition, and if I should give to the poor, I should not do it with a right spirit, and so should get nothing by it.

ANSWER. First, we have shown already that a temporal blessing is promised to a moral bounty and liberality. This is the way to be prospered. This is the way to increase. We find in Scripture many promises of temporal blessings to moral virtues, such as to diligence in our business, to justice in our dealings, to faithfulness, and to temperance. So there are many blessings promised to bounty and liberality.

Second, you may as well make the same objection against any other duty of religion. You may as well object against keeping the Sabbath, against prayer, public worship, or against doing anything at all in religion. For while in a natural condition you do not any of these duties with a right spirit. If you say that you do these duties because God has commanded or required them of you, and you shall sin greatly if you neglect them, you shall increase your guilt and so expose yourselves to the greater damnation and punishment. The same may be said of the neglect of this duty; the neglect of it is as provoking to God.

If you say that you read, and pray and attend public worship because that is the appointed way for you to seek salvation, so is bounty to the poor as much as those. The appointed way for us to seek the favor of God and eternal life is the way of the performance of all known duties, of which giving to the poor is one as much known, and as necessary as reading the Scriptures, praying, or any other. Showing mercy to the poor as much belongs to the appointed way of seeking salvation as any other duty whatever. Therefore this is the way in which Daniel directed Nebuchadnezzar to seek mercy. Daniel 4:27: "Wherefore, O king, let my counsel be acceptable to thee, and break off thy sins by righteousness, and thine iniquities by showing mercy to the poor."

OBJECTION 2. If I am liberal and bountiful, I shall only make a righteousness of it, and so it will do me more hurt than good.

ANSWER. First, the same answer may be made to this as to the former objection. You may as well make the same objection against doing any religious or moral duty at all. If this is a sufficient objection against deeds of charity, then it is a sufficient objection to prayer. For nothing is more common than for persons to make a righteousness of their prayers.

So it is a good objection against your keeping the Sabbath, attending any public worship, or ever reading in the Bible. For of all these things you are in danger of making a righteousness. Yea, if the objection is good against deeds of charity, then it is as good against acts of justice. And you may neglect to speak the truth, neglect to pay your debts, and neglect acts of common humanity; for of all those things you are in danger of making a righteousness. So that if your objection is good, you may throw off all religion and live like heathens or atheists, and may be thieves, robbers, fornicators, adulterers, murderers, and commit all the sins that you can think of lest, if you should do otherwise, you should make a righteousness of your conduct.

Second, your objection implies that it is not best for you to do as God commands and counsels you to do. We find many commands in Scripture to be charitable to the poor. The Bible is full of them, and you are not excepted from those commands. God makes no exception of any particular kinds of persons who are especially in danger of making a righteousness of what they do. And God often directs and counsels persons to this duty. Now will you presume to say that God has not directed you to the best way? He has advised you to do this, but you think it not best for you, but that it would do you more hurt than good if you should do it. You think there is other counsel better than God's, and that it is the best way for you to go contrary to God's commands.

OBJECTION 3. I have in times past given to the poor, but never found myself the better for it. I have heard ministers preach that giving to the poor was the way to prosper. But I do not perceive that I am more prosperous than I was before. Yea, I have met with many misfortunes, crosses, and disappointments in my affairs since.

And some will say, "That very year, or soon after the very time I had been giving to the poor, hoping to be blessed for it, I met with great losses, and things went harshly for me. Therefore I do not find what I hear preached about giving to the poor as being the way to be blessed and prosperous agreeable to my experience."

ANSWER. First, perhaps you looked for the fulfillment of the promise too soon, before you had fulfilled the condition. Particularly, perhaps you have been so sparing and grudging in your kindness to the poor that what you have done has been rather a discovery of a covetous, niggardly spirit than of any bounty or liberality. The promises are not made to everyone who gives anything at all to the poor, let it be ever so little, and after whatever manner given. You mistook the promises if you understood them so. A man may give something to the poor and yet be entitled to no promise, either temporal or spiritual. The promises are made to mercy and liberality. But a man may give something and yet be so niggardly and begrudging in it that what he gives may be, as the apostle calls it, a matter of covetousness. What he does may be more a manifestation of his covetousness and closeness than anything else. But there are no promises made to men's expressing their covetousness.

Perhaps what you gave was not freely given, but, as it were, of necessity. It was given grudgingly; your hearts were grieved when you gave. And if you gave once or twice what was considerable, yet that does not answer the rule. It may be, for all that, that in the general course of your lives you have been far from being kind and liberal to your neighbors. Perhaps you thought that because you once or twice gave a few shillings to the poor that then you stood entitled to the promises of being blessed in all your concerns, and of increasing and being established by liberal things, though in the general you have lived in a faulty neglect of the duty of charity. You raise objections from experience before you have made trial. To give once, twice, or three times is not to make trial, though you give considerably. You cannot make any trial unless you become a liberal person, or unless you become such that you may be truly said to be of a liberal and bountiful practice. Let one who is truly such, and has been such in the general course of his life, tell what he has found by experience.

Second, if you have been liberal to the poor and have met with calamities since, yet how can you tell how much greater calamities and losses you might have met with if you had been otherwise? You say you have met with crosses, disappointments, and frowns. If you expected to meet with no trouble in the world because you gave to the poor, you mistook the matter. Though there are many and great promises made to the liberal, yet God has nowhere promised that they shall not find this world a world of trouble. It will be so to all. Man is born to sorrow, and must expect no other than to meet with sorrow here. But how can you tell how much greater sorrow you would have met with if you had been close and unmerciful to the poor? How can you tell how much greater losses you would have met with, how much more vexation and trouble would have followed you? Have none ever met with greater frowns in their outward affairs than you have?

Third, how can you tell what blessings God has yet in reserve for you if you continue in well-doing? Although God has promised great blessings for liberality to the poor, yet He has not limited Himself as to the time of the bestowment. If you have not yet seen any evident fruit of your kindness to the poor, yet the time may come when you shall see it remarkably, and that at a time when you most stand in need of it. You cast your bread upon the waters and looked for it, and expected to find it again presently. And sometimes it is so. But this is not promised. What is promised is this: "Thou shalt find it again after many days." God knows how to choose a time for you better than you yourselves. You should therefore wait His time. If you go on in well-doing, God may bring it to you when you stand most in need.

It may be that there is some winter coming, some day of trouble. And God keeps your bread for you against that time. Then God will give you good measure, pressed down, shaken together, and running over. We must trust in God's Word for the bestowment of the promised reward whether we can see in what manner it is done or not. Pertinent to the present purpose are those words of the wise man in Ecclessiastes 11:4: "He that observeth the winds shall not sow; and he that re-gardeth the clouds shall not reap." In this context the wise man in speaking of charity to the poor and comparing it to sowing seed; he advises us to trust Providence for success in that as we do in sowing seed. He who regards the winds and clouds, to prognosticate thence prosperity to seed, and will not trust Providence with it, is not likely to sow, nor to have corn. So he who will not trust Providence for the reward of his charity to the poor will go without the blessing. After the words now quoted follows this advice in Ecclessiastes 11:6: "In the morning sow thy seed, and the evening withhold not thine hand; for thou knowest not whether shall prosper, either this or that, or whether they both shall be alike good." Therefore Galatians 6:9: "Let us not be weary in well doing, for in due season we shall reap, if we faint not." You think you have not reaped yet. Whether you have or not, go on still in giving and doing good; and, if you do so, you shall reap in due time. God only knows the due time, the best time, for you to reap.

OBJECTION 4. I am not obliged to give them anything, for though they are needy yet they are not in extremity. It is true they meet with difficulty, yet not so but that they can live, though they suffer some hardships.

ANSWER. But that objection does not answer the rules of Christian charity, to relieve those only who are reduced to extremity, as might be abundantly shown. I shall at this time mention but two things as evidences of it.

First, we are commanded to love and treat one another as brethren. 1 Peter 3:8: "Have compassion one of another; love as brethren; be pitiful." Now is it the part of brethren to refuse to help one another, and to do anything for each other's comfort, and for the relief of each other's difficulties, only when they are in extremity? Does it not become brothers and sisters to have a more friendly disposition one towards another than this comes to? Are we not to be ready to compassionate one another under difficulties, though they are not extreme?

The rule of the gospel is that when we see our brother under any difficulty or burden, we should be ready to bear the burden with him. Galatians 6:2: "Bear ye one another's burdens, and so fulfill the law of Christ." So we are commanded "by love to serve one another" (Galatians 5:13). The Christian spirit will make us apt to sympathize with our neighbor when we see him under any difficulty. Romans 12:15: "Rejoice with them that do rejoice, and weep with them that weep." When our neighbor is in difficulty, he is afflicted; and we ought to have such a spirit of love for him as to be afflicted with him in his affliction. And if we ought to be afflicted with him, then it will follow that we ought to be ready to relieve him. Because if we are afflicted with him, in relieving him we relieve ourselves. His relief is so far our own relief as his affliction is our affliction. Christianity teaches us to be afflicted in our neighbor's affliction. And nature teaches us to relieve ourselves when afflicted.

We should behave ourselves one towards another as brethren who are fellow travelers. For we are pilgrims and strangers here on earth, and are on a journey. Now, if brethren are on a journey together, and one meets with difficulty in the way, does it not become the rest to help him, not only in the extremity of broken bones or the like, but as to provision for the journey if his own falls short? It becomes his fellow travelers to afford him a supply out of their stores, and not to be over nice, exact, and fearful lest they give him too much; for it is but provision for a journey. And all are supplied when they get to their journey's end.

Second, that we should relieve our neighbor only when in extremity is not agreeable to the rule of loving our neighbor as ourselves. That rule implies that our love towards our neighbor should work in the same manner, and express itself in the same ways, as our love towards ourselves. We are very sensible of our own difficulties. We should also be readily sensible of theirs. From love to ourselves, when we are under difficulties and suffer hardships, we are concerned for our relief, are wont to seek relief, and lay ourselves out for it. And as we would love our neighbor as ourselves, we ought in like manner to be concerned when our neighbor is under difficulty and to seek his relief. We are wont to be much concerned about our own difficulties, though we are not reduced to extremity, and are willing in those cases to lay ourselves out for our own relief. So, as we would love our neighbor as ourselves, we should in like manner lay out ourselves to obtain relief for him though his difficulties are not extreme.

OBJECTION 5. That person is an ill sort of person. He does not deserve that people should be kind to him. He is of a very ill temper, of an ungrateful spirit, and particularly, because he has not deserved well of them, but has treated them ill, has been injurious to them, and even now entertains an ill spirit against them.

ANSWER. But we are obliged to relieve persons in want notwithstanding these things, by both the general and particular rules of God's Word.

First, we are obliged to do so by the general rules of Scripture. We are to love our neighbor as ourselves. A man may be our neighbor though he is an ill sort of man, and even our enemy, as Christ Himself teaches us by His discourse with the lawyer in Luke 10. A certain lawyer came to Christ, and asked Him what he should do to inherit eternal life? Christ asked him how it was written in the law. The young lawyer answered, "Thou shalt love the Lord thy God with all thy heart, and all thy soul, and with all thy strength, and with all thy mind, and thy neighbor as thyself." Christ told him that if he did this he would live. But then the lawyer asked Him who his neighbor was. It was received doctrine among the Pharisees that no man was their neighbor but their friends, and those of the same people and religion. Christ answered him by a parable or story of a certain man who went down from Jerusalem to Jericho, and fell among thieves, who stripped him of his raiment, wounded him, and departed from him, leaving him half dead. Soon after there came a priest that way who saw the poor man who had been thus cruelly treated by the thieves, but passed by without affording him any relief. The same as done by a Levite. But a certain Samaritan, coming that way, as soon as he saw the half-dead man, had compassion on him, took him up, bound up his wounds, set him on his own beast, carried him to the inn, and took care of him, paying the innkeeper money for his past and future expense, and promising him still more if he should find it necessary to be at more expense on behalf of the man.

Then Christ asked the lawyer which of these three, the priest, the Levite, or the Samaritan, was neighbor to the man who fell among the thieves. Christ proposed this in such a manner that the lawyer could not help owning that the Samaritan did well in relieving the Jew, that he did the duty of a neighbor to him. Now there was an inveterate enmity between the Jews and the Samaritans. They hated one another more than any other nation in the world. And the Samaritans were a people exceedingly troublesome to the Jews. Yet we see that Christ teaches that the Jews ought to do the part of neighbors to the Samaritans, to love them as themselves. For it was that of which Christ was speaking.

And the consequence was plain. If the Samaritan was neighbor to the distressed Jew, then the Jews, by a parity of reason, were neighbors to the Samaritans. If the Samaritan did well in relieving a Jew who was his enemy, then the Jews would do well in relieving the Samaritans, their enemies. What I particularly observe is that Christ here plainly teaches that our enemies, those who abuse and injure us, are our neighbors, and therefore come under the rule of loving our neighbor as ourselves.

Another general rule that obliges us to the same thing is that wherein we are commanded to love one another as Christ has loved us. John 13:34: "A new commandment I give unto you, that ye love one another; as I have loved you, that ye also love one another." Christ calls it a new commandment, with respect to that old commandment of loving our neighbor as ourselves. This command of loving our neighbor as Christ has loved us opens our duty to us in a new manner, and in a further degree than that one did. We must not only love our neighbor as ourselves, but as Christ has loved us. We have the same in John 15:12: "This is My commandment, that ye love one another as I have loved you."

The meaning of this is not that we should love one another to the same degree that Christ loved us, though there ought to be a proportion, considering our nature and capacity, but that we should exercise our love one to another in like manner. For instance, Christ has loved us so as to be willing to deny Himself, and to suffer greatly, in order to help us; so should we be willing to deny ourselves in order to help one another. Christ loved us and showed us great kindness though we were far below Him; so should we show kindness to those of our fellow men who are far below us. Christ denied Himself to help us though we are not able to recompense Him; so should we be willing to lay out ourselves to help our neighbor freely, expecting nothing again. Christ loved us, was kind to us, and was willing to relieve us, though we were very evil and hateful, of an evil disposition, not deserving any good, but deserving only to be hated and treated with indignation; so we should be willing to be kind to those who are of an ill disposition, and are very undeserving. Christ loved us, and laid Himself out to relieve us, though we were His enemies and had treated him ill. So we, as we would love one another as Christ has loved us, should relieve those who are our enemies, hate us, have an ill spirit toward us, and have treated us ill.

Second, we are obliged to this duty by many particular rules. We are particularly required to be kind to the unthankful and to the evil. Therein we follow the example of our heavenly Father, who causes His sun to rise on the evil and on the good, and sends rain on the just and the unjust. We are obliged not only to be kind to them who are so to us, but to them who hate and despitefully use us. I need not mention the particular places which speak to the effect.

But when persons are virtuous and pious, of a grateful disposition, and are friendly disposed towards us, they are more the objects of our charity for it, and our obligation to kindness to them is the greater. Yet if things are otherwise, that does not render them unfit objects of our charity, nor set us free from obligation to kindness towards them.

OBJECTION 6. I have nothing to spare. I have nothing more than enough for myself.

ANSWER. It must doubtless be allowed that in some cases persons, by reason of their own circumstances, are not obliged to give to others. For instance, if there is a contribution for the poor, they are not obliged to join in the contribution who are in as much need as those are for whom the contribution is made. It savors of ridiculous vanity in them to contribute with others for such as are not more needy than they. It savors of a proud desire to conceal their own circumstances, and an affectation of having them accounted about what they in truth are.

Second, there are scarcely any who may not make this objection depending on how they interpret it. There is no person who may not say that he has nothing more than enough for himself, depending on what he may mean by "enough." He may intend that he has not more than he desires, or more than he can dispose of to his own advantage; or not so much but that, if he had anything less, he should look upon himself in worse circumstances than he is in now. He will own that he could live if he had less. But then he will say he could not live so well. Rich men may say they have not more than enough for themselves, depending on what they may mean by it. They need it all, they may say, to support their honor and dignity, as is proper for the place and degree in which they stand. Those who are poor, to be sure, will say, they have not too much for themselves. Those who are of the middle sort will say that they have not too much for themselves. And the rich will say that they have not too much for themselves. Thus there will be none found to give to the poor.

Third, in many cases we may, by the rules of the gospel, be obliged to give to others when we cannot do it without suffering ourselves. If our neighbor's difficulties and necessities are much greater than our own, and we see that he is not likely to be otherwise relieved, we should be willing to suffer with him and to take part of his burden on ourselves. Else how is that rule of bearing one another's burdens fulfilled? If we are never obliged to relieve others' burdens but when we can do it without burdening ourselves, then how do we bear our neighbor's burdens when we bear no burden at all? Though we may not have a superfluity, yet we may be obliged to afford relief to others who are in much greater necessity. This appears by that rule from Luke 3:11: "He that hath two coats, let him impart to him that hath none; and he that hath meat, let him do likewise." Yea, they who are very poor may be obliged to give for the relief of others in much greater distress than they. If there is no other way of relief, those who have the lightest burden are obliged still to take some part of their neighbor's burden, to make it the more supportable. A brother may be obliged to help a brother in extremity though they are both very much in want. The apostle commends the Macedonian Christians for being liberal to their brethren though they themselves were in deep poverty. 2 Corinthians 8:1–2: "Moreover, brethren, we do you to wit of the grace of God bestowed on the churches of Macedonia, how in a great trial of affliction, the abundance of their joy, and their deep poverty, abounded unto the riches of their liberality."

Fourth, those who have not too much for themselves are willing to spare seed to sow so that they may have fruit hereafter.

Perhaps they need that which they scatter in the field and seem to throw away. They may need it for bread for their families. Yet they will spare seed to sow so that they may provide for the future and may have increase. But we have already shown that giving to the poor is in Scripture compared to sowing seed, and is as much the way to increase as the sowing of seed is. It does not tend to poverty, but the contrary. It is not the way to diminish our substance, but to increase it. All the difficulty in this matter is in trusting God with what we give, in trusting His promises. If men could but trust the faithfulness of God to His own promises, they would give freely.

OBJECTION 7. I do not certainly know whether he is an object of charity or not. I am not perfectly acquainted with his circumstances. Neither do I know what sort of man he is. I do not know whether he is in want as he pretends. How do I know how he came to be in want? Perhaps it was by his own idleness or prodigality. I cannot be obliged till I certainly know these things.

ANSWER. First, this is Nabal's objection, for which he is greatly condemned in Scripture (see 1 Samuel 25). In his exiled state, David came and begged relief from Nabal. Nabal objected in 1 Samuel 25:10–11: "Who is David? And who is the son of Jesse? There be many servants nowadays that break away every man from his master. Shall I then take my bread and my water, and my flesh that I have killed for my shearers, and give it unto men, whom I know not whence they be?" His objection was that David was a stranger to him. He did not know who he was, nor what his circumstances were. He did not know but that he was a runaway, and he was not obliged to support and harbor a runaway. He objected that he did not know if he was a proper object of charity or not.

But Abigail in no way countenanced his behavior herein,

but greatly condemned it. She called him a man of Belial, and says that he was as his name was. Nabal was his name, and folly was with him. Her behavior was very contrary to his, and she is greatly commended for it. The Holy Ghost tells us in 1 Samuel 25:3 that "she was a woman of a good understanding." At the same time God exceedingly frowned on Nabal's behavior on this occasion. We are informed that about ten days after God smote Nabal he died (verse 38).

This story is doubtless told us partly to discountenance too great a scrupulosity as to the object on whom we bestow our charity, and making it an objection against charity to others that we do not certainly know their circumstances. It is true, when we have opportunity to be certainly acquainted with their circumstances, it is well to embrace it. And to be influenced in a measure by probability in such cases is not to be condemned. Yet it is better to give to several who are not objects of charity than to send away empty one who is.

Second, we are commanded to be kind to strangers whom we do not know, nor their circumstances. This is commanded in many places, but I mention only Hebrews 13:2: "Be not forgetful to entertain strangers; for thereby some have entertained angels unawares." By strangers here the apostle means one whom we do not know, and whose circumstances we do not know, as is evident by these words: "for thereby some have entertained angels unawares." Those who entertained angels unawares did not know the persons whom they entertained, nor their circumstances. Else how could it be unawares?

OBJECTION 8. I am not obliged to give to the poor till they ask. If any man is in necessity, let him come and make known his straits to me, and then it will be time enough for me to give him. Or if he needs a public contribution, let him come and ask. I do not know that the congregation or church is obliged to relieve till they ask relief.

ANSWER. First, it surely is the most charitable to relieve the needy in that way wherein we shall do them the greatest kindness. Now it is certain that we shall do them a greater kindness by inquiring into their circumstances and relieving them, without putting them upon begging. There is none of us but who, if it were their case, would look upon it more kind in our neighbors to inquire into our circumstances and help us of their own accord. To put our neighbors upon begging in order to get relief is painful. It is more charitable, more brotherly, more becoming Christians and the disciples of Jesus, to do it without that. I think this is self-evident, and needs no proof.

Second, this is not agreeable to the character of the liberal man given in Scripture: he who devises liberal things (Isaiah 32:8). It is not to devise liberal things if we neglect all liberality till the poor come begging to us. But to inquire who stand in need of our charity, and to contrive to relieve them in the way that shall do them the greatest kindness, that is to devise liberal things.

Third, we would not commend a man for doing so to his own brother. If a man had a brother or sister in great straits, and he were well able to supply them under the pretense that, if he or she want anything, let them come and ask and I will give them, we would hardly think such an one behaved like a brother. Christians are commanded to love as brethren, to look upon one another as brethren in Christ, and to treat one another as such.

Fourth, we would commend others for taking a method contrary to that which is proposed by the objector. If we heard or read of people who were so charitable—who took such care of the poor, and were so concerned that none among them should suffer, who were proper objects of charity—that they were wont diligently to inquire into the circumstances of their neighbors to find out who were needy, and liberally supplied them of their own accord; I say, if we should hear or read of such a people, would it not appear well to us? Would not we have the better thought of that people, on that account?

OBJECTION 9. That person has brought himself to want by his own fault.

ANSWER. But what do you mean by "his own fault?"

First, if you mean a lack of a natural faculty to manage affairs to advantage, that is to be considered as his calamity. Such a faculty is a gift that God bestows on some and not on others—and it is not owing to themselves. You ought to be thankful that God has given you such a gift which He has denied to the person in question. And it will be a very suitable way for you to show your thankfulness to help those to whom that gift is denied, and let them share the benefit of it with you. This is as reasonable as that he to whom Providence has imparted sight should be willing to help him to whom sight is denied, and that he should have the benefit of the sight of others who has none of his own. He to whom God has given wisdom should be willing that the ignorant should have the benefit of his knowledge.

Second, if they have been reduced to want by some oversight, and are to be blamed that they did not consider better for themselves, yet that does not free us from all obligation to charity towards them. If we should forever refuse to help men because of that, it would be for us to make their inconsiderateness and imprudent act an unpardonable crime, quite contrary to the rules of the gospel, which insist so much upon forgiveness. We would not be disposed so highly to resent such an oversight in any for whom we have a dear affection, such as our children or our friends. We would not refuse to help them in that necessity and distress which they brought upon themselves by their own inconsiderateness. But we ought to have a dear affection and concern for the welfare of all our fellow Christians, whom we should, love as brethren, and as Christ has loved us.

Third, if they have come to want by a vicious idleness and prodigality, yet we are not thereby excused from all obligation to relieve them unless they continue in those vices. If they do not continue in those vices, the rules of the gospel direct us to forgive them. And if their fault is forgiven, then it will not remain to be a bar in the way of our charitably relieving them. If we do otherwise, we shall act in a manner very contrary to the rule of loving one another as Christ has loved us. Now Christ has loved us, pitied us, and greatly laid out Himself to relieve us from that want and misery which we brought on ourselves by our own folly and wickedness. We foolishly and perversely threw away those riches with which we were provided, upon which we might have lived and been happy to all eternity.

Fourth, if they continue in the same courses still, yet that does not excuse us from charity to their families that are innocent. If we cannot relieve those of their families without their having something of it, yet that ought not to be a bar in the way of our charity. It is supposed that those of their families are proper objects of charity. And those who are so, we are bound to relieve. The command is positive and absolute. If we look upon that which the heads of the families have of what we give to be entirely lost, yet we had better lose something of our estate than suffer those who are really proper objects of charity to remain without relief.

OBJECTION 10. Others do not do their duty. If others did their duty, the poor would be sufficiently supplied. If others did as much as I have in proportion to their ability and obligation, the poor would have enough to help them out of their straits.

Or some may say, it belongs to others more than it does to us. They have relations who ought to help them. There are others to whom it more properly belongs than to us.

ANSWER. We ought to relieve those who are in want though brought to it through others' fault. If our neighbor is poor, though others are to blame, yet that does not excuse us from helping him. If it belong to others more than to us, yet if those others neglect their duty and our neighbor therefore remains in want, we may be obliged to relieve him. If a man is brought into straits through the injustice of others, perhaps by thieves or robbers, as the poor Jew whom the Samaritan relieved, yet we may be obliged to relieve him though it be not through our fault that he is in want, but through that of other men. And whether that fault is a commission or a neglect does not alters the case.

As to the poor Jew who fell among thieves between Jerusalem and Jericho, it more properly belonged to those thieves who brought him into that distress to relieve him than to any other person. Yet seeing they would not do it, others were not excused. The Samaritan did no more than his duty, relieving him as he did, though it properly belonged to others. Thus if a man has children or other relations to whom it most properly belongs to relieve him, yet, if they will not do it, the obligation to relieve him falls upon others. So for the same reason we should do more for the relief of the poor because others neglect to do their proportion or what belongs to them. By the neglect of others to do their portion, they need more; their necessity is greater.

OBJECTION 11. The law makes provision for the poor, and obliges the respective towns in which they live to provide for them. There is no occasion for particular persons to exercise any charity this way. The case is not the same with us now as it was in the primitive church. For then Christians were under a heathen government. And however the charity of Christians in those times is much to be commended, yet now, by reason of our different circumstances, there is no occasion for private charity. In the state in which Christians now are, provision is made for the poor otherwise.

ANSWER. This objection is built upon two suppositions, both of which I believe are false.

First, towns are obliged by law to relieve everyone who otherwise would be an object of charity. This I suppose to be false, unless it is supposed that none are proper objects of charity but those who have no estate left to live upon, which is very unreasonable, and what I have already shown to be false in answer to the fourth objection in showing that it does not answer the rules of Christian charity to relieve only those who are reduced to extremity.

Nor do I suppose it was ever the design of the law in requiring the various towns to support their own poor to cut off all occasion for Christian charity. Nor is it fitting there should be such a law. It is fitting that the law should make provision for those who have no estates of their own. It is not fitting that persons who are reduced to that extremity should be left to so precarious a source of supply as a voluntary charity. They are in extreme necessity of relief, and therefore it is fitting that there should be something sure for them to depend on. But a voluntary charity in this corrupt world is an uncertain thing. Therefore the wisdom of the legislature did not think fit to leave those who are so reduced upon such a precarious foundation for subsistence. But I do not suppose that it was ever the design of the law to make such provision for all who are in want as to leave no room for Christian charity.

This objection is built upon another supposition which is equally false, that there are in fact none who are proper objects of charity but those who are relieved by the town. Let the design of the law be what it will, yet if there are in fact persons who are so in want as to stand in need of our charity, then that law does not free us from obligation to relieve them by our charity. For as we have just now shown in answer to the last objection, if it more properly belongs to others to relieve them than us, yet if they do not do it, we are not free. So that if it is true that it belongs to the town to relieve all who are proper objects of charity; yet if the town in fact does not do it, we are not excused.

If one of our neighbors suffers through the fault of a particular person, at the hand of a thief or robber, or of a town, it does not alters the case. But if he suffers and is without relief, it is an act of Christian charity in us to relieve him. Now it is too obvious to be denied that there are in fact persons so in want that it would be a charitable act in us to help them, notwithstanding all that is done by the town. A man must hide his mental eyes to think otherwise.

CHAPTER FIFTEEN

The Sin of Theft
and Injustice

(July, 1740)

"Thou shalt not steal."

EXODUS 20:15

Subject: An unjust usurping of our neighbor's property without his consent is forbidden by the eighth commandment.

This is one of the ten commandments which constitute a summary of man's duty as revealed by God. God made many revelations to the children of Israel in the wilderness by Moses; but this one made in the Ten Commandments is the chief. Most of those other revelations contained ceremonial or judicial laws, but this contains the moral law. The most of those other laws respected the Jewish nation, but here is a summary of laws binding on all mankind. Those were to last till Christ should come and set up the Christian church. These are of perpetual obligation and last to the end of the world. God everywhere, by Moses and the prophets, manifests a far greater regard to the duties of these commands than to any of the rites of the ceremonial law.

These commands were given at Mount Sinai before any of the precepts of the ceremonial or judicial laws. They were delivered by a great voice out of the midst of fire, which made all the people in the camp tremble; and afterwards were engraven on tables of stone and laid up in the ark. The first table contained the four first commandments, which teach our duty to God; the second table contained the six last, which teach our duty to man. The sum of the duties of the first table is contained in that which Christ says is the first and great commandment of the law. Matthew 22:37: "Thou shalt love the Lord thy God with all thy heart, and with all thy soul, and with all thy mind." The sum of what is required in the second table is what Christ calls the second command, like unto the first. Verse 39: "The second is like unto it, Thou shalt love thy neighbor as thyself."

Of the commands of this second table of the law, the first (which is the fifth of the ten) refers to that honor which is due to our neighbor; the second respects his life; the third his chastity; the fourth his estate; the fifth his good name; the sixth and last respects his possessions and enjoyments in general. It is that command which respects our neighbor's estate, and which is the fourth command of the second table, and the eighth of the whole decalogue, on which I am now to insist. And here I shall make the command itself, as the words of it lie before us in the decalogue, my subject, and as the words of the commandment are in the form of a prohibition, forbidding a certain kind of sin. So I shall consider particularly what it is that this command forbids. The sin that is forbidden in this command is called stealing; yet we cannot reasonably understand it only of that act that in the more ordinary and strict sense of the word, is called stealing. But the iniquity that this command forbids may be summarily expressed thus: It is an unjust usurping of our neighbor's property without his consent.

So much is doubtless comprehended in the text; yet this comprehends much more than is implied in the ordinary use of the word "stealing," which is only a secret taking of that which is another's from his possession without either his consent or knowledge. But the Ten Commands are not to be limited to the strictest sense of the words, but are to be understood in such a latitude as to include all things that are of that nature or kind. Hence Christ reproves the Pharisees' interpretation of the sixth command (Matthew 5:21–22), and also their interpretation of the seventh command (see verses 27–28). By this it appears that the commands are not to be understood as forbidding only these individual sins that are expressly mentioned in the strictest sense of the expressions, but all other things of the same nature or kind. Therefore, what is forbidden in this command is all unjust usurpation of our neighbor's property. Here it may be observed that an unjust usurpation of our neighbor's property is twofold: it may be either by withholding what is our neighbor's, or by taking it from him.

The dishonesty of withholding what is our neighbor's

There are many ways in which persons may unjustly usurp their neighbor's property by withholding what is his due. But I shall particularize only two things:

First, the unfaithfulness of men in not fulfilling their engagements. Ordinarily, when men promise anything to their neighbor, or enter into engagements by undertaking any business with which their neighbor entrust them, their engagements invest their neighbor with a right to that which is engaged; so if they withhold it, they usurp that which belongs to their neighbor. Such is also the case when men break their promises because they find them to be inconvenient, and they cannot fulfill them without difficulty and trouble, or merely because they have altered their minds since they promised. They think they have not consulted their own interest in the promise that they have made, and that if they had considered the matter as much before they promised as they have since, they would not have promised. Therefore they take the liberty to set their own promises aside. Besides, sometimes persons violate this command by neglecting to fulfill their engagements through a careless, negligent spirit.

They violate this command in withholding what belongs to their neighbor when they are not faithful in any business which they have undertaken to do for their neighbor. If their neighbor has hired them to labor for him for a certain time, and they are not careful to husband the time; if they are hired to do a day's labor and are not careful to improve the day, as they have reason to think that he who hired justly expected of them; or if they be hired to accomplish such a piece of work and are not careful to do it well, do not do it as if it were for themselves, or as they would have others do for them, when they in like manner betrust them with any business of theirs; or if they are entrusted with any particular affair that they undertake, but do not use that care, contrivance, and diligence to manage it so as will be to the advantage of him who entrusts them, and as they would manage it, or would insist that it should be managed, if the affair was their own—in all these cases they unjustly withhold what belongs to their neighbor.

Second, another way in which men unjustly withhold what is their neighbor's is in neglecting to pay their debts. Sometimes this happens because they run so far into debt that they cannot reasonably hope to be able to pay their debts; and this they do either through pride and affectation of living above their circumstances, or through a grasping, covetous disposition, or some other corrupt principle. Sometimes they neglect to pay their debts from carelessness of spirit about it, little concerning themselves whether they are paid or not, taking no care to go to their creditor or to send for him. And if they see him from time to time, they say nothing about their debts. Sometimes they neglect to pay their debts because it would put them to some inconvenience. The reason why they do not do it is not because they cannot do it, but because they cannot do it as conveniently as they desire. And so they rather choose to put their creditor to inconvenience by being without what properly belongs to him than to put themselves to inconvenience by being without what does not belong to them, and what they have no right to detain. In any of these cases they unjustly usurp the property of their neighbor.

Sometimes persons have that by them with which they could pay their debts if they would; but they want to lay out their money for something else, to buy fine clothing for their children, or to advance their estates, or for some such end. They have other designs in hand that must fail if they pay their debts. When men thus withhold what is due, they unjustly usurp what is not their own. Sometimes they neglect to pay their debts, and their excuse for it is that their creditor does not need it; that he has a plentiful estate, and can well bear to lie out of his money. But if the creditor is never so rich, that gives no right to the debtor to withhold from him that which belongs to him. If it is due, it ought to be paid; for that is the very notion of its being due. It is no more lawful to withhold from a man what is his due without his consent, because he is rich and able to do without it, than it is lawful to steal from a man because he is rich and able to bear the loss.

The dishonesty of unjustly taking a neighbor's property

The principal ways of doing this seem to be these four: by negligence, by fraud, by violence, or by stealing, strictly so called.

The first way of unjustly depriving our neighbor of that which is his is by negligence, by carelessly neglecting that which is expected by neighbors one of another, and is necessary to prevent our neighbor's suffering in his estate by us, or by anything that is ours; and necessary in order that neighbors may live one by another, without suffering in their lawful interests, rights, and possessions, one by another.

For instance, when proper care is not taken by men to prevent their neighbor's suffering in the produce of his fields or enclosures, from their cattle or other brute creatures (which may be either through negligence with regard to their creatures themselves in keeping those that are unruly and giving them their liberty, though they know that they are not fit to have their liberty, and are commonly wont to break into their neighbor's enclosures greatly to his damage) or through a neglect of that which is justly expected of them, to defend others' fields from suffering by the neighborhood of their own—in such cases men are guilty of unjustly taking from their neighbor what is his property.

It is said in the law of Moses: "If a man shall cause a field or vineyard to be eaten, and shall put in his beast, and shall feed in another man's field; of the best of his own field, and of the best of his vineyard, shall he make restitution" (Exodus 22:5).

Now a man may be unjustly the cause of his neighbor's field or vineyard being eaten, either by putting in his beast, and so doing what he should not do, or by neglecting to do what he should do to prevent his beast from getting into his field. What is said in the Psalm 144, the two last verses, supposes that a people who carry themselves as becomes a people whose God is the Lord will take thorough care that beasts do not break into their neighbor's enclosures: "That our oxen may be strong to labor; that there be no breaking in, nor going out; that there be no complaining in our streets. Happy is that people that is in such a case; yea happy is that people whose God is the Lord."

Second, taking away that which is our neighbor's by fraud, or by deceiving him, is another mode of usurping our neighbor's property. This is the case when men in their dealings take advantage of their neighbor's ignorance, oversight, or mistake to get something from him; or when they make their gains by concealing the defects of what they sell, putting off bad for good, though this is not done by speaking falsely, but only by keeping silence. It also happens when they take a higher price for what they sell than it is really worth, and more than they could get for it if the concealed defects were known; or when they sell that as good that indeed is not merchantable, which is condemned in Amos 8:6: "Yea, and sell the refuse of the wheat."

If a man sells something to another with defects that are concealed, knowing that the other receives it as good, and pays such a price for it under a notion of its having no remarkable defect but what he sees, and takes the price which the buyer under that notion offers—the seller knows that he takes a price from the buyer for that which the buyer did not get from him; for the buyer is deceived, and pays for those things which he finds wanting in what he buys. It is just the same as if a man should take a payment that another offers him through a mistake, for that which he never had of him, thinking that he had it of him when he did not.

So a man fraudulently takes away that which is his neighbor's when he gets his money from him by falsely commending what he has to sell, above what he knows to be the true quality of it, and attributes those good qualities to it that he knows it does not have; or if he does not do that, yet he sets forth the good qualities in a degree beyond what he knows to be the true degree, or speaks of the defects and ill qualities of what he has to sell, as if they were much less than he knows they are.

On the contrary, if the buyer cries down what he is about to buy, contrary to his real opinion of the value of it, these things, however common they are in men's dealings one with another, are nothing short of iniquity, fraud, and a great breach of the commandment upon which we are discoursing. Proverbs 20:14: " 'It is nought, it is nought,' saith the buyer; but when he is gone his way then he boasteth." There are many other ways whereby men deceive one another in their trading, and whereby they fraudulently and unjustly take away that which is their neighbor's.

Third, another mode of unjustly invading and taking away our neighbor's property is by violence. This violence may be done in different degrees. Men may take away their neighbor's goods either by mere open violence, either making use of superior strength, forcibly taking away anything what is his, or by express or implicit threatenings, forcing him to yield up what he has into their hands, as is done in open robbery and piracy. Or he may make use of some advantages that they have over their neighbor in their dealings with him, constrain him to yield to their gaining unreasonably of him, as when they take advantage of their neighbor's poverty to extort unreasonably from him those things that he is under a necessity of procuring for himself or family. This is an oppression against which God has shown a great displeasure in His Word. Leviticus 25:14: "And if thou sell ought unto thy neighbor, or buyest ought of thy neighbor, ye shall not oppress one another." Proverbs 22:22–23: "Rob not the poor because he is poor, neither oppress the afflicted in the gate; for the Lord will plead their cause, and spoil the soul of those that spoiled them." And Amos 4:1–2: "Hear this word, ye kine of Bashan, that are in the mount of Samaria, which oppress the poor, which crush the needy, the Lord hath sworn in his holiness, that he will take you away with hooks, and your posterity with fishhooks."

When the necessity of poor, indigent people is the very thing whence others take occasion to raise the price of provisions, even above the market, this is such an oppression. There are many poor people whose families are in such necessity of bread that they, in their extremity, will give almost any price for it rather than go without it. Those who have to sell, though hereby they have an advantage in their hands, yet surely should not take the advantage to raise the price of provisions. We would doubtless think we had just cause to complain if we were in such necessity as they are, and were reduced to their straits, and were treated in this manner. And let us remember that it is owing only to the distinguishing goodness of God to us that we are not in their circumstances. And whatever our present circumstances are, yet we know not but that the time may still come when their case may be ours.

Men may oppress others, though they are not poor, if they will take advantage of any particular necessities of their neighbor to extort unreasonably from him. The case may be so at particular seasons that those who are not poor may stand in particular and extraordinary need of what we have or what we can do for them. So it would be greatly to their disadvantage or loss to be without it. Now to take advantage of their urgent circumstances, to get from them an unreasonable price, is a violent dealing with our neighbors.

It is very unreasonable to say, "Such men are so rich, and get money so much more easily than I, that it is no hurt for me to take advantage when they are in special need, and make them give me, for work that I do for them a great deal more than I would desire to ask of other men." Let such consider whether, if they should by any means hereafter get forward in the world and come to have plentiful estates, they would like for persons to act upon such principles towards them. That men are rich gives us no more right to take away from them what is theirs in this way than it does to steal from them because they come easily by their property, and can do without it better than we.

Another thing that is a kind of violent taking from our neighbor what is his is taking the advantage of the law to gain from others, when their cause in honesty and conscience is just and good. The circumstances of mankind, their rights, possessions, and dealings one with another, are so various that it is impossible that any body of human laws should be contrived to suit all possible cases and circumstances. Hence the best laws may be abused and perverted to purposes contrary to the general design of laws, which is to maintain the rights and secure the properties of mankind. Human laws have a regard due to them, but always in subordination to the higher laws of God and nature. Therefore, when it so happens that we have an advantage by the law to gain what the laws of moral honesty do not allow, it is an oppression and violence to take the advantage. That human laws allow it will not excuse us before God, the Judge of the world, who will judge us another day by His own laws and not by the laws of the commonwealth.

The fourth way of unjustly taking from our neighbor that which is his is stealing, so called. All unjust ways of taking away, invading, or usurping what is our neighbor's are called stealing in the most extensive use of the word, and all is included in the expression in this command. Yet the word "stealing," as it is more commonly used, is not of so great extent, and does not intend all unjust invasion of our neighbor's property, but only a particular kind of unjust taking. So in common speech, when we speak of fraudulent dealings, of extortion, unfaithfulness in our trust, and of stealing, we understand different sins by these expressions, though they are a usurpation of what is our neighbor's.

Stealing, strictly so called, may be thus defined: It is a designed taking of our neighbor's goods from him without his consent or knowledge. It is not merely withholding what is our neighbor's, but taking it away; and therein it differs from unfaithfulness in our undertakings and betrustments, and also from negligence in the payment of debts. It is a designed or willful depriving our neighbor of what is his, and so differs from wronging our neighbor in his estate through carelessness or negligence. It is taking our neighbor's goods without his knowledge. It is a private, clandestine taking away, and so differs from robbery by open violence.

So it differs from extortion, for in that the person knows what is taken from him. The aim of him who takes is no other than that he should know it; for he makes use of other means than his ignorance to obtain what is his neighbors, that is, violence to constrain him to give it up. It also differs from fraudulent dealing or trading; for though in fraudulent dealing the lawful possessor does not understand the ways and means by which he parts with his goods, and by which his neighbor becomes possessed of them; yet he knows the fact. The deceiver designedly conceals the manner only. But in stealing, strictly so called, he who takes does not intends that it shall be known that he takes it. It also differs from extortion and fraudulent dealing in that it is wholly without the consent of the owner; for in extortion, though there is no free consent, yet the consent of the owner is in some sort gained, though by oppressive means. In fraudulent dealing, consent is in some sort obtained, though it is by deceit; but in stealing, no kind of consent is obtained.

A person may steal from another, yet not take his goods without the knowledge of the owner; because he may know of it accidentally. He may see what is done, unawares to the thief. Therefore I have defined stealing as a designed taking without the consent or knowledge of the owner. If it is accidentally known, yet it is not known in the design and intention of the thief. The thief is so far at least private in it that he gives no notice to the owner at the time. It must be also without the consent of the owner. A person may take without the knowledge of the owner, and yet not take without his consent. The owner may not know of his taking at the time, or of his taking any particular things; yet there may be his implicit consent. There may have been a general consent, if not expressed, yet implied. The circumstances of the affair may be such that his consent may well be presumed upon, either from an established custom allowed by all, or from the nature of the case, the thing being of such a nature that it may well be presumed that none would refuse their consent. An example would be the case of a person's accidentally passing through his neighbor's vineyard in Israel and eating his fill of grapes, or from the circumstances of the persons, as is the case in many instances, of the freedom which near neighbors and intimate friends often take, and of that boldness which they use with respect to each other's goods.

In all such cases, though the owner does not particularly know what is done, yet he who takes does not do it with any contrived designed concealment. And though there is no express, particular consent, yet there is a consent either implied or justly presumed upon. And he who takes does not do it designedly without consent.

It may happen in some cases that one may take the goods of another both without his knowledge and consent, either explicit or implicit, but through mistake; yet he may not be guilty of stealing. Therefore the design of him who takes must come into consideration. When he designedly takes away that which is his neighbor's, without his consent or knowledge, then he steals. So that if it should happen that he has both his consent and knowledge, without his design, he steals. And if it so happen that he takes without either his neighbor's consent or knowledge, and yet without his own design, he does not steal. I desire therefore that this that I take to be the true definition of theft or stealing may be borne in mind, that is, a designed taking of our neighbor's goods without his consent or knowledge, because it is needful to clear up many things which I have yet to say on this subject.

Dishonest excuses

Here I shall particularly take notice of some things by which persons may be ready to excuse themselves in privately taking their neighbor's goods; these, however, cannot be a just excuse for it, nor will they make such a taking to be stealing.

First, they think that the person whose goods are privately taken owes or is in debt to him who takes them. Some may be ready to say that they do not take that which is their neighbor's, they take that which is their own; because as much is due to them, their neighbor owes them as much, and unjustly detains it, and they do not know whether ever they shall get their due from him. Their neighbor will not do them right, and therefore they must make it right themselves.

But such pleas as these will not justify a man in going in a private and clandestine manner to take away anything of his neighbor's from his possession without his consent or knowledge; his doing this is properly stealing. For though something of his neighbor's, that is as valuable as what he takes, may be due to him; that does not give him such a right to his neighbor's goods that he may take anything that is his, according to his own pleasure, and at what time and in what manner he pleases. That his neighbor is in debt to him does not give him a right to take it upon himself to be his own judge, so that he may judge for himself which of his neighbor's goods shall be taken from him to discharge the debt; and that he may act merely according to his own private judgment and pleasure in such a case, without so much as acquainting his neighbor with the affair.

In order to warrant such a proceeding as this, everything that his neighbor has must be his. A man may not take indifferently what he pleases out of a number of goods without the consent or knowledge of any other person, unless all is his own, to be disposed of as he pleases. Such a way of using goods according to our own pleasure, taking what we will and at what time we will, can be warranted by nothing but a dominion over the whole. And though he who is in debt may be guilty of great injustice in detaining what is due to another, yet it does not then follow but that he who takes from him may also be guilty of great injustice towards him. The course he takes to right himself may be very irregular and unreasonable; and such a course, if universally allowed and pursued in such cases, would throw human society into confusion.

When men obtain a property in any of the professions of this life, they are at the same time also invested with a right to retain a possession of them till they are deprived of them in some fair and regular proceeding. Every man has a right to hold his estate and keep possession of his properties, so that no other can lawfully use them as his own until he either parts with them of his own accord, or until it be taken from him according to some established rule in a way of open justice. Therefore he who, under pretense of having just demands upon his neighbor, privately takes his goods without his consent, takes them unjustly and is guilty of stealing.

Second, much less will it make such a private taking not to be stealing that he who takes has, in way of kindness or gift, done for the person from whom he takes as much is equivalent to the value of what he takes. If a man does his neighbor some considerable kindness, whether in labor or in something that he gives him, what he does or gives is supposed to be done voluntarily; and he is not to make his neighbor a debtor for it. And therefore, if anything is privately taken away upon any such consideration, it is gross stealing.

For instance, when any person needs to have any services done for him, where a considerable number of hands are necessary, it is common for the neighborhood to meet together and join in helping their neighbor; and frequently some provision is made for their entertainment. If any person who has assisted on such an occasion, and is a partaker at such an entertainment, shall think within himself, "The service I have done is worth a great deal more than what I shall eat and drink here," and therefore shall take liberty privately to take the provision set before him to carry away with him, purposely concealing the matter from him who has entertained him, this is gross stealing. And it is a very ridiculous plea which they make to excuse so unmanly and vile an act.

Persons in such cases may say to themselves that the provision is made for them and set before them, that it is a time wherein considerable liberty is given; and they think, seeing that they have done so much for their host, they may take something more than they eat and drink there. But then let them be open in it; let them acquaint those with it who make the entertainment, and let it not be done in any way in a secret, clandestine manner, with the least design or attempt to avoid their notice. On the contrary, let care be taken to give them notice and obtain their consent.

When persons do such things in a private manner, they condemn themselves by their own act. Their doing what they do secretly shows that they are conscious that they go beyond what it is expected they should do, and do what would not be allowed, if it were known. Such an act, however light they may make of it, is abominable theft, and what any person of religion or any sense of the dignity of their own nature would abhor and detest to the greatest degree.

Third, it is not sufficient to make a private taking without consent not to be stealing that it is but a small matter that is taken. If the thing is of little value, yet if it is worth purposely concealing it from the owner, the value is great enough to render the taking of it proper theft. If it is pretended that the thing is of so small consequence that it is not worth asking for, then surely it is not worth purposely concealing it from the owner when it is taken. He who, under this pretense, conceals his taking, in the very act contradicts his own pretense; for his action shows that he apprehends, or at least suspects, that, as small a matter as it is, the owner would not like the taking of it if he knew it; otherwise the taker would not desire to conceal it.

The owner of the goods, and not other people, is the proper judge whether what he owns is of such a value that it is worth his while to keep it, and to refuse his consent to the taking of it from him. He who possesses, not he who takes away, has a right to judge of what consequence his possessions are to him. He has a right to set what value he pleases on them, and to treat them according to that value. Besides, merely that a thing is of small value cannot give a right to others to purposely and designedly take it away without the knowledge or consent of the owner. Because if this only gives a right, then all have a right to take things of small value; and at this rate a great number of persons, each of them taking from a man that which is of small value, might take away all he has.

Therefore, it will not justify persons, in purposely taking such things as fruit from the trees, gardens, or fields of their neighbors, without their knowledge or consent, that the things which they take are things of small value. Nor is that sufficient to render such an act to not be an act of theft, properly so called. This shows also that the smallness of the value of what is privately taken at feasts and entertainments does not render the taking of such things not to be stealing.

The small value of a thing may in some cases justify an occasional taking of things, so far as we may from thence, and from what is generally allowed, reasonably presume that the owner gives his consent. But if that is the case, and persons really take, as supposing that the owner consents to such occasional taking, then he who takes will not at all endeavor to do what he does secretly, nor in any measure to avoid notice. But merely the smallness of the value of a thing can never justify secretly taking what is another's.

The subject applied and the dishonest warned

The first use I would make of this doctrine is to warn against all injustice and dishonesty, as to what appertains to our neighbor's temporal goods or possessions. Let me warn all to avoid all ways of unjustly invading or usurping what is their neighbor's, and let me press that exhortation of the apostle from Romans 12:17: "Provide things honest in the sight of all men." This implies that those things that we provide for ourselves and use as our own should be such as we come honestly by; and especially that we should avoid all clandestine or underhand ways of obtaining anything that is our neighbor's, either by fraudulent dealing or by that taking without our neighbor's knowledge and consent, of which we have been speaking.

I warn you to beware of dishonesty in withholding what is your neighbor's, either by unfaithfulness to your trust in any business which you undertake, or by withholding your neighbor's just and honest dues. Consider that saying of the apostle from Romans 13:8: "Owe no man anything, but to love one another." Be also warned against wronging your neighbor or injuring him in his enclosures, or in any of his just rights and properties, through careless neglect of what is reasonably expected by neighbors from one another, in order that they may live one by another without mutual injury. Let all beware that they bring no guilt on their souls in the sight of God by taking an advantage to oppress any person. Especially beware of taking advantage of others' poverty to extort from them. For God will defend their cause, and you will be no gainers by such oppression.

Beware also of all injustice by deceitful and fraudulent dealing. You doubtless meet with abundance of temptation to fraud, and have need to keep a strong guard on yourselves.

There are many temptations to falsehood in trading, both about what you would buy and what you have to sell. There are in buying temptations to do as in Proverbs 20:14: " 'It is nought, it is nought,' saith the buyer." There are many temptations to take indirect courses, to blind those with whom you deal, about the qualities of what you have to sell, to diminish the defects of your commodities, or to conceal them, and to put off things for good, which are bad. And there are doubtless many other ways that men meet with temptations to deceive others that your own experience will better suggest to you than I can.

But here I shall take occasion to speak of a particular kind of fraud that is very aggravated, and is rather a defrauding of God than man. What I mean is giving that which is bad for good in public contributions. Though it is a matter of great shame and lamentation that it should be so, yet it is to be feared, from what has sometimes been observed, that there are some who, when there is a public contribution to be made for the poor, or some other pious and charitable use, sometimes take that opportunity to put off their bad money—that which they find or think their neighbors will refuse to take at their hands because they will have opportunity to see what is offered them, and to observe the badness of it, even that they therefore take opportunity to put off to God.

Hereby they endeavor to save their credit, for they apprehend that they shall be concealed. They appear with others to go to the contribution, as it is not known but that they put in that which is good. But they cheat the church of God, and defraud the expectations of the poor, or rather they lie to God; for those who receive what is given stand as Christ's receivers, and not as acting for themselves in this matter.

They who do thus do that which is very much of the same nature with that sin against which God denounces that dreadful curse in Malachi 1:14: " 'Cursed be the deceiver which hath in his flock a male, and voweth and sacrificeth unto the Lord a corrupt thing; for I am a great King,' saith the Lord of hosts, 'and My name is dreadful among the heathen.' " He who has in his flock a male means he who has in his flock that which is good and fit to be offered to God. For it was the male of the flock principally that was appointed, in the law of Moses, to be offered in sacrifice. He has in his flock that which is good, but he vows and sacrifices to the Lord "the torn, the lame, and the sick." It is said in the foregoing verse, "Ye said also, 'Behold what a weariness is it,' and ye have snuffed at it, saith the Lord of hosts; and ye brought that which was torn, and the lame, and the sick; thus ye brought an offering: should I accept this of your hands? saith the Lord."

Contributions in the Christian church come in the room of sacrifices in the Jewish church. Mercy comes in the room of sacrifice, and what is offered in the way of mercy is as much offered to God as the sacrifices of old were. For what is done to the poor is done to Christ, and he who has pity on the poor lends to the Lord (Proverbs 19:17). The Jews who offered the sick and lame of the flock knew that if they had offered it to their governor, and had attempted to put it off as part of the tribute or public taxes due to their earthly rulers, it would not be accepted; and therefore they were willing to put it off to God. "And if ye offer the blind for sacrifice, is it not evil? And if ye offer the lame and sick, is it not evil? Offer it now unto thy governor; will he be pleased with thee, or accept thy person? saith the Lord of hosts."

So those persons who purposely put bad money into contributions know that what they put in would not be accepted if they should offer to pay their public taxes. Yea, they know that their neighbors would not accept it at their hands; and therefore they are willing to save themselves by putting it off to God.

This practice has also very much of the nature of the sin of Ananias and Sapphira. What they offered was by way of contribution for charitable uses. The brethren sold what they had and brought it into a common stock, and put all under the care of deacons so that the poor might every one be supplied. Ananias and Sapphira brought a part of their possessions and put it into the common stock. And their sin was that they put it in for more than it really was. It was but a part of what they had, and they put it in, and would have it accepted as if it had been all. So those among us, of whom I am speaking, put off what they put into the charitable stock for more than it is. For they put it in under the notion that it is something of some value. They intend that it shall be so taken by the church that sees them go to the contribution, when indeed they put in nothing at all.

Ananias and Sapphira were charged with lying to God, and doing an act of fraud towards God Himself in what they did. Acts 5:4: "Whilst it remained, was it not thine own? And after it was sold, was it not in thine own power? Why hast thou conceived this thing in thine heart? Thou hast not lied unto men, but unto God." So those who knowingly put bad money for good into a contribution for a charitable use, as much as in them lies commit an act of fraud and deceit towards God. For the deacons who receive what is contributed do not receive it in their own names, but as Christ's receivers. I hope these things may be sufficient to deter every reader from ever daring to do such a thing for the future.

Another thing I would warn you against is stealing, properly and strictly so called, or designedly taking away any of your neighbor's goods without his consent or knowledge. And especially I would now take occasion to warn against a practice which is very common in the country, particularly among children and young people, and that is stealing fruit from their neighbor's trees or enclosures. There is a licentious liberty taken by many children and young people in making bold with their neighbor's fruit. And it is to be feared that they are too much countenanced in it by their parents and many elderly people.

I am sensible that the great thing which is pleaded, and made very much the ground of this liberty which is taken and so much tolerated, is a very abusive and unreasonable construction and application of that text of Scripture in Deuteronomy 23:24: "When thou comest into thy neighbor's vineyard, then thou mayest eat grapes thy fill. But thou shalt not put any in thy vessel." Because this text seems to be so much mistaken and misimproved, I shall therefore endeavor particularly to state the matter of persons taking their neighbor's fruit, and set it in a just and clear light as concerning this text.

It was to eat their fill of grapes when they occasionally came into or passed through their neighbor's vineyard, and not that they should go there on purpose to eat grapes. This is manifest by the manner of expression: "When thou comest into thy neighbor's vineyard, thou mayest eat," that is, when you have come there on some other occasion. If God had meant to give them leave to come there for no other end, it would not have been expressed so, but rather thus: "Thou mayest come into thy neighbor's vineyard and eat grapes thy fill." Such were the circumstances of that people; and vineyards among them were so common that there was no danger that this liberty would be attended with ill consequence. It is manifest throughout the history of Israel that vineyards among them were so common that the people in general had them. Every husbandman among them was a vinedresser; and a great part of the business of a husbandman among them consisted in dressing and taking care of his vineyards. Grapes seem to have been the most common sort of fruit that they had. Besides, there was no liberty given for persons to go to a vineyard to eat the fruit of it. So that there was no danger of neighbors suffering one by another by any such liberty. The liberty did not tend to any such consequence as the flocking of a great number to eat grapes, whereby the fruit of the vineyard might be much diminished.

Such were the circumstances of the case that the consent of the owners of vineyards in general might well be presumed upon, though no such express liberty had been given. You may remember that in the definition of stealing, I observed that explicit consent is not always necessary because the case may be so circumstanced that consent may be well presumed on. And the reason why consent might well be presumed on in the case of eating grapes, of which we are now speaking, is, that there could be no sensible injury, nor any danger of any ill consequences, by which a man would sensibly suffer in the benefit of his vineyard. Hence it is the more easy to determine what would and would not be justified by this text among us.

Suppose a particular person among us had a vineyard of the same kind as those that the children of Israel had; it would not justify others in using the same liberty when occasionally passing through it because it would be a rare thing, and the rarity and scarcity of the fruit would render it of much greater value. Besides, if one man was distinguished by such a possession, to allow of such a liberty would have a much greater tendency to ill consequences than if they were common, as they were in the land of Canaan. There would be danger of many persons falsely pretending and making occasions to pass through the vineyard for the sake of such rare fruit.

Nor would it be a parallel case if men in general among us

had each of them a few vines. That would be a very different thing from persons in general having large vineyards. Nor would this text, in such a case, warrant men's eating their fill of grapes when occasionally passing by. And though all in general had vineyards, as they had in the land of Canaan, this text would not justify men in going into their neighbor's vineyard to eat the fruit. No such liberty is given in the text. If there had been such liberty, it might have been of ill consequence. For the sake of saving their own grapes, men might make a practice of going and sending their children into their neighbor's vineyard to eat their fill from time to time.

But the liberty given in this text to the children of Israel seems to be very parallel with the liberty taken among us to take an apple or two and eat as we are occasionally passing through a neighbor's orchard; this, as our circumstances are, we may do and justly presume that we have the owner's consent. This is a liberty that we take, and find no ill consequences. It was very much so with vineyards in the land of Canaan as it is with orchards among us. Apples in some countries are a rare fruit. And there it would by no means be warrantable for persons to take the same liberty when occasionally passing by their neighbor's apple tree that we warrantably take here when going through a neighbor's orchard.

The consideration of these things will easily show the great abuse that is made of this text when it is brought to justify such a resorting of children and others to their neighbor's fruit trees, as is sometimes, to take and eat the fruit. Indeed, this practice is not only not justified by the law of Moses, but it is in itself unreasonable and contrary to the law of nature. The consequences of it are pernicious, so that a man can have no dependence on enjoying the fruit of his labor or the benefit of his property in those things that may possibly have very much value. He can have no assurance but that he shall be mainly deprived of what he has, and that others will not have the principal benefit of it; and so that his end in planting and cultivating that from which he expected those fruits of the earth, that God has given for the use, comfort, and delight of mankind, will not be in the main frustrated.

An exhortation to honesty

Under this use, I shall confine myself to two particulars, as many other things having been already spoken to.

First, I shall hence take occasion to exhort parents to restrain the children from stealing, and particularly from being guilty of theft in stealing the fruits of their neighbor's trees or fields. Christian parents are obliged to bring up their children in the nurture and admonition of the Lord. But how much otherwise do they act who bring them up in theft! And those parents are guilty of this who, though they do not directly teach them to steal by example and setting them about it, yet tolerate them in it.

Parents should take effectual care not only to instruct their children better, and to warn them against any such thievish practices, but also thoroughly to restrain them. Children who practice stealing make themselves vile. Stealing, by the common consent of mankind, is a very vile practice. Therefore those parents who will not take thorough care to restrain their children from such a practice will be guilty of the same sin that God so highly resented, and awfully punished, in Eli, of which we read in 1 Samuel 3:13: "For I have told him that I will judge his house forever, for the iniquity which he knoweth; because his sons made themselves vile, and he restrained them not."

Second, I exhort those who are conscious that they have heretofore wronged their neighbor to make restitution. This is a duty, the obligation to which is exceedingly plain. If a person was wronged in taking away anything that was his, certainly he is wronged also in detaining it. And all the while that a person who has been guilty of wronging his neighbor neglects to make restitution, he lives in that wrong. He not only lives impenitent as to that first wrong of which he was guilty, but he continually wrongs his neighbor. A man who has gotten anything from another wrongfully goes on to wrong him every day that he neglects to restore it, when he has opportunity to do it. The person injured not only suffered wrong from the other when his goods were first taken from him, but he suffers new injustice from him all the while they are unjustly kept from him.

Therefore I counsel you who are conscious that you have heretofore wronged your neighbor, either by fraud, oppression, unfaithfulness, or stealing, whether lately or formerly, though it may have been a great while ago, speedily to go and make restitution for all the wrong your neighbor has suffered at your hands. That it was done long ago does not acquit you from your obligation to restore. This is a duty with which you must comply; you cannot be acquitted without it. As long as you neglect it, it will be unreasonable in you to expect any forgiveness of God. For what ground can you have to think that God will pardon you as long as you willfully continue in the same wrong, and wrong the same man every day by detaining from him that which is his? In your prayers you ask of God that He would forgive all your sins; but your very prayers are mockery if you still willfully continue in those sins. Indeed, if you go and confess your faults to your neighbor, and he freely acquits you from making restitution, you will be acquitted from the obligation. For in so doing, your neighbor gives you what before was his—but otherwise you cannot be acquitted.

I would leave this advice with all, for direction in their

behavior on their deathbeds. Indeed, you should not by any means put it off till you come to die; and you will run the most fearful risk in so doing. But if you will not do it now, while you are in health, I will leave it with you to remember when you shall come to lie on your deathbeds. Doubtless, then, if you have the use of your reason, you will be concerned for the salvation of your poor souls. And let this be one thing then remembered, as being absolutely necessary in order to your salvation, that before you die you must make restitution for whatever wrong you shall have done to any of your neighbors; or at least leave orders that such restitution be made. Otherwise you will, as it were, go out of the world, and go before your great Judge, with stolen goods in your hands. And certainly it will not be very comfortable or safe to bring them into His infinitely holy and dreadful presence, when He sits on His throne of judgment with His eyes as a flame of fire, being more pure than to look on iniquity; when He is about to sentence you to your everlasting unalterable state.

Everyone here present, who has been guilty of wronging his neighbor and has not made restitution, must die. Let all such therefore remember this counsel now given them on the day when death shall approach, if they shall be so foolish as to neglect it till that time.

CHAPTER SIXTEEN

Unresolvedness in Religion Is Very Unreasonable

(June, 1734)

"And Elijah came unto all the people, and said,
'How long halt ye between two opinions? If the Lord be God,
follow Him; but if Baal, then follow him.'
And the people answered him not a word."

1 Kings 18:21

t is the manner of God, before He bestows any signal mercy on the people, first to prepare them for it, and before He removes any awful judgments which He has brought upon them for their sins, first to cause them to forsake the sins that procured those judgments. We have an instance of this in the context. It was a time of sore famine in Israel. There

301

had been neither rain nor dew for the space of three years and six months. This famine was brought upon the land for their idolatry. But God was now about to remove this judgment. And therefore, to prepare them for it, He sends Elijah to convince them of the folly of idolatry, and to bring them to repentance for it. In order to this Elijah, by the command of the Lord, goes and shows himself to Ahab, and directs him to send and gather all Israel to him at Mount Carmel, and all the prophets of Baal, four hundred and fifty, and the prophets of the groves that ate at Jezebel's table, four hundred, that they might determine the matter and bring the controversy to an issue, whether Jehovah or Baal were God. To this end, Elijah proposes that each should take a bullock, that he should take one and the prophets of Baal another, that each should cut his bullock to pieces, lay it on the wood and put no fire under it, and that the God who answered by fire would be concluded to be God.

The text contains an account of what Elijah said to all the people at their first meeting, and of their silence: "And Elijah came unto all the people, and said, 'How long halt ye between two opinions? If the Lord be God, follow Him; but if Baal, then follow him.'" To this the people, it seems, made no reply. In these words, we may observe:

1. How Elijah expostulates with the people about their halting so long between two opinions, in which expostulation may be observed:

First, what the two opinions were between which they halted, that is, whether the Lord or Baal was God. The case in Israel seems to have been this: there were some who were altogether for Baal and wholly rejected the true God—of this number, to be sure, were Jezebel and the prophets of Baal. And there were some among them who were altogether for the God of Israel and wholly rejected Baal. God told Elijah that He had "yet left in Israel seven thousand that had not bowed the knee to Baal, and whose mouths had not kissed him" (1 Kings 19:18).

But the rest of the people halted between two opinions. They saw that some were for one and some for the other, and they did not know which to choose; and, as is commonly the case when a difference of opinion prevails, there were many who had no religion at all. They were not settled in anything. The different opinions prevalent in Israel distracted and confounded them. Many who professed to believe in the true God were yet very cold and indifferent, and many were wavering and unsettled. They saw that the king and queen were for Baal, and Baal's party was the prevailing party. But their forefathers had been for the Lord. And the people did not know who were right. Thus they halted between two opinions.

Second, in this expostulation is implied the unreasonableness of their thus halting between two opinions. "How long halt ye between two opinions? If the Lord be God, follow Him; but if Baal, then follow him." This implies that they ought to determine one way or the other.

2. We may observe their silence on this occasion: "And the people answered him not a word," being convicted in their own consciences of the unreasonableness of their being for so long a time wavering and unresolved. They had nothing to reply in excuse for themselves.

DOCTRINE: Unresolvedness in religion is very unreasonable.

PROPOSITION 1. Many persons remain exceedingly undetermined with respect to religion. They are very much undetermined in themselves whether to embrace religion or reject it. Many who are baptized and make a profession of religion, and who seem to be Christians, are yet in their own minds halting between two opinions. They never yet fully came to a conclusion whether to be Christians or not. They are taught the Christian religion in their childhood and have the Bible, the Word preached, and the means of grace all their days. Yet they continue and grow up, and many grow old, in an unresolvedness whether to embrace Christianity or not. Many continue unresolved as long as they live.

First, there are some persons who have never come to a settled determination in their own minds whether there is any truth in religion. They hear of the things of religion from their childhood all their days, but never come to a conclusion in their own minds whether they are real or merely fancies. Particularly, some have never come to any determination in their own minds whether there is any such thing as conversion. They hear much talk about it, and know that many pretend to be the subjects of it, but they are never resolved whether all is not merely designed hypocrisy and imposture.

Some never come to any determination whether the Scriptures are the Word of God or whether they are the invention of men, and whether the story concerning Jesus Christ is anything but a fable. They fear it is true, but sometimes very much doubt it. Sometimes, when they hear arguments for it, they assent that it is true; but upon every little objection or temptation that arises, they call it into question and are always wavering and never settled about it.

So it seems to have been with many of the Jews in Christ's time. They were always at a loss what to make of Him, whether He was indeed the Christ, whether He was Elijah, one of the old prophets, or a mere impostor. John 10:24–25: "Then came the Jews round about Him and said unto Him, 'How long dost Thou make us to doubt? If Thou be the Christ, tell us plainly.' Jesus answered them, 'I told you, and ye believed not.'" Some have never so much as come to a resolution in their own minds whether there is a God or not. They do not know that there is, and oftentimes very much doubt it.

Second, there are some who never have come to any determination in their own minds whether to embrace religion in the practice of it. Religion does not consist merely or chiefly in theory or speculation, but in practice. It is a practical thing. The end of it is to guide and influence us in our practice. And considered in this view, there are multitudes who never have come to a conclusion whether to embrace religion or not. It is probably pretty general for men to design to be religious some time or other before they die—for none intend to go to hell—but they still keep it at a distance. They put it off from time to time, and never come to any conclusion which determines them in their present practice. And some never so much as fix upon any time; they design to be religious sometime before they die, but they do not know when.

There are many who have always continued unresolved about the necessity of striving and being earnestly engaged for salvation. They flatter themselves that they may obtain salvation, though they are not so earnestly engaged, though they mind the world and their worldly affairs more than their salvation. They are often told how necessary it is that they make haste and do not delay, that they do whatever their hand finds to do with their might, and that a dull slack way of seeking salvation is never likely to be effectual. But of these things they are never thoroughly convinced. Some seem to resolve to be in earnest, and seem to set out with some engagedness of mind. But soon they fail because they have never been fully convinced of its necessity.

Many have never come to a determination what to choose for their portion. There are but two things which God offers to mankind for their portion: One is this world, with the pleasures and profits of sin, together with eternal misery ensuing; the other is heaven and eternal glory, with a life of self-denial and respect to all the commands of God. Many, as long as they live, come to no settled determination which of these to choose. They must have one or the other. They cannot have both. But they always remain in suspense and never make their choice.

They would fain have heaven and this world too. They would have salvation and the pleasures and profits of sin too. But considering heaven and the world, as God offers them, they will have neither. God offers heaven only with the self-denial and difficulty which are on the way to it; and they are not willing to have heaven on these conditions. God does not offer the world and the pleasures of sin to men alone, but with eternal misery in connection with them. And so neither are they willing to have the world. They would fain divide heaven from the holiness and self-denial, which are the way to it, and from the holiness which reigns in it, and then they would be glad to have heaven. They would fain divide sin from hell, and then they would fully determine forever to cleave to sin.

But God will not make such a division for them. They must have one or the other of these for their portion as God offers them. And therefore they never make any choice at all. Indeed, practically and in effect they choose sin and hell. But they do not come to any resolution in their own minds which they will have for their portion, whether heaven and holiness or the world and hell. They are always wavering and halting between two opinions. Sometimes they seem to determine for the one and sometimes for the other. When they meet with no difficulty or temptation, and can, as they say, do their duty without hurting themselves or much crossing their carnal inclinations, they seem to choose heaven and holiness. At other times, wherein they meet with difficulty in the way of duty, and great temptations of worldly profits or pleasures are laid before them, then they choose the world and let heaven and holiness alone. There are among us vast multitudes before whom these two things have been set hundreds of times, who have never to this day come to a determination which to have.

So they have never yet determined which shall be their master, God or mammon. There are but few who have undertaken the service of God, and have come to a resolution and preparedness of mind to serve God and follow Christ at all times, and to whatever difficulties it may expose them. Yet, at the same time, neither are they determined that they will continue to serve Satan. They are afraid to draw up such a conclusion. Thus many spend their lives without making their choice, though in the mean time they practically choose the service of Satan. These are the persons of whom the Apostle James speaks in James 1:8: "The double-minded man is unstable in all his ways."

2. To continue thus undetermined and unresolved in the things of religion is very unreasonable, and that upon the following accounts:

First, in the things of religion we are to be interested to the highest degree. The truth or falsehood of the doctrines of religion concerns us to the highest degree possible. It is no matter of indifference to us whether there is a God or not, whether the Scriptures are the Word of God, whether Christ is the Son of God, or whether there is any such thing as conversion. It makes an infinite difference to us whether these things are so or not. Therefore we are under the greatest obligation in point of interest to resolve in our minds whether they are true or false. They who are undetermined whether there is any truth in religion, and are content to be so, not inquiring nor thoroughly using the means to be determined, act very unreasonably. They remain in doubt whether there is any such thing as heaven or hell; they are quiet and easy to continue ignorant in this matter; they are not engaged in their minds to come to a determination; they do not search and inquire what arguments there are to prove any such things, nor diligently weigh and consider the force of them. Rather they busy their minds about other things of infinitely less importance, and act as if they thought it did not much concern them whether there is a future and eternal state.

If they think that there is not, yet it is a matter of so great importance that no wise man would rest until he had satisfied himself, because if there is such a future state as the Scriptures assert, then we must have our part in it, in either a state of eternal rewards or a state of eternal punishment. So it is no matter of indifference to us what we have for our portion, whether this world with hell or a life of holiness and self-denial with heaven. These opposite portions relate not merely to a few days in this world, but to eternity. It is infinite madness therefore not to come to a determination.

So it is no matter of indifference what master we serve, whether God or mammon, or what interest we will pursue, whether our temporal or eternal interest; or which we prefer, the commands of God, or our pleasures, ease, and convenience. We ought therefore to come to some determination which we will choose.

Second, God has made us reasonable creatures, and capable of rationally determining for ourselves. Doubtless God has made man capable of discovering the truth in matters of religion, of coming to a good determination in these questions, whether the Scriptures are the Word of God, whether there is a future state, and the like. The resolution of these questions, which it so much concerns us to determine, is not above our capacities. God has not set these things beyond the extent of our faculties.

God has made us capable of making a wise choice for ourselves as to the life we shall choose to lead. He has given man so much understanding as to make him capable of determining which is best: to lead a life of self-denial and enjoy eternal happiness, or to take our swing in sinful enjoyments and burn in hell forever. The question is of no difficult determination. It is so far from being a matter too hard for our reason that the reason of a child is sufficient to determine this matter. Therefore men, in remaining undetermined in these matters, do not act as reasonable creatures, but make themselves like "the horse and the mule, which have no understanding" (Psalm 32:9).

Third, God puts into our hands a happy opportunity to determine for ourselves. What better opportunity can a man desire to consult his own interest than to have liberty to choose his own portion? God sets life and death before us. Deuteronomy 30:19: "I call heaven and earth to record this day against you, that I have set before you life and death, blessing and cursing; therefore choose life, that thou and thy seed after thee may live." See also Ezekiel 18:31–32 and 33:11. What better opportunity can we desire to secure for ourselves the greatest good than to have eternal life and unchangeable happiness set before us and offered to our choice? Therefore those who neglect coming to a resolution act unreasonably because they stand so much in their own light and neglect so glorious an opportunity.

Fourth, the things about which we are to make our choice are but few in number. There are but two portions set before us, one of which must be our portion: either life or death, either blessing or cursing; either a life of universal and persevering obedience with eternal glory, or a worldly, carnal, wicked life with eternal misery. If there were many terms in the offer made us, many things of nearly and equal value, one of which we must choose, to remain long in suspense and undetermined would be more excusable. There would be more reason for long deliberation before we should fix our minds on one or the other. But there are only two terms; there are but two states in another world, in one or the other of which we must be fixed to all eternity.

And there are but two states in this world: a state of sin and a state of holiness, a natural state and a converted state. There is but one way in which we can come to life, which renders the determination of reason much easier. There are but two masters, to one of which we must be reputed the servants: Baal and Jehovah, God and mammon. There are but two competitors for the possession of us: Christ and the devil. There are but two paths, in one of which you are to travel: either in the straight and narrow way that leads to life, or the broad way that leads to destruction.

This shows the unreasonableness of those who live under light and have the offers of the gospel made to them, and yet remain from year to year unfixed and undetermined, halting between two opinions.

Fifth, God has given us all needed helps to make our determination as to the truth of the things of religion, such as whether there is a God, whether the Scriptures are the Word of God, whether there is a future state, and so on. We are not left in the dark as to these things as the poor heathens are, who are under great disadvantages to come to the knowledge of the truth—though they are not under any impossibility, for "they may haply feel after God and find Him" (Acts 17:27). But we have a clear sunshine to guide us. We have a particular description of those things that are set before us for truth and have great opportunity to examine them. The Scripture lies open before us, and all the doctrines of the gospel are particularly set forth, with the reasons on which their evidence is founded. We may search and try their force and sufficiency as we please.

We have great helps to a wise and rational determination in our choice, to determine whether it is best for us to choose a life of sin or a life of holiness, the service of God or the service of Baal. We have very plainly set before us the advantages of both sides. The losses and gains are particularly stated. Christ has dealt with us faithfully, and has told us what we shall get and what we shall lose by being His followers. He has also told us what we shall get and what we shall lose by a life of sin. He has not dealt with us deceitfully. He has not pretended greater advantages in godliness than there really are, nor greater disadvantages or dangers in sin. John 14:2: "In My Father's house are many mansions. If it were not so, I would have told you."

He has told us plainly that we must take up the cross daily and follow Him, that we must hate father and mother, wife and children, brethren and sisters, and our own life also in order to become His disciples, and that we must cut off our rights hands and pluck out our right eyes in order to enter into heaven. Thus we have a fair opportunity to count the costs on both sides, and are directed so to do (Luke 14:28). How unreasonable therefore is it for men, who have all these helps and advantages, to remain in suspense, and to come to no conclusion whether they will be Christians or heathens, whether they will be for God or the devil, though they have lived under the preaching of the Word and the offers of the gospel for many years.

Sixth, we have no reason to expect to be under better advantages to determine hereafter than we are now. We never shall have a clearer revelation of gospel truth. Never shall we have the advantages and disadvantages of both sides more plainly set before us than they are already in the Word of God. Nor are we ever likely to be under better advantages to know what will be best for us, and most for our interest. Those therefore who delay gain nothing by their delays, but give Satan more opportunity to darken their minds, to deceive them, and to lead them astray in their choice. Therefore their delay of coming to a resolution is unreasonable.

Seventh, if they do not come to a determination in this life, God will determine for them, and will appoint them their portion with the wicked. If sinners, by refusing to choose either life or death, either heaven or hell, could thereby avoid both, or if in this case the matter would remain undetermined till they should determine it, the folly and unreasonableness of delaying a determination would not be so great—but that is not the case. If they go on halting between two opinions, God will determine for them, and that quickly. He will determine where their portion shall be, that is, among the unbelievers, in the lake that burns with fire and brimstone forever. God will not always wait upon them to see what they will choose, but He will put a resolution to the matter by His unalterable sentence. Therefore it becomes all, if they are afraid to have their lot assigned them in hell, to come soon to a determination.

Eighth, delay in this case is unreasonable because those who delay do not know how soon the opportunity of choosing for themselves will be past. The opportunity will last no longer than life. Once life is past, they will no more have the offer made to them. The sentence will be past; the matter will be closed.

Those who delay their choice in this world will be glad to choose afterwards. Then they will not be at a loss which to choose; they will be able easily to determine. The judgments of sinners after this life are soon resolved as to whether there is any truth in religion or not. They can soon determine which is most eligible: a life of obedience and self-denial, with heaven for a reward, or a life of irreligion and sin, with hell for a punishment. They no longer halt between two opinions. But it is too late. Their opportunity is past. They would give all the world for another opportunity to choose. They would then soon come to a determination, but it will not be granted to them.

APPLICATION

USE OF EXAMINATION. Let this put everyone upon examining himself, whether or not he has ever yet come to a full determination in the affair of religion. First, inquire whether you have yet come to a full determination with respect to the truth of the things of religion. Have you ever been fully convinced? Is it a question which has been answered and determined with you whether there is a future state, or does it yet remain an unresolved question with you? Are you not yet to seek whether there is any future state, and whether or not the story about Jesus Christ is any more than a fable? Here I desire you to note two things:

First, if the main reason you assent to the truth of religion is that others believe so and you have been so instructed from your childhood, you are of those with whom the truth of religion yet remains undetermined. Tradition and education will never fix and settle the mind in a satisfactory and effectual belief of the truth. Though men, taking religion upon trust, may seem to give a full assent to the truth of religion and not call it into question, yet such a faith will not stand a shock. A temptation easily overthrows it. The reason of man in times of trial will not rest on so poor an evidence.

There are multitudes who seem to grant the truth of religion, with whom the main foundation of their faith is the tradition of their fathers or the profession of their neighbors. And it is to be feared that it is so with many who count themselves good Christians. But as to all such persons as never have seen any other evidence to satisfy them, either of the truth or falsehood of religion, they only halt between two opinions. The same may be said of those who are unstable in their disposition with regard to Christ or the things He taught.

Second, if you have fully come to a determination that the things of religion are true, they will be of weight with you above all things in the world. If you are really convinced that these things are not fables, but are reality, it is impossible but that you must be influenced by them above all things in the world. For these things are so great, and so infinitely exceed all temporal things, that it cannot be otherwise. He who really is convinced that there is a heaven, a hell, and an eternal judgment; that the soul, as soon as it is parted from the body, appears before the judgment seat of God; and that the happiness and misery of a future state is as great as the Scriptures represents it; or that God is as holy, just, and jealous as He has declared concerning Himself in His Word; I say, He who is really convinced and has settled it with himself that these things are certainly true—will be influenced by them above all things in the world. He will be more concerned by far how he shall escape eternal damnation, and have the favor of God and eternal life, than how he shall get the world, gratify the flesh, please his neighbors, get honor, or obtain any temporal advantage whatsoever. His main inquiry will not be what he shall eat and what he shall drink, but he will seek first the kingdom of God and His righteousness.

Examine yourselves therefore by this: Are not your hearts chiefly set upon the world and the things of it? Is it not more your concern, care, and endeavor to further your outward interest than to secure an interest in heaven? And is not this the very reason that you have never seen the reality of eternal things?

Inquire whether you have ever yet come to a determination about religion with respect to the practice of it; whether you have chosen heaven with the way to it, that is, the way of obedience and self-denial, before this world and the ways of sin; whether you have determined upon it as most eligible, to devote yourselves to the service of God.

Here I shall mention four things which are signs that men halt between two opinions in the matter:

1. They put off duty till hereafter. When persons love to keep their duty at a distance, do not engage in it for the present, but think of engaging when they shall be under better conveniences for it; when they are very good intenders concerning what they will do tomorrow, but very poor performers today; when they say, as Felix, "Go thy way for this time, when I have a convenient season I will call for thee"—it is a sign that they halt between two opinions, and have never as yet come to a full determination with respect to the practice of religion. Those who have fully determined that religion is necessary and eligible will not desire to put it off, but will make it their present and immediate business.

2. It is a sign of the same thing when persons are strict and conscientious in some things, but not universal in their obedience. They do some duties, but live in the omission of others; they avoid some sins, but allow themselves in others; they are conscientious with respect to the duties of worship public and private, but not in their behavior to their neighbors; they are not just in their dealings, nor conscientious in paying their debts. Nor do they do unto others as they would that they

should do to them, but have crooked perverse ways in their dealings with mankind.

The same may be said when they are just in their dealings and trade with men, but are not conscientious in other things, such as indulging sensual appetites, drinking to excess, allowing themselves in wanton practices; or are honest and temperate, but licentious in using their tongues, backbiting and reproaching their fellowmen (see 2 Timothy 3:6–7).

3. It is a sign that you halt between two opinions if you sometimes are wont to be considerably engaged in religion, but at other times neglect it; if you sometimes form a resolution to be in good earnest, then drop it again; if you sometimes seem to be really engaged in seeking salvation and are very earnest in religious duties, but at other times are wholly taken up about the things of the world, while religion is neglected and religious duties are omitted.

These things show that you are yet unsettled and have never yet come to a full determination concerning religion, but are halting between two opinions, and therefore are thus unstable in all your ways and proceed thus by fits and starts in religion. James 1:6–8: "But let him ask in faith, nothing wavering; for he that wavereth is like a wave of the sea, driven with the wind and tossed. For let not that man think that he shall receive anything of the Lord. A double-minded man is unstable in all his ways." If your determination were fixed in religion, you would be more steady in your practice.

4. It is a sign that you are halting between two opinions if it is your manner to balk at your duty whenever any notable difficulty comes in the way that is considerably cross to your interest, or very inconsistent with your ease or convenience, or your temporal honor. Whatever zeal you may seem to have,

whatever concern about the things of religion, and however strict you are ordinarily, you have never, if this is your manner, come to a full determination; you have never fully made choice of religion and the benefits of it for your only portion. At best you have gotten no further than King Agrippa, who was almost persuaded to be a Christian (Acts 26:28). You are in the state of the stony-ground hearers: you have no root in yourselves and, like a tree without roots, are easily blown down by every wind.

USE OF EXHORTATION. I shall conclude with an earnest exhortation to all no longer to halt between two opinions, but immediately to come to a determination whether to be Christians or not. Let me insist upon it, that you now make a choice whether you will have heaven, with a life of universal and persevering obedience, for your portion, or hell, with a life spent in the pursuit of this world. Consider those things which have been said, showing the unreasonableness of continuing in such irresolution about an affair of infinite importance to you, and as to which you have so short an opportunity to make your choice. Consider two things in addition to what has already been said:

First, those who live under the gospel, and thus continue undetermined about religion, are more abominable to God than the heathen. He hates those persons who continue from year to year under the calls, warnings, instructions, and entreaties of God's Word, who yet can be brought to nothing, who will come to no determination at all, who will neither be Christians nor heathens. These are they who are spoken of in Revelation 3:15–16: " I know thy works, that thou are neither cold nor hot. I would thou wert cold or hot. So then, because thou art lukewarm, and neither cold nor hot, I will spew thee out of My mouth." And Ezekiel 20:39: "As for you, O house of

Israel, thus saith the Lord God, 'Go ye, serve ye every one his idols; and hereafter also, if ye will not hearken unto Me, but pollute ye My holy name no more with your gifts, and with your idols." These are like those spoken of in 2 Timothy 3:7, "ever learning, and never coming to the knowledge of the truth."

Second, if you still refuse to come to a determination whether to be Christians or not, how just will it be if God shall give you no further opportunity! If you refuse to make any choice at all, after all that has been done to bring you to it, in setting life and death so often before you, in calling and warning you, how just will it be if God shall wait no longer upon you but shall, by His unalterable sentence, determine the case Himself, fix your state with the unbelievers, and teach you the truth and eligibleness of religion by sad and fatal experience, when it will be too late for you to choose your portion.

CHAPTER SEVENTEEN

Temptation And Deliverance

Joseph's Great Temptation and Gracious Deliverance (1738)

J

*"And he left his garment in her hand,
and fled, and got him out."*

GENESIS 39:12

W e have here, and in the context, an account of that remarkable behavior of Joseph in Potiphar's house that was the occasion of both his great affliction and his high advancement and prosperity in the land of Egypt.

We read in the beginning of the chapter how Joseph, after he had been so cruelly treated by his brethren and sold into Egypt as a slave, was advanced in the house of Potiphar, who had bought him. Joseph was one who feared God, and therefore God was with him, and so influenced the heart of Potiphar his master that, instead of keeping him as a mere slave, to which purpose he was sold, he made him his steward and overseer over his house, and all that he had was put into his hands, insomuch that we are told in verse 6 that "he left all that he had in his hand; and he knew not ought that he had, save the bread which he did eat." While Joseph was in these prosperous circumstances, he met with a great temptation in his master's house. We are told that, he being a goodly person and well-favored, his mistress cast her eyes upon and lusted after him, and used all her art to tempt him to commit uncleanness with her.

Concerning this temptation, and his behavior under it, many things are worthy to be noted. Particularly:

• We may observe how great the temptation was that he was under. It is to be considered that Joseph was now in his youth, a season of life when persons are most liable to be overcome by temptations of this nature. And he was in a state of unexpected prosperity in Potiphar's house, which has a tendency to lift persons up, especially young ones, whereby commonly they more easily fall before temptations.

• And then, the superiority of the person who laid the temptation before him rendered it much greater. She was his mistress, and he a servant under her.

• Note the manner of her tempting him. She not only carried herself towards Joseph so as to give him cause to suspect that he might be admitted to such criminal converse with her, but she directly proposed it to him, plainly manifesting her disposition to it. So there was no such thing as suspicion of her unwillingness to deter him, but a manifestation of her desire to entice him to it. Yea, she appeared greatly engaged in the matter.

• There was not only her desire manifested to entice him, but her authority over him to enforce the temptation. She was his mistress, and he might well imagine that if he utterly refused to comply, he would incur her displeasure. And she, being his master's wife, had power to do much to his disadvantage, and to render his circumstances more uncomfortable in the family.

• The temptation was the greater in that she not only tempted him once, but frequently, day by day (verse 10). And at last she became more violent with him: She caught him by his garment, saying, 'Lie with me."

His behavior was very remarkable under these temptations. He absolutely refused any compliance with them. He made no reply that manifested that the temptation had gained at all upon him, so much as to hesitate about it or at all deliberate upon it. He complied in no degree, either to the gross act she proposed or anything tending towards it, or that should at all be gratifying to her wicked inclination. And he persisted resolute and unshaken under her continual solicitations, as in verse 10: "And it came to pass as she spake to Joseph day by day, that he hearkened not unto her, to lie by her, or to be with her." He, to his utmost, avoided so much as being where she was.

The motives and principles from which he acted, manifested by his reply to her solicitations, are remarkable. First, he sets before her how injuriously he would be acting against his master if he should comply with her proposal: "Behold, my master . . . hath committed all that he hath to my hand; there is none greater in this house than I; neither hath he kept back any thing from me but thee, because thou art his wife." But he then proceeded to inform her of that which, above all things, deterred him from a compliance, that it would be great wickedness and sin against God: "How shall I do this and sin against God?" He would not do any such thing, as he would not injure his master; but that which influenced more than all on this occasion was the fear of sinning against God. On this account he persisted in his resolution to the last.

In the text we have an account of his behavior under the last and greatest temptation that he had from her. This temptation was great, as it was at a time when there was nobody in the house but he and his mistress (verse 11). There was an opportunity to commit the fact with the greatest secrecy. And at this time it seems that she was more violent than ever before. She caught him by the garment. She laid hold on him, as though she were resolute to attain her purpose of him.

Under these circumstances he not only refused her, but fled from her, as he would have done from one who was going to assassinate him. He escaped, as for his life. He not only would not be guilty of such a fact, but neither would he by any means be in the house with her where he would be in the way of her temptation. This behavior of Joseph's is doubtless recorded for the instruction of all. Therefore, from the words, I observe this:

DOCTRINE: It is our duty not only to avoid those things that are themselves sinful, but also, as far as may be, those things that lead and expose to sin.

Section 1: Why we should avoid what tends to sin.

Thus did Joseph: he not only refused actually to commit uncleanness with his mistress who enticed him, but refused to be there where he would be in the way of temptation (verse 10). He refused to lie by her or be with her. And in the text we are told that "he fled and got him out." He would by no means be in her company. It was no sin in itself for Joseph to be in the house where his mistress was; but under these circumstances it would expose him to sin. Joseph was sensible that he naturally had a corrupt heart that tended to betray him to sin; and therefore he would by no means be in the way of temptation, but with haste he fled; he ran from the dangerous place. Inasmuch as he was exposed to sin in that house, he fled out of it with as much haste as if it had been on fire or was full of enemies who stood ready with drawn swords to stab him to the very heart. When she took him by the garment, he left his garment in her hands. He would rather lose his garment than stay a moment where he was in such danger of losing his chastity.

I said that persons should avoid things that expose to sin, as far as may be, because it is possible that persons may be called to expose themselves to temptation; and when it is so, they may hope for divine strength and protection under temptation.

It may be a man's indispensable duty to undertake an office or a work that is attended with a great deal of temptation. Ordinarily a man ought not to run into the temptation of being persecuted for the true religion, lest the temptation should be too hard for him, but should avoid it as much as may be. Therefore Christ thus directed His disciples in Matthew 10:23: "When ye be persecuted in one city, flee to another." Yet, the case may be that a man is called not to flee from persecution, but to run the venture of such a trial, trusting in God to uphold him under it. Ministers and magistrates may be obliged to continue with their people in such circumstances, as Nehemiah says in Nehemiah 6:11: "Should such a man as I flee?" So it was with the apostles. Yea, some may be called to go into the midst of it, to those places where they cannot reasonably expect but to meet with such temptations. So Paul went up to Jerusalem, where he knew beforehand that there bonds and affliction awaiting him (Acts 20:23).

In some other cases, the necessity of affairs may call upon men to engage in some business that is peculiarly attended with temptations. But when it is so, they are indeed least exposed to sin, for they are always safest in the way of duty. Proverbs 10:9: "He that walketh uprightly, walketh surely." And though there are many things by which they may have extraordinary temptations in the affairs they have undertaken, yet if they have a clear call, it is no presumption to hope for divine support and preservation in it.

But for persons to needlessly expose themselves to temptation and do those things that tend to sin is unwarrantable and contrary to that excellent example set before us. That we ought to avoid not only those things that are in themselves sinful, but also those things that lead and expose to sin, is manifest by the following arguments:

ARGUMENT 1. It is very evident that we ought to use our utmost endeavors to avoid sin, which is inconsistent with needlessly doing those things that expose and lead to sin. And the greater any evil is, the greater care and the more earnest endeavors it requires to avoid it. Those evils that appear to us as very great and dreadful, we use proportionably great care to avoid. And therefore the greatest evil of all requires the greatest and utmost care to avoid it.

Sin is an infinite evil because it is committed against an infinitely great and excellent Being, and so is a violation of infinite obligation. Therefore, however great our care is to avoid sin, it cannot be more than proportionable to the evil we would avoid. Our care and endeavor cannot be infinite as the evil of sin is infinite. We ought to use every method that tends to the avoiding of sin. This is manifest to reason and, not only so, but is positively required of us in the Word of God. Joshua

22:5: "Take diligent heed to do the commandment and the law which Moses, the servant of the Lord charged you, to love the Lord your God, and to walk in all His ways, and to keep His commandments, and to cleave unto Him, and to serve Him with all your soul." Deuteronomy 4:15–16: "Take ye therefore good heed unto yourselves, lest ye corrupt yourselves." Chapter 12:30: "Take heed to thyself, that thou be not ensnared." Luke 12:15: "Take heed and beware of covetousness." 1 Corinthians 10:12: "Let him that thinketh he standeth take heed lest he fall." Deuteronomy 4:9: "Take heed to thyself, keep thy soul diligently." These and many other texts of Scripture plainly require of us the utmost possible diligence and caution to avoid sin.

But how can he be said to use the utmost possible diligence and caution to avoid sin who voluntarily does those things that naturally expose and lead to sin? How can he be said with the utmost possible caution to avoid an enemy who voluntarily lays himself in his way? How can he be said to use the utmost possible caution to preserve the life of his child who suffers it to go on the edge of precipices or pits, to play on the borders of a deep gulf, or to wander in a wood that is haunted by beasts of prey?

ARGUMENT 2. It is evident that we ought to avoid those things that expose and lead to sin because a due sense of the evil of sin and a just hatred of it will necessarily have this effect upon us to cause us so to do. If we were duly sensible of the evil and dreadful nature of sin, we would have an exceeding dread of it upon our spirits. We would hate it worse than death, would fear it worse than the devil himself, and would dread it even as we dread damnation. But those things that men exceedingly dread, they naturally shun; and they avoid those things that they apprehend expose them to those things. A child that has been greatly terrified by the sight of any wild beast will by no means be persuaded to go where it apprehends that it shall fall into its way.

As sin in its own nature is infinitely hateful, so in its natural tendency it is infinitely dreadful. It is the tendency of all sin to eternally undo the soul. Every sin naturally carries hell in it! Therefore, all sin ought to be treated by us as we would treat a thing that is infinitely terrible. If any one sin, yea, the least sin, does not necessarily bring eternal ruin with it, this is owing to nothing but the free grace and mercy of God to us, and not to the nature and tendency of sin itself. But certainly we ought not to take the less care to avoid sin or all that tends to it for the freeness and greatness of God's mercy to us, through which there is hope of pardon; for that would be indeed a most ungrateful and vile abuse of mercy. Were it made known to us that if we ever voluntarily committed any particular act of sin, we would be damned without any remedy or escape, should we not exceedingly dread the commission of such? Would we not be very watchful and careful to stand at the greatest distance from that sin, and from everything that might expose us to it, and that has any tendency to stir up our lusts or to betray us to such an act of sin? Let us then consider that, though the next voluntary act of known sin shall not necessarily and unavoidably issue in certain damnation, yet it will certainly deserve it. We shall thereby really deserve to be cast off without any remedy or hope. And it can only be owing to free grace that it will not certainly and remedilessly be followed with such a punishment. And shall we be guilty of such a vile abuse of God's mercy to us as to take encouragement from it, the more boldly to expose ourselves to sin?

ARGUMENT 3. It is evident that we ought not only to avoid sin, but things that expose and lead to sin, because this is the way we act in things that pertain to our temporal interest. Men avoid not only those things that are themselves the hurt or ruin of their temporal interest, but also the things that tend or expose to it. Because they love their temporal lives, they will not only actually avoid killing themselves, but they are very careful to avoid those things that bring their lives into danger though they do not certainly know but they may escape.

They are careful not to pass rivers and deep waters on rotten ice, though they do not certainly know that they shall fall through and be drowned. They will not only avoid those things that would be in themselves the ruin of their estates—such as setting their own houses on fire and burning them up with their substance, taking their money and throwing it into the sea, and so on—but they carefully avoid those things by which their estates are exposed. They have their eyes about them and are careful with whom they deal; they are watchful that they are not overreached in their bargains, and that they do not lay themselves open to knaves and fraudulent persons.

If a man is sick with a dangerous distemper, he is careful to avoid everything that tends to increase the disorder—not only what he knows to be mortal, but other things that he fears may be prejudicial to him. Men are in this way wont to take care of their temporal interest. And therefore, if we are not as careful to avoid sin as we are to avoid injury in our temporal interest, it will show a regardless disposition with respect to sin and duty, or that we do not much care if we sin against God. God's glory is surely of as much importance and concern as our temporal interest. Certainly we should be as careful not to be exposed to sin against the Majesty of heaven and earth as men are wont to be of a few pounds; yea, the latter are but mere trifles compared with the former.

ARGUMENT 4. We are wont to do this by our dear earthly friends. We not only are careful of those things wherein the destruction of their lives, or their hurt and calamity in any respect, directly consist, but are careful to avoid those things that but remotely tend to it. We are careful to prevent all occasions of their loss, and are watchful against that which tends in any way to deprive them of their comfort or good name; and the reason is because they are very dear to us. In this manner, men are wont to be careful of the good of their own children, and dread the approaches of any mischief that they apprehend they are or may be exposed to. And we would take it hard if our friends did not do thus by us.

And surely we ought to treat God as a dear Friend. We ought to act towards Him as those who have a sincere love and unfeigned regard for Him; so we ought to watch and be careful against all occasions of that which is contrary to His honor and glory. If we do not have a temper and desire to do so, it will show that, whatever our pretenses are, we are not God's sincere friends and have no true love for Him. If we should be offended at any who have professed friendship to us, if they have treated us in this manner and were no more careful of our interest, surely God may justly be offended that we are no more careful of His glory.

ARGUMENT 5. We would have God, in His providence towards us, not to order those things that tend to our hurt or expose our interest; therefore certainly we ought to avoid those things that lead to sin against Him.

We desire and love to have God's providence such towards us as that our welfare may be well secured. No man loves to live exposed, uncertain, and in dangerous circumstances. While he is so, he lives uncomfortably in that he lives in continual fear. We desire that God would so order things concerning us that we may be safe from fear of evil, and that no evil may come nigh our dwelling because we dread calamity. So we do not love the appearance and approaches of it, and love to have it at a great distance from us. We desire to have God to be to us as a wall of fire round about us to defend us, and that He would surround us as the mountains do the valleys, to guard us from every danger or enemy so that no evil may come nigh us.

Now this plainly shows that we ought, in our behavior towards God, to keep at as great a distance from sin, and from all that exposes to it, as we desire God, in His providence to us, should keep calamity and misery at a great distance from us, and not to order those things that expose our welfare.

ARGUMENT 6. Seeing that we are to pray that we may not be led into temptation, certainly we ought not to run ourselves into it. This is one request that Christ directs us to make to God in that form of prayer which He taught His disciples: "Lead us not into temptation." And how inconsistent shall we be with ourselves if we pray to God that we should not be led into temptations, and at the same time we are not careful to avoid temptation, but bring ourselves into it by doing those things that lead and expose to sin. What self-contradiction is it for a man to pray to God that he may be kept from that which he takes no care to avoid! By praying that we may be kept from temptation, we profess to God that being in temptation is a thing to be avoided; but by running into it we show that we choose the contrary, that is, not to avoid it.

ARGUMENT 7. The apostle directs us to avoid those things that are in themselves lawful, but tend to lead others into sin. Surely then we should avoid what tends to lead ourselves into sin. The apostle directs us in 1 Corinthians 8:9: "Take heed lest . . . this liberty of yours become a stumbling block to them that are weak." Romans 14:13: "That no man put a stumbling block, or an occasion to fall, in his brother's way." Verse 15: "But if thy brother be grieved with thy meat, now walkest thou not charitably. Destroy not him with thy meat." Verses 20–21: "For meat, destroy not the work of God. All things indeed are pure; but it is evil for that man who eateth with offense. It is good neither to eat flesh nor to drink wine, nor anything whereby thy brother stumbleth, or is offended, or is made weak." Now if this rule of the apostle is agreeable to the word of Christ, as we must suppose, or expunge what He says out of the canon of Scripture, then a like rule obliges more strongly in those things that tend to lead ourselves into sin.

ARGUMENT 8. There are many precepts of Scripture that directly and positively imply that we ought to avoid those things that tend to sin. This very thing is commanded by Christ in Matthew 26:41, where He directs us to "watch lest we enter into temptation." But certainly running ourselves into temptation is the reverse of watching against it. We are commanded to abstain from all appearance of evil; that is, we are to do by sin as a man does by a thing the sight or appearance of which he hates, and therefore will avoid anything that looks like it, and will not come near or in sight of it.

Again, Christ commanded us to separate from those things that are stumbling blocks or occasions of sin, however dear they are to us. Matthew 5:29–30: "If thy right eye offend thee, pluck it out and cast it from thee. And if thy right hand offend thee, cut if off." By the right hand offending us is not meant its paining us; but the word in the original signifies being a stumbling block, if your right hand proves to be a stumbling block or an occasion to fall, an occasion to sin. Those things are called offenses or stumbling blocks in the New Testament that are the occasions of falling into sin. Yea, Christ tells us that we must avoid them, however dear they are to us, though as dear as our right hand or right eye. If there is any practice that naturally tends and exposes us to sin, we must be done with it, though we love it never so well and are never so loath to part with it; though it is as contrary to our inclination as to cut off our own right hand or pluck out our own right eye—and that upon pain of damnation—for it is intimated that if we do not, we must go with two hands and two eyes into hell fire.

Again, God took great care to forbid the children of Israel those things that tended to lead them into sin. For this reason He forbade them marrying strange wives. Deuteronomy 7:3–4: "Neither shalt thou make marriages with them . . . for they will turn away thy sons from following Me that they may serve other gods." For this reason they were commanded to destroy all those things, that the nations of Canaan had used in their idolatry; and if any were enticed over to idolatry, they were to be destroyed without mercy, though ever so near and dear friends. They were not only to be parted with, but stoned with stones; yea, they themselves were to fall upon them and put them to death, though son or daughter, or their bosom friend. Deuteronomy 13:6: "If thy brother . . . or thy son, or thy daughter, or the wife of thy bosom, or thy friends, which is as thine own soul, entice thee secretly, saying, 'Let us go and serve other gods,' thou shalt not consent unto him . . . neither shall thine eye pity him, neither shalt thou spare, neither shalt thou conceal him. But thou shalt surely kill him; thine hand shall be first upon him to put him to death."

Again, the wise man warns us to avoid those things that tend and expose us to sin, especially the sin of uncleanness. Proverbs 6:27: "Can a man take fire in his bosom and his clothes not be burnt? Can one go upon hot coals and his feet not be burnt? So, whosoever touches her shall not be innocent." This is the truth held forth: avoid those customs and practices that naturally tend to stir up lust. There are many examples in Scripture that have the force of precept, and are recorded as not only worthy, but that demand our imitation. The conduct of Joseph is one. That recorded of King David is another. Psalm 39:1–2: "I said I will take heed to my ways, that I sin not with my tongue; I will keep my mouth with a bridle, while the wicked is before me. I was dumb with silence. I held my peace, even from good." When he says, "even from good," that is, he was so watchful over his words, and kept at such a great distance from speaking what might in any way tend to sin, that he avoided, in certain circumstances, speaking what was in itself lawful lest he should be betrayed into that which was sinful.

ARGUMENT 9. A prudent sense of our own weakness and exposedness to yield to temptation obliges us to avoid that which leads or exposes to sin. Whoever knows himself, and is sensible how weak he is; his constant exposedness to run into sin; how full of corruption his heart is that, like fuel, is ready to catch fire and bring destruction upon him; how much he has in him to incline him to sin, and how unable he is to stand of himself; who is sensible of this, and has any regard for his duty—will he not be very watchful against everything that may lead and expose to sin? On this account Christ directed us in Matthew 26:41 to "watch and pray, lest ye enter into temptation." The reason is added that "the flesh is weak!" He who, in confidence of his own strength, boldly runs the venture of sinning by going into temptation, manifests great presumption and a sottish insensibility of his own weakness. "He that trusteth in his own heart is a fool" (Proverbs 28:26).

The wisest and strongest, and some of the most holy men in the world, have been overthrown by such means. Such was David; such was Solomon: his wives turned away his heart. If such persons so eminent for holiness were in this way led into sin, surely it should be a warning to us. "Let him that thinketh he standeth, take heed lest he fall."

Section 2: What things lead and expose to sin

If anything be made out clearly, from reason and the Word of God, to be our duty, this would be enough with all Christians. Will a follower of Christ stand objecting and disputing against what is irrefragably proved and demonstrated to be his duty?

QUESTION. How shall we know what things lead and expose to sin? Let a man do what he will, he cannot avoid sinning as long as he has such a corrupt heart within him. And there is nothing a man can do but he may find some temptation in it. And though it be true that a man ought to avoid those things which have a special tendency to expose men to sin, yet how shall we judge and determine what things have a natural tendency to sin, or do especially lead to it?

ANSWER. I would answer in some particulars which are plain and easy, and which cannot be denied without the greatest absurdity.

1. That which borders on those sins to which the lusts of men's hearts strongly incline them is of this sort. Men come into the world with many strong and violent lusts in their hearts, and are exceedingly prone of themselves to transgress, even in the safest circumstances in which they can be placed. And surely so much the nearer they are to that sin to which they are naturally inclined, so much the more are they exposed. If any of us who are parents should see our children near the brink of some deep pit, or close by the edge of the precipice of a high mountain; and not only so, but if we were to see that the ground upon which the child stood was slippery and steeply descended directly toward the precipice, would we not reckon a child exposed in such a case? Would we not be in haste to remove the child from its very dangerous situation?

It was the manner among the Israelites, to build their

houses with flat roofs, so that persons might walk on the tops of their houses. And therefore God took care to make it a law among them, that every man should have battlements upon the edges of their roofs; lest any person should fall off and be killed. Deut. 22:8, "When thou buildest a new house, then thou shalt make a battlement for thy roof, that thou bring not blood upon thine house, if any man fall from thence." And certainly we ought to take the like care that we do not fall into sin; which carries in it eternal death. We should, as it were, fix a battlement, a guard, to keep us from the edge of the precipice. Much more ought we to take care, that we do not go upon a roof that is not only without battlements, but when it is steep, and we shall naturally incline to fall. — Men's lusts are like strong enemies, endeavoring to draw them into sin. If a man stood upon a dangerous precipice, and had enemies about him, pulling and drawing him, endeavoring to throw him down; would he, in such a case, choose or dare to stand near the edge? Would he look upon himself as safe being close on the brink? Would he not endeavor, for his own safety, to keep at a distance?

2. Those things that tend to feed lusts in the imagination are of this kind. They lead and expose men to sin. Those things that have a natural tendency to excite in the mind the imagination of that which is the object of the lust certainly tend to feed and promote that lust. What can be more evident than that presenting the object tends to stir up the appetite? Reason and experience teach this. Therefore all things, whether words or actions, that have a tendency and expose to sin, tend also to raise in the mind imaginations of what the lust tends to. It is certainly wrong to feed a lust, even in the imagination. It is quite contrary to the holy rules of God's Word. Proverbs 24:9: "The thought of foolishness is sin." Matthew 5:28: "Whosoever looketh on a woman to lust after her . . . hath committed adultery." A man, by

gratifying his lusts in his imagination and thoughts, may make his soul in the sight of God to be a hold of foul spirits, and like a cage of every unclean and hateful bird. And sinful imaginations tend to sinful actions, and outward behavior in the end. Lust is always first conceived in the imagination, and then brought forth in the outward practice. You may see the progress of it in James 1:15: "Then when lust hath conceived, it bringeth forth sin." Such things are abominable in the sight of a pure and holy God. We are commanded to keep at a great distance from spiritual pollution, and to hate even the very "garment spotted with the flesh" (Jude 23).

3. Those things that the experience and observation of mankind show to be ordinarily attended or followed with sin are of this sort. Experience is a good rule to determine by in things of this nature. How do we know the natural tendency of anything but by observation and experience? Men observe and find that some things are commonly attended and followed with other things; and hence mankind pronounces that they have a natural tendency to them. We have no other way to know the tendency of anything. Thus men, by observation and experience, know that the warmth of the sun and showers of rain are attended with the growth of plants; and hence they learn that they have a tendency to it. So they find by experience that the bite of some kinds of serpents is commonly followed with illness, and often with death; and hence they learn that the bite of such serpents has a natural tendency to bring disorder upon the body and expose it to death. And so, if experience and common observation show that any particular practice or custom is commonly attended with that which is very sinful, we may safely conclude that such a practice tends to sin, that it leads and exposes to it.

Thus we may determine that tavern haunting and gaming

are things that tend to sin because common experience and observation show that those practices are attended with a great deal of sin and wickedness. The observation of all ages and all nations, with one voice, declares it. It shows that where taverns are much frequented for drinking and the like, they are special places of sin, of profaneness, and other wickedness; and it shows that those towns where there is much of this are places where no good generally prevails. It also shows that those persons who are given to much frequenting of taverns are most commonly vicious persons; and so of gaming, such as playing cards. Experience shows that those persons who practice this generally fall into much sin. Hence these practices have become infamous among all sober, virtuous persons.

4. Another way by which persons may determine some things that lead and expose to sin is by their own experience, or what they have found in themselves. This surely is enough to convince them that such things actually lead and expose to sin. For what will convince men if their own experience will not? Thus, if men have found by undeniable experience that any practice or custom stirs up lust in them, and has betrayed them into foolish and sinful behavior, or sinful thoughts, they may determine that they lead to sin. If they, upon examining themselves, must own that a custom or practice has disposed them to the omission of known duty, such as secret or family prayer, and has indisposed them to reading and religious meditation; or if they find, since they have complied with such a custom, that they are less watchful of their hearts, less disposed to anything that is serious; that the frame of their mind is more light, and their hearts less disposed on the things of another world, and more after vanity—these are sinful effects. And therefore, if experience shows a custom or practice to be attended with these things, then experience shows that they

lead and expose to sin.

5. We may determine whether a thing is of an evil tendency or not by the effect that an outpouring of the Spirit of God, and a general flourishing of religion, has with respect to it. If this puts a stop to any practice or custom and roots it out, surely it argues that practice or custom is of no good tendency. For if there is no hurt in it, and it tends to no hurt, why should the Spirit of God destroy it? The Spirit of God has no tendency to destroy anything that is neither sinful nor has any tendency to sin. Why should it? Why should we suppose that He is an Enemy to that which has no hurt in it; nor has any tendency to that which is hurtful?

The flourishing of religion has no tendency to abolish or expel anything that is in no way against religion. That which is not against religion, religion will not appear against. It is a rule that holds in all contraries and opposites. The opposition is equal on both sides. So contrary as light is to darkness, so contrary is darkness to light. So contrary as the flourishing of religion is to any custom, just so contrary is that custom to the flourishing of religion. That custom that religion tends to destroy, that custom, if it prevails, tends also to destroy religion. Therefore, if the flourishing of religion and the outpouring of the Spirit of God tend to overthrow any custom that takes place or prevails, we may surely determine that custom is either in itself sinful, or tends and exposes to evil.

6. We may determine by the effect that a general decay of religion has with respect to them whether they are things of a sinful tendency or not. If they are things that come with a decay of religion, that creep in as that decays, we may determine they are things of no good tendency. The withdrawing of good does not let in good but evil. Evil, not good, comes in as

good gradually ceases.

Therefore, if there is any decay of religion in the town, or in particular persons, and upon this any certain customs or practices take place and are allowed that were wholly abstained from and renounced when religion was in a more flourishing state; we may safely conclude that such customs and practices are contrary to the nature of true religion and are therefore in themselves sinful, or tending to sin.

7. We may in good things determine whether any custom is of a good tendency by considering what the effect would be if it was openly and universally owned and practiced. There are many things that persons practice somewhat secretly, and that they plead not to be hurtful, but which, if they had suitable consideration to discern the consequence of everybody openly practicing the same, would soon show a most woeful state of things. If therefore there is any custom that will not bear universal open practice and profession, we may determine that custom is of an ill tendency. For if it is neither sinful in itself, nor tends to anything sinful, then it is no matter how open it is; for we need not be afraid of that custom being too prevalent and universal that has no ill tendency in it.

Section 3: A serious warning to all, and especially young people

Thus I have mentioned some general rules by which to determine and judge what things are of a bad and sinful tendency. And these things are so plain that for a person to deny them would be absurd and ridiculous.

I would now, in the name of God, warn all persons to avoid such things as appear by these rules to lead and expose to sin. Particularly, I would take occasion to warn young people, as they would approve themselves fearers of God, to avoid all such things in company that, being tried by these rules, will appear to have a tendency to sin. Avoid all such ways of talking and acting as have a tendency to this; and follow the example of Joseph. Not only gross acts of uncleanness, but all acts of lasciviousness, in both talking and acting, are strictly forbidden in Scripture as what should not be so much as once named among saints or Christians. Galatians 5:19: "Now the works of the flesh are manifest, adultery, fornication, uncleanness, lasciviousness." Ephesians 5:3–5: "But fornication, and all uncleanness, let it not be once named among you as becometh saints; neither filthiness, nor foolish talking, nor jesting, which are not convenient; for this ye know, that no whoremonger, nor unclean person, hath any inheritance in the kingdom of Christ, and of God." We should hate even the garment spotted with the flesh; that is, we should hate and shun all that, in the least degree, approaches to any such thing.

And I desire that certain customs, too common among young people, may be examined by those rules that have been mentioned. That custom in particular of young people of different sexes reclining together—however little is made of it, and however ready people may be to laugh at its being condemned—if it is examined by the rules that have been mentioned, it will appear, past all contradiction, to be one of those that lead and expose to sin. And I believe experience and fact abundantly bear witness to it. It has been one main thing that has led to the growth of uncleanness in the land. And there are other customs and liberties, customarily used among young people in company, that they who use them know that they lead to sin. They know that they stir up their lusts; and this is the very end for which they do it, to gratify their lusts in some measure. Little do such persons consider what a holy God they are soon to be judged by, who abominates the impurities of their hearts. If therefore they actually stir up and feed lust, then certainly they tend to further degrees and more gross acts. That which stirs up lust makes it more violent, and therefore certainly more exposes persons to be overcome by it. How evident and undeniable are these things; and how strange that any should make a derision of them!

Possibly you may be confident of your own strength, and may think with yourself that you are not in danger, that there is no temptation in these things but what you are able easily to overcome. But you should consider that the most self-confident are most in danger. Peter was very confidant that he would not deny Christ, but how dreadfully otherwise was the event! If others who have fallen into gross sins should declare how it was with them, doubtless they would say that they at first thought there was no danger. They were far from the thought that ever they should commit such wickedness; but yet, by venturing further and further, they fell at last into the foulest and grossest transgressions. Persons may long withstand temptation, and be suddenly be overcome at last. None are so much in danger as the most bold. They are most safe who are most sensible of their own weakness, most distrustful of their own hearts, and most sensible of their continual need of restraining grace.

Young persons, with respect to the sin of uncleanness, are dealt with by the devil, just as some give an account of serpents charming the birds and other animals down into their mouths. If the serpent takes them with his eyes, though they seem to be frightened by it, yet they will not flee away, but will keep the serpent in sight, and approach nearer and nearer to him, till they fall prey.

Another custom that I desire may be examined by the aforementioned rules is that of young people of both sexes getting together in companies for mirth, and spending the time together till late in the night in their jollity. I desire our young people to suffer their ears to be open to what I have to say upon this point, as I am the messenger of the Lord of hosts to them, and not determine that they will not hearken before they have heard what I shall say. I hope there are but few persons among us so abandoned as to determine that they will go on in a practice, whether they are convinced that it is unlawful or not, or though it should be proved to them to be unlawful by undeniable arguments.

Let us then examine this custom and practice by what has been said. It has been proved undeniably that we ought not to go on in a practice that leads and exposes to sin; and rules have been laid down to judge what thus exposes and leads to it, that I think are plain and undeniable. Certainly a Christian will not be unwilling to have his practices examined and tried by the rules of reason and God's Word; but will rather rejoice in it. I desire particularly that the practice may be tried by that sure touchstone of experience. This is one of the rules of trial that have been mentioned, that any custom that the experience and observation of mankind show to be ordinarily attended with sin may be concluded to be unlawful. And if we look abroad in the country, I doubt not but these two things will be found:

First, that as to those places where there is most of this carried on among young people (as there is more of it in some places than others), it will be found as a thing that universally holds, that the young people there are commonly a loose, vain, and irreligious generation, little regarding God, heaven, or hell, or anything but vanity. And commonly in those towns where most frolicking is carried on, there are the most frequent breakings out of gross sins; fornication in particular.

Second, if we go though the country, we shall for the most

part find that those persons who are most addicted to this practice are the furthest from serious thought, and are the vainest and loosest upon other accounts. And why would this be if such a practice was not sinful, or did not have a natural tendency to lead persons into sin.

Now I appeal to those who have made pretenses to serious religion and saving piety. You have formerly pretended to keep up religion in your closets, and in your own souls. Now seriously ask yourselves whether or not you have not found that this practice has indisposed you to serious religion, and taken off your minds from it? Has it not tended to your neglect of secret prayer? And, if you have not wholly neglected it, have you not found that you have been abundantly more ready to turn it off in any manner, and glad to have done with it, more backward to reading and serious meditation, and such things; and that your mind has been exceedingly diverted from religion, and that for some time? I do not send you far off to find out whether this custom is not of bad tendency—not beyond the sea, but your own breast; there let the matter be determined.

Let us now try this custom by the effect which the outpouring of the Spirit of God on a people has with respect to it. This we are under great advantage to do because there has lately been, in this place, the most remarkable outpouring of the Spirit of God that has ever been in New England, and it may be in the world, since the apostles' days. It is well known that before then the custom prevailed in the town; but afterwards the custom was altogether laid aside, and was so for several years. No account can be given why the Spirit of God, and the flourishing of religion, would abolish such a custom unless that custom is, in either its nature or tendency, an enemy to the Spirit of God and to religion.

The fruits of the Spirit of God are good, and therefore it is good that this custom should be removed; for this is plainly one of the effects. And if so, it is because the custom is bad in either its nature or tendency. Otherwise there would be no good in its being removed. The Spirit of God abolished this custom for this reason, because, if it had been kept up in the town, it would have had a direct tendency to hinder that work that the Spirit was about to do among us. This was undeniably the reason.

Supposing such a custom had been begun and set up by the young people all over the town in the midst of the time of the late outpouring of the Spirit, all of a sudden; would any wise persons who truly have the cause of religion at heart rejoiced at it? Would not everyone have concluded, without any hesitation, that there was great danger that it would take off people's minds from religion and make them vain, and so put an end to the flourishing of religion? Would not every considerate person have thought thus of it? And if such a custom would have had an ill tendency then, so it will now.

OBJECTION. The town is not in such circumstances now as it was then. It might have done hurt then by putting an end to the great concern, but now it may do no hurt; for there is now no such great concern to be interrupted by it.

ANSWER. Though the town is not in such circumstances now as it was then, yet there ought to be as much engagedness of mind about religion, as much concern among sinners, and as much engagedness among the godly, as then. It is to our shame that there is not. And if such a practice would have tended to destroy such a religious concern then, it certainly tends to prevent it now. It is a rule that will hold that what has a tendency to destroy a thing when it is, tends to prevent when it is not. And are we not praying from Sabbath to Sabbath, and from day to day, for such a concern again? And do not those who pretend to be converted, and yet have lately set up this custom, pray for the same? Are you a convert, a saint, and yet not desire that there should be any more pouring out of the Spirit of God? The town has cause to be ashamed of such converts, if it has any such. And if you do, why do you do what tends to prevent it?

Let this practice be tried by the effect that a general decay of religion has with respect to it. Now we have a trial. It is now a time that religion is greatly decayed among us; and the effect is that this custom comes in with this decay. Young people begin again to set up their old custom of frolicking (as it is called), and spending a great part of the night in it, to the violation of family order. What is the reason, if this custom is not bad, in either its nature or tendency, that it did not come in before when religion was lively? Why does it stay till it can take the advantage of the withdrawal of religion? This is a sign that it is a custom that shuns a spirit of lively religion, as darkness shuns the light, and never comes in till light withdraws.

Here again I would send persons to their own experience. How did this practice come in with you in particular, you who two or three years ago seemed to be so engaged in religion? Did it not come in, did you not begin to practice it, as the sense of religion wore off? And what is the matter? Why did not you set up the practice then, when your heart was taken up about reading, meditation, and secret prayer to God? If this does not at all stand in the way of them, and is no hindrance to them, why were you not engaged in both together? What account can you give of it? Why did you leave off this practice and custom, or abstain from it? To what purpose is this change, one while it must be avoided as evil, and another while practiced and pleaded for as good? Making such an alteration does not look well, nor will it be for the honor of religion in the eye of the world; for whether the practice is lawful or not, yet such a thing will surely be improved to our disadvantage. For your avoiding it then has this appearance in the eye of the country, that then you condemned it. And therefore your returning now to it will appear to them as backsliding in you. Such change-lings are evermore, in the eye of the world, greatly to the dishonor of their profession, let it be what it will.

Indeed, this custom, as it is practiced, not only tends to sin, but is in itself very disorderly, sinful, and shameful. For it is attended late in the night, and in the dead of the night, to the neglect of family prayer, and violating all family order—which is disorder and profaneness. Is it lawful to rob God of His ordinary sacrifices for the sake of your pleasure, diversion, and jollity? Are you of that mind, that it is a decent thing that the stated worship of the great God should give way to your mirth and your diversions? Is this the way of God's holy children?

Those works that are commonly done in the dead of night seem to have a black mark set upon them by the apostle, and Christians are exhorted to avoid them. Romans 13:12–13: "Let us cast off the works of darkness, and let us put on the armor of light. Let us walk honestly, as in the day; not in rioting and drunkenness; not in chambering and wantonness." The word here rendered "rioting" is of far different significance from the term as it is used in our laws for the forcible doing of an unlawful thing by three or more persons assembled together for that purpose. But the word here properly signifies a disorderly convention of persons in order to spend their time together in pleasure and jollity. So the word is commonly used in Scripture. Proverbs 23:20: "Be not amongst riotous eaters of flesh." Proverbs 28:7: "He that is a companion of riotous men shameth his father." Luke 15:13: "Wasted his substance with riotous living." Again, a black mark seems to be set on such in Scripture, as in 1 Thessalonians 5:5-7: "Ye are all the children of light, and the children of the day; we are not of the night, nor of darkness. Therefore let us not sleep, as do others; but let us watch and be sober. For they that sleep, sleep in the night; and they that be drunken are drunken in the night."

Many of you who have lately set up this practice of frolicking and jollity profess to be children of the light and of the day, and not to be the children of darkness. Therefore walk as in the day, and do not do those works of darkness that are commonly done at unseasonable hours of the night. Such things are not only condemned by the apostle, but are looked upon as infamous in all ages among sober people, as all past writings manifest. Therefore it is a thing of bad report, and so is forbidden. Philippians 4:8: "Whatsoever things are of good report, if there be any virtue . . . any praise, think on these things."

OBJECTION. But the wise man allows for this practice when he says, "There is a time to mourn and a time to dance" (Ecclesiastes 3:4).

ANSWER. This is nothing to the purpose; for the most that any can pretend it proves is that it may be used under some circumstances, but not at all that dancing and other things used by our young people in their frolics are lawful, in those circumstances—any more than what is said in the verse 3 of that same chapter ("there is a time to kill") proves that it is lawful for a man to commit murder. To deny that dancing, under any circumstances whatever, was lawful would be absurd; for there was a religious dancing in the Jewish church that was a way of expressing their spiritual mirth. So David danced before the Lord, and he calls upon others to praise God in the dance. There may be other circumstances wherein dancing may not be unlawful. But all this amounts to nothing to the present purpose, to prove that this particular custom is not of a bad tendency. Besides, when the wise man says, "there is a time to dance," it does not prove that the dead of the night is the time for it. The same wise man does not justify carnal mirth, but condemns it. Ecclesiastes 2:2: "I said of laughter, it is mad; and of mirth, what doth it?"

OBJECTION. If we avoid all such things, it will be the way for our young people to be ignorant how to behave themselves in company.

ANSWER. But consider what this objection comes to. It certainly comes to this, that the pouring out of the Spirit of God upon a people tends to banish all good conduct, good breeding, and decent behavior from among them, and to sink them down into clownishness and barbarity! The Spirit of God actually put an end to this practice among us. But who is not ashamed to make such an objection? Will any of our young converts talk thus? Will you, who think you were converted by the late pouring out of the Spirit of God, and are made holy persons, heirs of eternal life, talk so blasphemously of it?

If our young people are resolute still to go on, notwithstanding all that has been said, I hope that those of them w ho call themselves converted will first find out some rational, satisfying answer to the arguments that have been used against it. This at least may be reasonably expected of them, seeing that they make such a profession. You have this day been partaking of the sacrament of the Lord's Supper, and therein solemnly renewed your profession. If after such light set before you, and such mercy given, you will go on, let it be known to you that your eating now and at other times will only prove to be eating and drinking judgment to yourselves.

And I desire heads of families, if they have any government over their children, or any command of their own houses, not to tolerate their children in such practices, nor suffer such conventions in their houses. I do not desire that young people should be abridged of any lawful and proper liberties; but this custom can be of no benefit or service in the world. It tends only to mischief.

Satan, doubtless, would be glad to have such an interest among us as he used to have, and is therefore striving to steal in while we are sleeping. But let us rouse ourselves up by vigorously opposing his encroachments. I shall repeat those words of the apostle from Romans 13:12–14, and leave them to the serious consideration of all persons, old and young: "The night is far spent; the day is at hand; let us therefore cast off the works of darkness, and let us put on the armor of light. Let us walk honestly as in the day, not in rioting and drunkenness, not in chambering and wantonness, not in strife and envying. But put ye on the Lord Jesus Christ, and make no provision for the flesh, to fulfill the lusts thereof."

CHAPTER EIGHTEEN

Ministers and Their People Must Meet One Another Before Christ's Tribunal on the Day of Judgment

(A farewell sermon preached July 1, 1750 in Northampton after Jonathan Edwards was voted out as the pastor)

"As also you have acknowledged us in part, that we are your rejoicing, even as ye also are ours in the day of the Lord Jesus."

2 CORINTHIANS 1:14

The apostle, in the preceding part of the chapter, declares what great troubles he met with in the course of his ministry. In the text, and the two foregoing verses, he declares what his comforts and supports

349

were under the troubles he met with. There are four things in particular:

1. He had approved himself to his own conscience. Verse 12: "For our rejoicing is this, the testimony of our conscience, that in simplicity and godly sincerity, not with fleshly wisdom, but by the grace of God, we have had our conversation in the world, and more abundantly to you-wards."

2. Another thing he speaks of as matter of comfort is that, as he had approved himself to his own conscience, so he had also to the consciences of his hearers, the Corinthians, to whom he now wrote, that they should approve of him at the day of judgment.

3. The hope he had of seeing the blessed fruit of his labors and sufferings in the ministry, in their happiness and glory, on that great day of accounts.

4. In his ministry among the Corinthians, he had approved himself to his Judge, who would approve and reward his faithfulness on that day.

These three last particulars are signified in my text and the preceding verse; and, indeed, all four are implied in the text. It is implied that the Corinthians had acknowledged him as their spiritual father, and as one who had been faithful among them, and as the means of their future joy and glory at the day of judgment. It is implied that the apostle expected at that time to have a joyful meeting with them before the Judge, and with joy to behold their glory as the fruit of his labors; and so they would be his rejoicing. It is implied also that he then expected to be approved by the great Judge when he and they would meet together before Him, and that He would then acknowledge his fidelity, that this had been the means of their glory, and that thus he would, as it were, give them to

Him as his crown of rejoicing. But the apostle could not hope for this unless he had the testimony of his own conscience in his favor. And therefore the words imply, in the strongest manner, that he had approved himself to his own conscience.

There is one thing implied in each of these particulars, and in every part of the text, which I shall make the subject of my present discourse:

DOCTRINE: Ministers, and the people who have been under their care, must meet one another before Christ's tribunal at the Day of Judgment.

Ministers, and the people who have been under their care, must be parted in this world, however well they have been united. If they are not separated before, they must be parted by death; and they may be separated while life is continued. We live in a world of change, where nothing is certain or stable, and where a little time, a few revolutions of the sun, brings to pass strange things, surprising alterations, in particular persons in families, in towns and churches, in countries and nations. It often happens that those who seem most united in a little time are most disunited and at the greatest distance. Thus ministers and people, between whom there has been the greatest mutual regard and strictest union, may not only differ in their judgments and be alienated in affection, but one may rend from the other, and all relations between them be dissolved. The minister may be removed to a distant place, and they may never have any more to do one with another in this world. But if it is so, there is one more meeting that they must have, and that is on the last great day of accounts.

Here I would show in what manner ministers and the people who have been under their care shall meet one another on

the Day of Judgment, for what purposes; and for what reasons
God has so ordered it that ministers and their people shall then
meet together in such a manner and for such purposes.

1. I would show in some particulars in what manner ministers
and the people who have been under their care shall meet
one another at the day of judgment: First, they shall not meet
on the day merely as all the world must then meet together. I
would observe a difference in two things: There is a difference
as to a clear, actual view and a distinct knowledge and notice of
each other.

Although the whole world will then be present, all mankind
of all generations gathered in one vast assembly, with all of
the angelic nature, both elect and fallen angels, yet we need
not suppose that everyone will have a distinct and particular
knowledge of each individual of the whole assembled multitude,
that will undoubtedly consist of many millions of millions.
Though it is probable that men's capacities will be much
greater than in their present state, yet they will not be infinite.
Though their understanding and comprehension will be vastly
extended, yet men will not be deified. There will probably be
a very enlarged view that particular persons will have of the
various parts and members of that vast assembly, and so of the
proceedings of that great day. Yet it must be that, according to
the nature of finite minds, some persons and some things on
that day shall fall more under the notice of particular persons
than others. This, as we may well suppose, will be according as
they shall have a nearer concern with some than others in the
transactions of the day.

There will be a special reason why those who have had
special concerns together in this world, in their state of probation, and whose mutual affairs will then be tried and judged,

should especially be set in one another's view. Thus we may suppose that rulers and subjects, earthly judges and those whom they have judged, neighbors who have had mutual converse, dealings, and contests, heads of families and their children and servants, shall then meet and, in a peculiar distinction, be set together. Especially will it be thus with ministers and their people. It is evident by the text that these shall be in each other's view; they shall distinctly know each other, and shall have particular notice one of another at that time.

They shall meet together as having special concern one with another in the great transactions of that day. Although they shall meet the whole world at that time, yet they will not have any immediate and particular concern with all. Yea, the far greater part of those who shall then be gathered together will be such as they have had no intercourse with in their state of probation, and so will have no mutual concerns. But as to ministers and the people who have been under their care, they will be such as have had much immediate concern one with another in matters of the greatest importance. Therefore they especially must meet, and be brought together before the Judge as having special concern one with another in the design and business of that great day of accounts. Thus their meeting, as to the manner of it, will be diverse from the meeting of mankind in general.

Second, their meeting on the day of judgment will be very diverse from their meetings one with another in this world. Ministers and their people, while their relationship continues, often meet together in this world. They are wont to meet from Sabbath to Sabbath, and at other times, for the public worship of God, the administration of ordinances, and the solemn services of God's house. Besides these meetings, they have also occasions to meet to determine and manage their ecclesiastical affairs, for the exercise of church discipline, and for settling and adjusting those things that concern the purity and good order of public administrations. But their meeting on the Day of Judgment will be exceedingly diverse in its manner and circumstances from any meetings and interviews they have one with another in the present state. I would observe how in a few particulars:

• Now they meet together in a preparatory, mutable state, but then in an unchangeable state. Now sinners in the congregation meet their minister in a state wherein they are capable of a saving change, capable of being turned, through God's blessing on the ministrations and labors of their pastor, from the power of Satan unto God, and being brought out of a state of guilt, condemnation, and wrath to a state of peace and favor with God, to the enjoyment of the privileges of His children, and a title to their eternal inheritance. And saints now meet their minister with great remains of corruption, and sometimes under great spiritual difficulties and affliction, and therefore are yet the proper subjects of means for a happy alteration of their state, which they have reason to hope for in the attendance on ordinances, and of which God is pleased commonly to make His ministers the instruments. Ministers and their people now meet in order to bring to pass such happy changes; they are the great benefits sought in their solemn meetings.

But when they shall meet together on the Day of Judgment, it will be far otherwise. They will all meet in an unchangeable state. Sinners will be in an unchangeable state. They who then shall be under the guilt and power of sin, and have the wrath of God abiding on them, shall be beyond all remedy or possibility of change, and shall meet their ministers without any hopes of relief or remedy, or getting any good by their means. As for the saints, they will already be perfectly delivered from all their corruption, temptation, and calamities of every kind, and set forever out of their reach; and no deliverance, no happy alteration, will remain to be accomplished in the use of means of grace under the administrations of ministers. It will then be pronounced, "He that is unjust, let him be unjust still; and he that is filthy, let him be filthy still; and he that is righteous, let him be righteous still; and he that is holy, let him be holy still."

• Then they shall meet together in a state of clear, certain, and infallible light. Ministers are set as guides and teachers, and are represented in Scripture as lights set up in the churches, and in the present state meet their people from time to time in order to instruct and enlighten them, to correct their mistakes, and to be a voice behind them, when they turn aside to the right hand or the left, saying, "This is the way, walk ye in it"; to evince and confirm the truth by exhibiting the proper evidences of it. They are to refute errors and corrupt opinions, to convince the erroneous, and establish the doubting.

But when Christ shall come to judgment, every error and false opinion shall be detected. All deceit and delusion shall vanish away before the light of that day, as the darkness of the night vanishes at the appearance of the rising sun. Every doctrine of the Word of God shall then appear in full evidence, and none shall remain unconvinced. All shall know the truth with the greatest certainty, and there shall be no mistakes to rectify.

Now ministers and their people may disagree in their judgments concerning some matters of religion; they may sometimes meet to confer together concerning those things wherein they differ, and to hear the reasons that may be offered on one side and the other—and all may be ineffectual as to any conviction of the truth. They may meet and part again no more agreed than before, and the side that was in the wrong may remain so still.

Sometimes the meetings of ministers with their people, in such a case of disagreeing sentiments, are attended with unhappy debate and controversy, managed with much prejudice and want of candor, not tending to light and conviction, but rather to confirm and increase darkness, and establish opposition to the truth and alienation of affection one from another. But when they shall meet together on the Day of Judgment, before the tribunal of the great Judge, the mind and will of Christ will be made known, and there shall no longer be any debate or difference of opinions. The evidence of the truth shall appear beyond all dispute, and all controversies shall be finally and forever decided.

Now ministers meet their people in order to enlighten and awaken the consciences of sinners, setting before them the great evil and danger of sin, the strictness of God's law, their own wickedness of heart and practice, the great guilt they are under, the wrath that abides upon them, and their impotence, blindness, poverty, and helpless and undone condition—but all is often in vain. They remain still, notwithstanding all their ministers can say, stupid and unawakened, and their consciences unconvinced. But it will not be so at their last meeting on the Day of Judgment. When sinners shall meet their minister before their great Judge, they will not meet Him with a stupid conscience. They will then be fully convinced of the truth of those things that they formerly heard from him concerning the greatness and terrible majesty of God, His holiness and hatred of sin, His awful justice in punishing it, the strictness of His law, the dreadfulness and truth of His threatenings, and their own unspeakable guilt and misery. And they shall never more be insensible of these things. The eyes of conscience will now be fully enlightened, and never shall be blinded again. The mouth of conscience shall now be opened, and never shall be shut any more.

Now ministers meet with their people in public and in private to enlighten them concerning the state of their souls, to open and apply the rules of God's Word to them, in order to their searching their own hearts and discerning their state. But now ministers have no infallible discernment of the state of their people; and the most skillful of them are liable to mistakes, and often are mistaken in things of this nature. Nor are the people able certainly to know the state of their minister, or one another's state; very often those pass among them for saints, and it may be eminent saints, who are grand hypocrites.

On the other hand, those are sometimes censured, or hardly received into their charity, who are indeed some of God's jewels. And nothing is more common than for men to be mistaken concerning their own state. Many who are abominable to God, and the children of His wrath, think highly of themselves as His precious saints and dear children. Yea, there is reason to think that often some who are most bold in their confidence of their safe and happy state, and think themselves not only true saints, but the most eminent saints in the congregation, are in a peculiar manner a smoke in God's nostrils. Thus it undoubtedly often is in those congregations where the Word of God is most faithfully dispensed, notwithstanding all that ministers can say in their clearest explications and most searching applications of the doctrines and rules of God's Word to the souls of their hearers.

But on the Day of Judgment, they shall have another sort of meeting. Then the secrets of every heart shall be made manifest, and every man's state shall be perfectly known. 1 Corinthians 4:5: "Therefore judge nothing before the time until the Lord come, who both will bring to light the hidden things of darkness, and will make manifest the counsels of the hearts: and then shall every man have praise of God." Then none shall be deceived concerning his own state, nor shall be any more in doubt about it. There shall be an eternal end to all the self-conceit and vain hopes of deluded hypocrites, and all the doubts and fears of sincere Christians. And then shall all know the state of one another's souls. The people shall know whether their minister has been sincere and faithful, and the minister shall know the state of every one of their people, and to who the Word and ordinances of God have been a savor of life unto life, and to whom a savor of death unto death.

Now in this present state it often happens that when ministers and people meet together to debate and manage their ecclesiastical affairs, especially in a state of controversy, they are ready to judge and censure with regard to each other's views, designs, and the principles and ends by which each is influenced, and are greatly mistaken in their judgment and wrong one another in their censures. But at that future meeting, things will be set in a true and perfect light, and the principles and aims that everyone has acted from shall be certainly known. There will be an end to all errors of this kind, and all unrighteous censures.

In this world, ministers and their people often meet together to hear of and wait upon an unseen Lord. But at the judgment, they shall meet in His most immediate and visible presence. Ministers who now often meet their people to preach to them the King eternal, immortal, and invisible, to convince them that there is a God and declare to them what manner of being He is, to convince them that He governs and will judge the world, and that there is a future state of rewards and punishments, and to preach to them a Christ in heaven, at the right hand of God, in an unseen world, shall then meet their people in the most immediate, sensible presence of this great God, Savior, and

Judge, appearing in the most plain, visible, and open manner, with great glory, with all His holy angels, before them and the whole world. They shall not meet them to hear about an absent Christ, an unseen Lord, and future Judge, but to appear before that Judge, being set together in the presence of that supreme Lord, in His immense glory and awful majesty, of whom they have heard so often in their meetings together on earth.

• The meeting at the last day of ministers and the people who have been under their care will not be attended by anyone with a careless, heedless heart. With such a heart are their meetings often attended in this world by many persons, having little regard for Him whom they pretend unitedly to adore in the solemn duties of His public worship, taking little heed to their own thoughts or frame of their minds, not attending to the business they are engaged in or considering the end for which they have come together. But at that great day there will not be one careless heart—no sleeping, no wandering of mind from the great concern of the meeting, no inattentiveness to the business of the day, no regardlessness of the presence they are in or of those great things that they shall hear from Christ, or that they formerly heard from Him and of Him by their ministers in their state of trial, or that they shall now hear their ministers declaring concerning them before their Judge.

2. Having observed these things concerning the manner and circumstances of this future meeting, before the tribunal of Christ at the day of judgment, I now proceed to observe to what purposes they shall then meet.

Their first purpose will be to give an account before the great Judge of their behavior one to another in the relationship they bore to each other in this world. Ministers are sent forth by Christ to their people on His business. They are His servants and messengers, and, when they have finished their service, they must return to their Master to give Him an account of what they have done, and of the entertainment they have had in performing their ministry. Thus we find in Luke 14:16-21 that when the servant who was sent forth to call the guests to the great supper had finished his appointed service, he returned to his master and gave him an account of what he had done, and of the entertainment he had received. And when the master, being angry, sent his servant to others, he returned again and gave his master an account of his conduct and success. So we read in Hebrews 13:17 of ministers or rulers in the house of God, that "they watch for souls, as those that must give account." And we see by the forementioned Luke 14 passage that ministers must give an account to their Master not only of their own behavior in the discharge of their office, but also of their people's reception of them, and of the treatment they have met with among them.

Faithful ministers will then give an account with joy concerning those who have received them well and made a good improvement of their ministry; and these will be given them on that day as their crown of rejoicing. And, at the same time, they will give an account of the ill treatment of such as have not well received them and their messages from Christ. They will meet these not as they used to do in this world, to counsel and warn them, but to bear witness against them, as their judges and assessors with Christ to condemn them. On the other hand, the people on that day will rise up in judgment against wicked and unfaithful ministers who have sought their own temporal interest more than the good of the souls of their flock.

Second, at that time ministers and the people who have been under their care shall meet together before Christ so that He may judge between them as to any controversies that have subsisted between them in this world. It often comes to pass in this evil world that great differences and controversies arise between ministers and the people under their pastoral care. Though they are under the greatest obligations to live in peace, above persons in almost any relationship whatever, and although contests and dissensions between persons so related are the most unhappy and terrible in their consequences on many accounts of any sort of contentions, yet how frequent have such contentions been! Sometimes a people contest with their ministers about their doctrine, sometimes about their administrations and conduct, and sometimes about their maintenance. Sometimes such contests continue a long time, and sometimes they are decided in this world, according to the prevailing interest of one party or the other rather than by the Word of God and the reason of things. And sometimes such controversies never have any proper determination in this world.

But on the Day of Judgment there will be a full, perfect, and everlasting decision of them. The infallible Judge, the infinite Fountain of light, truth, and justice, will judge between the contending parties, and will declare what is the truth, who is in the right, and what is agreeable to His mind and will. And in order hereto, the parties must stand together before Him on the last day, which will be the great day of finishing and determining all controversies, rectifying all mistakes, and abolishing all unrighteous judgments, errors, and confusions that have before subsisted in the world of mankind.

Third, ministers and the people who have been under their care must meet together at that time to receive an eternal sentence and retribution from the Judge, in the presence of each other, according to their behavior in the relationship they stood in to one another in the present state. The Judge will not only declare justice, but He will do justice between ministers and their people. He will declare what is right between them, approving him who has been just and faithful and condemning the unjust. Perfect truth and equity shall take place in the sentence which He passes, in the rewards He bestows, and in the punishments He inflicts. There shall be a glorious reward to faithful ministers, to those who have been successful. Daniel 12:3: "And they that be wise shall shine as the brightness of the firmament, and they that turn many to righteousness, as the stars forever and ever," and also to those who have been faithful and yet not successful. Isaiah 49:4: "Then I said, I have labored in vain, I have spent my strength for nought; yet surely my judgment is with the Lord, and my reward with my God."

And those who have well received and entertained them shall be gloriously rewarded. Matthew 10:40–41: "He that receiveth you receiveth Me; and he that receiveth Me receiveth Him that sent Me. He that receiveth a prophet in the name of a prophet shall receive a prophet's reward, and he that receiveth a righteous man in the name of a righteous man shall receive a righteous man's reward." Such people and their faithful ministers shall be each other's crown of rejoicing. 1 Thessalonians 2:19–20: "For what is our hope, or joy, or crown of rejoicing? Are not even ye in the presence of our Lord Jesus Christ at His coming? For ye are our glory and joy." And in the text, "We are your rejoicing, as ye also are ours, in the day of the Lord Jesus." But they who mistreat Christ's faithful ministers, especially in that wherein they are faithful, shall be severely punished. Matthew 10:14–15: "And whosoever shall not receive you, nor hear your words, when ye depart out of that house or city, shake off the dust of your feet. Verily I say unto you, it shall be more tolerable for the sinners of Sodom and Gomorrah in the day of judgment than for that city." Deuteronomy 33:8–11: "And of Levi he said, 'Let thy thummin and thy urim be with thy holy one. They shall teach Jacob Thy judgments and Israel Thy law.' Bless, Lord, his substance, and accept the work of his hands; smite through the loins of them that rise against him, and of them that hate him, that they rise not again." On the other hand, those ministers who are found to have been unfaithful, shall have a most terrible punishment (see Ezekiel 33:6; Matthew 23:1-33).

Thus justice shall be administered on the great day to ministers and their people; and to that end they shall meet together so that they may not only receive justice for themselves, but shall see justice done to the other party. For the end of that great day is to reveal or declare the righteous judgment of God (Romans 2:5). Ministers shall have justice done them, and they shall see justice done to their people. And the people shall receive justice themselves from their Judge, and shall see justice done to their minister. And so all things will be adjusted and settled forever between them, everyone being sentenced and recompensed according to his works, either in receiving and wearing a crown of eternal joy and glory, or in suffering everlasting shame and pain.

3. I come now to the next thing proposed, to give some reasons why we may suppose God has so ordered it that ministers and the people who have been under their care shall meet together on the Day of Judgment in such a manner and for such purposes. There are two things that I would now observe:

First, the mutual concerns of ministers and their people are of the greatest importance. The Scripture declares that God will bring every work into judgment, with every secret thing, whether it is good or whether it is evil. It is fitting that all the concerns and all the behavior of mankind, both public and private, should be brought at last before God's tribunal, and be finally determined by an infallible judge. But it is especially requisite that it should be thus as to affairs of very great importance.

Now the mutual concerns of a Christian minister and his church and congregation are of the vastest importance, in many respects of much greater importance than the temporal concerns of the greatest earthly monarchs and their kingdoms or empires. It is of vast consequence how ministers discharge their office and conduct themselves towards their people in the work of the ministry, and in affairs appertaining to it. It is also a matter of vast importance how a people receive and entertain a faithful minister of Christ, and what improvement they make of his ministry. These things have a more immediate and direct respect to the great and last end for which man was made, and the eternal welfare of mankind, than any of the temporal concerns of men, whether private or public. And therefore it is especially fitting that these affairs should be brought into judgment, and openly determined and settled in truth and righteousness and that, to this end, ministers and their people should meet together before the omniscient and infallible Judge.

Second, the mutual concerns of ministers and their people have a special relationship to the main things appertaining to the Day of Judgment. They have a special relationship to that great and divine Person who will then appear as Judge. Ministers are His messengers, sent forth by Him in their office and administrations among their people to represent His person, stand in His stead, as those who are sent to declare His mind, to do His work, and to speak and act in His name. And therefore it is especially fitting that they should return to Him to give an account of their work and success. The King is Judge of all His subjects; they are all accountable to Him. But it is more especially requisite that the King's ministers, who are especially entrusted with the administrations of His kingdom, and who are sent forth on some special negotiation, should return to Him to give an account of themselves, and their discharge of their trust, and the reception they have met with.

Ministers are not only messengers of the Person who at the last day will appear as Judge, but the errand they are sent upon and the affairs they have committed to them as His ministers most immediately concern His honor and the interest of His kingdom. The work they are sent upon is to promote the designs of His administration and government; therefore their business with their people has a near relation to the day of judgment. For the great end of that day is completely to settle and establish the affairs of His kingdom, to adjust all things that pertain to it, so that everything that is opposite to the interests of His kingdom may be removed, and that everything which contributes to the completeness and glory of it may be perfected and confirmed so that this great King may receive His due honor and glory.

Again, the mutual concerns of ministers and their people have a direct relationship to the concerns of the Day of Judgment, as the business of ministers with their people is to promote the eternal salvation of the souls of men and their escape from eternal damnation. The Day of Judgment is the day appointed for that end, openly to decide and settle men's eternal state, to fix some in a state of eternal salvation, to bring their salvation to its utmost consummation, and to fix others in a state of everlasting damnation and the most perfect misery. The mutual concerns of ministers and people have a most direct relationship to the Day of Judgment, as the very design of the work of the ministry is the people's preparation for that day. Ministers are sent to warn them of the approach of that day, to forewarn them of the dreadful sentence then to be pronounced on the wicked, to declare to them the blessed sentence then to be pronounced on the righteous, to use means with them that they may escape the wrath which is then to come on the ungodly, and to obtain the reward then to be bestowed on the saints.

And as the mutual concerns of ministers and their people have so near and direct a relationship to that day, it is especially fitting that those concerns should there be settled and issued, and that in order to this, that ministers and their people should meet and appear together before the great Judge on that day.

APPLICATION

The improvement I would make of the subject is to lead the people here present, who have been under my pastoral care, to some reflections, and to give them some suitable advice to our present circumstances, relating to what has been lately done in order to our being separated, but expecting to meet each other before the great tribunal on the Day of Judgment. The deep and serious consideration of our future most solemn meeting is certainly most suitable at such a time as this, that having so lately bee done that, in all probability, will (as to the relationship we have heretofore stood in) be followed with an everlasting separation.

How often have we met together in the house of God in this relationship! How often have I spoke to you, instructed, counseled, warned, directed, and fed you, and administered ordinances among you, as the people who were committed to my care, and of whose precious souls I had the charge! But in all probability this will never be again. The prophet Jeremiah (25:3) puts the people in mind of how long he had labored among them in the work of the ministry: "From the thirteenth year of Josiah, the son of Amon, king of Judah, even unto this day (that is, the three and twentieth year), the word of the Lord came unto me, and I have spoken unto you, rising early and speaking." I am not about to compare myself with the prophet Jeremiah, but in this respect I can say, as he did, that "I have spoken the Word of God to you, unto the three and twentieth year, rising early and speaking."

It was three and twenty years, the 15th day of last February, since I have labored in the work of the ministry, in the relation of a pastor to this church and congregation. And though my strength has been weakness, having always labored under great infirmity of body, besides my insufficiency for so great a charge in other respects, yet I have not spared my feeble strength, but have exerted it for the good of your souls. I can appeal to you, as the apostle does to his hearers in Galatians 4:13, "Ye know how, through infirmity of the flesh, I preached the gospel unto you." I have spent the prime of my life and strength in labors for your eternal welfare. You are my witnesses that, what strength I have had, I have not neglected in idleness, nor laid out in prosecuting worldly schemes and managing temporal affairs for the advancement of my outward estate, and aggrandizing myself and family. But I have given myself to the work of the ministry, laboring in it night and day, rising early and applying myself to this great business to which Christ appointed me.

I have found the work of the ministry among you to be a great work indeed, a work of exceeding care, labor, and difficulty. Many have been the heavy burdens that I have borne in it, to which my strength has been very unequal. God called me to bear these burdens. I bless His name that He has so supported me as to keep me from sinking under them, and that His power herein has been manifested in my weakness. So although I have often been troubled on every side, yet I have not been distressed; perplexed, but not in despair; cast down, but not destroyed. But now I have reason to think that my work is finished that I had to do as your minister; you have publicly rejected me, and my opportunities have ceased.

How highly, therefore, does it now become us to consider that time when we must meet one another before the chief Shepherd; when I must give an account of my stewardship, of the service I have done for, and the reception and treatment I have had among the people to whom He sent me.

And you must give an account of your own conduct towards me, and the improvement you have made of these three and twenty years of my ministry; for then both you and I must appear together, and we both must give an account in order for an infallible, righteous, and eternal sentence to be passed upon us by Him who will judge us with respect to all that we have said or done in our meeting here, and all our conduct one towards another in the house of God and elsewhere. He will try our hearts and manifest our thoughts, and the principles and frames of our minds. He will judge us with respect to all the controversies which have existed between us with the strictest impartiality, and will examine our treatment of each other in those controversies. There is nothing covered that shall not be revealed, nor hidden that shall not be known. All will be examined in the searching, penetrating light of God's omniscience and glory, and by Him whose eyes are as a flame of fire. Truth and right shall be made plainly to appear, being stripped of every veil. All error, falsehood, unrighteousness, and injury shall be laid open, stripped of every disguise. Every specious pretense, every cavil, and all false reasoning shall vanish in a moment, as not being able to bear the light of that day.

Then our hearts will be turned inside out, and the secrets of them will be made more plainly to appear than our outward actions do now. Then it shall appear what the ends are at which we have aimed, what have been the governing principles that we have acted from, and what have been the dispositions we have exercised in our ecclesiastical disputes and contests.

Then it will appear whether I acted uprightly, and from a truly conscientious, careful regard to my duty to my great Lord and Master, in some former ecclesiastical controversies that have been attended with exceedingly unhappy circumstances and consequences. It will appear whether there was any just cause for the resentment that was manifested on those occasions. And then our late grand controversy, concerning the qualifications necessary for admission to the privileges of members in complete standing in the visible church of Christ will be examined and judged in all its parts and circumstances, and the whole set forth in a clear, certain, and perfect light.

Then it will appear whether the doctrine that I have preached and published concerning this matter is Christ's own doctrine, whether He will not own it as one of the precious truths that have proceeded from His own mouth, and vindicate and honor it as such before the whole universe. Then it will appear what is meant by "the man that comes without the wedding garment," for that is the day spoken of in Matthew 22:13, wherein such a one shall be "bound hand and foot, and cast into outer darkness, where shall be weeping and gnashing of teeth." And then it will appear whether, in declaring this doctrine and acting agreeable to it, and in my general conduct in the affair, I have been influenced from any regard to my own temporal interest, or honor, or desire to appear wiser than others, or have acted from any sinister, secular views whatsoever, and whether what I have done has not been from a careful, strict, and tender regard to the will of my Lord and Master, and because I dare not offend Him, being satisfied what His will was after a long, diligent, impartial, and prayerful inquiry.

Then it will be seen whether I had this constantly in view and prospect, to engage me to great solicitude to not rashly determine the question, that such a determination would not be for my temporal interest, but in every way against it, bringing a long series of extreme difficulties, and plunging me into an abyss of trouble and sorrow. And then it will appear whether my people have done their duty to their pastor with respect to this matter; whether they have shown a right temper and spirit on this occasion; whether they have done me justice in hearing, attending to, and considering what I had to say in evidence of what I believed and taught as part of the counsel of God; whether I have been treated with that impartiality, candor, and regard that the just Judge esteemed due; and whether, in the many steps that have been taken, and the many things that have been said and done in the course of this controversy, righteousness, charity, and Christian decorum have been maintained—or, if it is otherwise, to how great a degree these things have been violated.

Then every step of the conduct of each of us in this affair, from first to last, and the spirit we have exercised in all, shall be examined and manifested; our own consciences shall speak plain and loud, each of us shall be convinced, and the world shall know; and never shall there be any more mistake, misrepresentation, or misapprehension of the affair to eternity.

This controversy is now probably brought to an issue between you and me as to this world. It has issued in the event of the week before last; but it must have another decision on that great day, that certainly will come, when you and I shall meet together before the great judgment seat. Therefore I leave it to that time, and shall say no more about it at present. But I would now proceed to address myself particularly to several sorts of persons:

1. To those who are professors of godliness among us. I would

now call you to a serious consideration of that great day wherein you must meet him who has heretofore been your pastor before the Judge whose eyes are as a flame of fire. I have endeavored, according to my best ability, to search the Word of God with regard to the distinguishing notes of true piety, those by which persons might best discover their state, and most surely and clearly judge themselves. These rules and marks I have from time to time applied to you, in preaching the Word to the utmost of my skill, and in the most plain and search manner that I have been able, in order to detect the deceived hypocrite and establish the hopes and comforts of the sincere. And yet it is to be feared that, after all that I have done, I now leave some of you in a deceived, deluded state; for it is not to be supposed that among several hundred professors none are deceived.

Henceforward I am likely to have no more opportunity to take the care and charge of your souls, to examine and search them. But still I entreat you to remember and consider the rules that I have often laid down to you during my ministry, with a solemn regard to the future day when you and I must meet together before our Judge, when the uses of examination you have heard from me must be rehearsed again before you, and those rules of trial must be tried; and it will appear whether they have been good or not. It will also appear whether you have impartially heard them and tried yourselves by them. The Judge Himself, who is infallible, will try both you and me. And after this none will be deceived concerning the state of their souls.

I have often put you in mind that, whatever your pretenses to experiences, discoveries, comforts, and joys have been, at that day everyone will be judged according to his works; and then you will find it to be so. May you have a minister of greater knowledge of the Word of God, and better acquaintance with soul cases, and of greater skill in applying himself to souls, whose discourses may be more searching and convincing, so that such of you as have held fast to deceit under my preaching may have your eyes opened by his, so that you may be undeceived before that great day.

What means and helps for instruction and self-examination you may hereafter have is uncertain. But one thing is certain, that the time is short; your opportunity for rectifying mistakes in so important a concern will soon come to an end. We live in a world of great changes. There is now a great change that has come to pass. You have withdrawn yourselves from my ministry, under which you have continued for so many years. But the time is coming, and will soon come, when you will pass out of time into eternity, and so will pass from under all means of grace whatsoever.

The greater part of you who are professors of godliness have (to use the phrase of the apostle) "acknowledged me in part." You have heretofore acknowledged me to be your spiritual father, the instrument of the greatest good to you that can be obtained by any of the children of men. Consider that day when you and I shall meet before our Judge, when it shall be examined whether you have had from me the treatment that is due to spiritual children, and whether you have treated me as you ought to have treated a spiritual father. As the relationship of a natural parent brings great obligations upon children in the sight of God, so much more, in many respects, the relationship of a spiritual father brings great obligations on such of whose conversation and eternal salvation they suppose God has made them the instruments. 1 Corinthians 4:15: "For though you have ten thousand instructors in Christ, yet have ye not many fathers; for in Christ Jesus, I have begotten you through the gospel."

2. Now that I am taking my leave of this people I would apply myself to such among them as I leave in a Christless, graceless

condition, and would call on such seriously to consider that solemn day when they and I must meet before the Judge of the world. My parting with you is, in some respects, in a peculiar manner, a melancholy parting inasmuch as I leave you in most melancholy circumstances, because I leave you in the gall of bitterness and bond of iniquity, having the wrath of God abiding on you, and remaining under condemnation to everlasting misery and destruction. Seeing that I must leave you, it would have been a comfortable and happy circumstance of our parting if I had left you in Christ, safe and blessed in that sure Refuge and glorious rest of the saints. But it is otherwise. I leave you far off, aliens and strangers, wretched subjects and captives of sin and Satan, and prisoners of vindictive justice, without Christ and without God in the world.

Your consciences bear me witness that, while I had opportunity, I have not ceased to warn you and set before you your danger. I have studied to represent the misery and necessity of your circumstances in the clearest manner possible. I have tried all the ways that I could think of tending to awaken your consciences, and make you sensible of the necessity of your improving your time and being speedy in flying from the wrath to come, and thorough in the use of means for your escape and safety. I have diligently endeavored to find out and use the most powerful motives to persuade you to take care for your own welfare and salvation. I have not only endeavored to awaken you, that you might be moved with fear, but I have used my utmost endeavors to win you. I have sought out acceptable words so that, if possible, I might prevail upon you to forsake sin, turn to God, and accept Christ as your Savior and Lord. I have spent my strength very much in these things. But yet, with regard to you whom I am addressing, I have not been successful, but have this day reason to complain in those words from Jeremiah 6:29: "The bellows are burnt, the lead is consumed of the fire, the founder melteth in vain, for the wicked are not plucked away."

It is to be feared that all my labors, as to many of you, have served no other purpose but to harden you, and that the word that I have preached, instead of being a savor of life unto life, has been a savor of death unto death. Though I shall not have any account to give for the future of such as have openly and resolutely renounced my ministry, as of a trust committed to me, yet remember that you must give account for yourselves, of your care of your own souls, and your improvement of all means past and future through your whole lives. God only knows what will become of your poor, perishing souls, what means you may hereafter enjoy, or what disadvantages and temptations you may be under. May God in His mercy grant that, however all past means have been unsuccessful, you may have future means that may have a new effect, and that the Word of God, as it shall be hereafter dispensed to you, may prove as the fire and the hammer that breaks the rock in pieces.

However, let me now at my parting exhort and beseech you not to wholly forget the warnings you have had while under my ministry. When you and I shall meet on the Day of Judgment, then you will remember them. The sight of me, your former minister, on that occasion will soon revive them in your memory, and that in a very affecting manner. Oh, do not let that be the first time that they are so revived.

You and I are now parting from one another as to this world. Let us labor so that we may not be parted after our meeting at the last day. If I have been your faithful pastor (which will that day appear whether I have or not), then I shall be acquitted, and shall ascend with Christ. Oh, do your part so that, in such a case, you may not be forced to eternally part from me, and all who have been faithful in Christ Jesus. This is a sorrowful parting, but that one would be more sorrowful. This you may perhaps bear without being much affected with it, if you are not glad of it, but such a parting in that day will most deeply, sensibly, and dreadfully affect you.

3. I would now address myself to those who are under some awakenings. Blessed be God that there are some such, and that (although I have reason to fear I leave multitudes in this large congregation in a Christless state) I do not leave them all in total stupidity and carelessness about their souls. Some of you whom I have reason to hope are under some awakenings have acquainted me with your circumstances, that has a tendency to cause me, now that I am leaving you, to take my leave with peculiar concern for you. What will be the issue of your present exercise of mind, I do not know; but it will be known on that day when you and I shall meet before the judgment seat of Christ. Therefore now be much in consideration of that day.

Now that I am parting with this flock, I would once more press upon you the counsels I have heretofore given, to take heed of slightly so great a concern, to be thorough and in good earnest in the affair, and to beware of backsliding, to hold on and hold out to the end. Cry mightily to God that these great changes that pass over this church and congregation do not prove to be your overthrow. There is great temptation in them, and the devil will undoubtedly seek to make his advantage of them, if possible, to cause your present convictions and endeavors to be abortive. You need to double your diligence, and watch and pray, lest you be overcome by temptation.

Whoever may hereafter stand related to you as your spiritual guide, my desire and prayer is that the great Shepherd of the sheep would have a special respect to you and be your Guide (for there is none who teaches like Him), and that He who is the infinite Fountain of light would "open your eyes, and turn you from darkness unto light, and from the power of Satan unto God; that you may receive forgiveness of sins, and inheritance among them that are sanctified, through faith that is in Christ," so that on that great day, when I shall meet you again before your Judge and mine, we may meet in joyful and glorious circumstances, never to be separated any more.

4. I would now apply myself to the young people of the congregation. Since I have been settled in the work of the ministry in this place, I have ever had a peculiar concern for the souls of the young people, and a desire that religion might flourish among them; and I have especially exerted myself in order to it because I knew the special opportunity they had beyond others, and that ordinarily those for whom God intended mercy were brought to fear and love him in their youth. And it has ever appeared to me a peculiarly amiable thing to see young people walking in the ways of virtue and Christian piety, having their hearts purified and sweetened with a principle of divine love. How exceedingly beautiful and conducive to the adorning and happiness of the town it would be if the young people could be persuaded, when they meet together, to converse as Christians and as the children of God, avoiding impurity, levity and extravagance, keeping strictly to rules of virtue, and conversing together of the things of God, and Christ, and heaven! This is what I have longed for, and it has been exceedingly grievous to me when I have heard of vice, vanity and disorder among our youth. And so far as I know my own heart, it was from hence that I formerly led this church to some measures to suppress vice among our young people, which gave such great offense, and by which I became so obnoxious to you. I have sought the good, not the hurt of our young people. I have desired their

truest honor and happiness, not their reproach, knowing that true virtue and religion tended not only to the glory and felicity of young people in another world, but their greatest peace and prosperity, and highest dignity and honor in this world, and above all things to sweeten, and render pleasant and delightful, even the days of youth.

But whether I have loved you and sought your good more or less, now committing your souls to Him who once committed the pastoral care of them to me, nothing remains but only (as I am now taking my leave of you) to earnestly beseech you, from love for yourselves if you have none for me, not to despise and forget the warnings and counsels I have so often given you. Remember the day when you and I must meet again before the great Judge of quick and dead, when it will appear whether the things I have taught you were true, whether the counsels I have given you were good, whether I truly sought your welfare, and whether you have well improved my endeavors.

I have, from time to time, earnestly warned you against frolicking (as it is called), and some other liberties commonly taken by young people in the land. And whatever some may say in justification of such liberties and customs, and may laugh at warnings against them, I now leave you my parting testimony against such things, not doubting but that God will approve and confirm it on that day when we shall meet before Him.

5. I would apply myself to the children of the congregation, the lambs of this flock, who have been so long under my care. I have just now said that I have had a peculiar concern for the young people, and in so saying I did not intend to exclude you. You are in youth, and in the most early youth. Therefore I have been sensible that if those who were young had a precious opportunity for their souls' good, you who are very young had, in many respects, a peculiarly precious opportunity. And

accordingly I have not neglected you. I have endeavored to do the part of a faithful shepherd, in feeding the lambs as well as the sheep. Christ once committed the care of your souls to me as your minister; and you know, dear children, how I have instructed you, and warned you from time to time. You know how I have often called you together for that end, and some of you, sometimes, have seemed to be affected with what I have said to you. But I am afraid it has had no saving effect as to many of you, but that you remain still in an unconverted condition, without any real, saving work wrought in your souls, convincing you thoroughly of your sin and misery, causing you to see the great evil of sin, and to mourn for it and hate it above all things, and giving you a sense of the excellency of the Lord Jesus Christ, bringing you with all your hearts to cleave to Him as your Savior, weaning your hearts from the world, causing you to love God above all, and to delight in holiness more than in all the pleasant things of this earth.

I must now leave you in a miserable condition, having no interest in Christ, and so under the awful displeasure and anger of God, in danger of going down to the pit of eternal misery. Now I must bid you farewell. I must leave you in the hands of God. I can do no more for you than to pray for you. Only I desire that you not forget, but often think of the counsels and warnings I have given you, and the endeavors I have used so that your souls might be saved from everlasting destruction.

Dear children, I leave you in an evil world that is full of snares and temptations. God only knows what will become of you. This the Scripture has told us, that there are but few saved, and we have abundant confirmation of it from what we see. This we see, that children die as well as others. Multitudes die before they grow up, and of those who grow up, comparatively few ever give good evidence of saving conversion to God. I pray

God to pity you, to take care of you, and to provide for you the best means for the good of your souls. I pray that God Himself would undertake for you to be your heavenly Father and the mighty Redeemer of your immortal souls. Do not neglect to pray for yourselves. Take heed that you are not of the number of those who cast off fear and restrain prayer before God. Constantly pray to God in secret, and often remember that great day when you must appear before the judgment seat of Christ and meet your minister there, who has so often counseled and warned you.